THE GURKHAS

THE GURKHAS

The Inside Story of the World's Most Feared Soldiers

JOHN PARKER

Bounty Books

Copyright © 1999 John Parker

The right of John Parker to be identified as the Author
of the Work has been asserted by him in accordance with
the Copyright, Designs and Patents Act 1988

First published in 1999 by
HEADLINE BOOK PUBLISHING

This edition published 2005 by Bounty Books,
a division of Octopus Publishing Group Ltd
Endeavour House,
189 Shaftesbury Avenue,
London WC2H 8JY

An Hachette UK Company
www.hachette.co.uk

Reprinted 2006, 2007, 2010, 2011

ISBN: 978-0-733712-93-1

A CIP catalogue record for this book is available
from the British Library

Printed and bound in China by Imago

CONTENTS

ACKNOWLEDGEMENTS

Many retired and current officers and men of the Gurkha regiments, both in Britain and Nepal, have assisted the author in compiling this work. The history of ten military regiments, spanning a period from the first formation in 1815 through to 1999, presented a vast panoply of activity to draw from, and a conventional military history would require several volumes. However, the story emerges after delving into key periods of action, and where possible I have relied on personal recall and much first-person testimony to link the progressive stages of its development. As will be apparent from the text, this has been achieved from more than 40 taped interviews I conducted in Britain and Nepal between 1997 and 1999, from extracts from the Gurkha tapes in the Sound Archive of the Imperial War Museum, from personal diaries, memoirs and correspondence and some gems from the archives of the Gurkha Museum, Winchester, a free 'must visit' for anyone interested in Gurkha history, and from whom all pictures in this book have been supplied, unless otherwise credited.

In the ensuing text I have deliberately not used the ranks of British officers because in general their recollections cover many years of service through which they have risen in rank, as with General Sir Walter Walker, CB, CBE, DSO, whose connections with the Gurkhas began as a junior officer and progressed through every rank to Major General, Brigade of Gurkhas, and eventually to Commander-in-Chief of Allied Forces in Northern Europe, 1969–72. Apart from his service with the Gurkhas, Sir Walter had been one of the great campaigners on their behalf, sometimes to the detriment of his own career, during the past half-century. His recollections may also be heard on tape in the Sound Archive of the Imperial War Museum. My gratitude also to: Major Gordon Corrigan, MBE, formerly OC Gurkha Training Wing, who led the trekking expedition to Nepal in 1998; Brigadier David Morgan, OBE; Brigadier John Thornton, OBE, MC; the late Brigadier E.D. 'Birdie' Smith, CBE, DSO; Lieutenant Colonel Tom Blackford; Lieutenant Colonel Anthony Harvey, OBE, MC (also on tape at the Imperial War Museum); Lieutenant Colonel R.H. Coleman, OC Gurkha Recruitment Centre, Pokhara; Major J.C. Palmer, Chief of Staff, Headquarters Brigade of Gurkhas; Brigadier C.J.D. Bullock, OBE, MC, curator of the Gurkha Museum, Winchester and museum archivist Gavin Edgerley-Harris; Major Michael Marshall (also on tape at the Imperial War Museum); Major Dal Bahadur Gurung, MVO, now with Himalayan Envpro Adventures, Kathmandu; Major Kulraj Limbu, secretary, Gurkha Welfare Memorial Trust, Kathmandu; the Hon. Captain Lalbahadur Gurung, MBE, Area Welfare Office, Gorkha; Lieutenant Lalbahadur Gurung; Lieutenant Hitman Gurung, OC Nepal Signal Troop, Brigade of Gurkhas, Nepal; RSM Debiram Rai and C/Sergeant Hombahadur Gurung, Headquarters Brigade of Gurkhas, Kathmandu; WO2 Shyam Kumar Thakuri, ex-6th Gurkha Rifles. Thanks also to Mrs Maureen Silver and to Holts Battlefields and History Tours, which arranged the 1998 trekking expedition to the Gurkha homelands.

GLOSSARY

QGO	Queen's Gurkha Officer
QGOO	Queen's Gurkha Orderly Officer
GCO	Gurkha Commissioned Officer; QGOs promoted to a full commission
Havildar	Indian army rank equivalent to sergeant
Havildar major	Indian army rank equivalent to sergeant major
Jemadar (or jemedar)	Indian army rank equivalent to lieutenant (QGO)
Lance naik	Indian army rank equivalent to lance corporal
LMG	Light machine gun
MMG	Medium machine gun
Naik	Indian army rank equivalent to corporal
PIAT	Projector Infantry AntiTank
Picquet (or piquet)	A small detachment of troops positioned to give an early warning of attack
Sepoy	A private soldier
Subadar (or subedar)	Indian army rank equivalent to captain (QGO)
Subadar major	Indian army rank equivalent to major (QGO), the senior Gurkha officer in a battalion

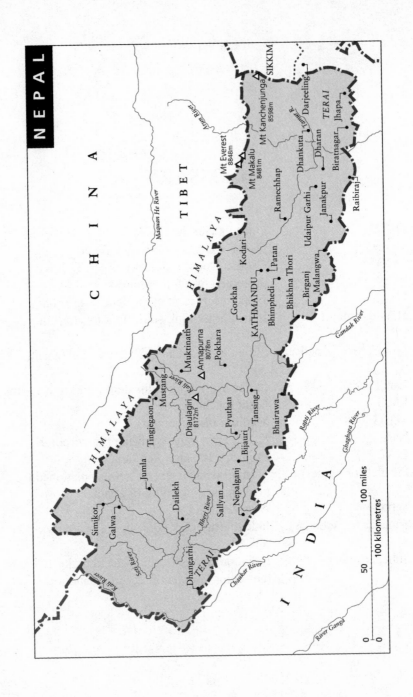

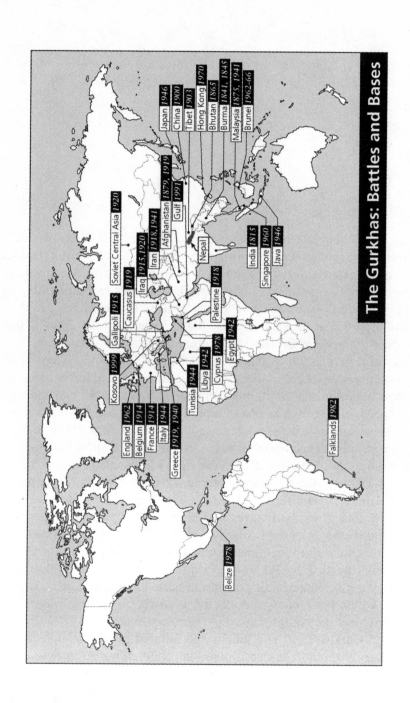

The Gurkhas: Battles and Bases

Japan 1946
China 1900
Tibet 1903
Hong Kong 1970
Bhutan 1865
Burma 1841, 1845
Malaysia 1875, 1941
Brunei 1962-66

Soviet Central Asia 1920
Afghanistan 1879, 1919
Gulf 1991

Iran 1918, 1941
Iraq 1918, 1920
Caucasus 1919

Gallipoli 1915

Nepal

India 1815
Singapore 1960
Java 1946

Palestine 1918

Kosovo 1999

Egypt 1942

Cyprus 1978
Libya 1942
Tunisia 1944

England 1962
Belgium 1914
France 1914
Italy 1944
Greece 1919, 1940

Falklands 1982

Belize 1978

PROLOGUE

As NATO aircraft screamed overhead in the final hours of their relentless 78-day bombing campaign against Serbia, crack British troops massed along the southern borders of Kosovo. Among them were a contingent of small but tough fighting men recruited from the hills of Nepal – affectionately known to all as the Gurkhas – and they had a particular mission. The 1st Battalion the Royal Gurkha Rifles was at the helm of the task force, alongside British Paratroopers, their partners in the 5th Airborne Brigade, and the SAS. They were collectively described as the 'elite' of the British armed forces and now they waited to lead a 40-mile column of NATO tanks and military vehicles into Kosovo as peacekeepers. It represented the single most ambitious military deployment since the 1991 Gulf War, followed in as they were by thousands of British, German, French and Italian troops, preparing to flood across the border from Macedonia.

At 4.22 a.m. the following morning, 12 June 1999, they were ready to move. As dawn flushed the dark skies, Operation Joint Guardian swung into action and waves of Chinook helicopters rose from the Macedonian side of the border in a cloud of dust. On the ground, the Gurkhas were given the signal to move out, and a detachment of 1RGR became the first NATO troops to cross the border into Kosovo to secure the heights against possible snipers. Two minutes later, Brigadier Adrian Freer, commander of the 5th Airborne Brigade was driven slowly over the border flanked by a protective cordon of 800 heavily armed Gurkhas, and now finally the tortured plight of hundreds of thousands of innocent men, women and children was to be relieved.

That the Gurkhas were at the forefront of this action was no surprise to military analysts. They have been front-line troops in many of the most significant campaigns involving the British military during the previous 184 years.

Statistics are perhaps hardly the way to begin what is a very human story, packed with tales of incredible courage and glowing tributes to a particular breed of small fighting men recruited from the foothills of the Himalayas into the service of a nation to whom they owed absolutely no allegiance. However, two sets of figures strike a particular chord. They bring us straight to the heart of this history of the Gurkhas, who are called mercenaries but for whom, it will be seen, money is not the only draw. For one thing, the British have never been especially generous in their payment. They began by handing out sufficient rewards to entice thousands of wild, young boys down from the hills of Nepal and away from their desperate lives in a closed, isolated and medieval society where until quite recently the average peasant male could not expect to live beyond early adulthood. But gradually the Gurkhas transcended the role of simple mercenary. Sheer kudos took hold, along with the deeply held family tradition of service in the British and Indian armies, which today can be traced back through four or five generations. Along the way, the Gurkhas have amassed a large hoard of some of the highest honours for bravery the British nation could bestow, the respect of successive British monarchs and the remarkable affection of its people.

And so . . . to the statistics:

It is 1914 . . . and at the beginning of the First World War, Britain canvassed support from the governments of her Empire and her friends. Among those who readily offered aid was one of the smallest and poorest, Nepal – a country still living in the Stone Age. She had no real need to do so, being far away from the battlefields of Europe and with no colonial ties. Nepal has always avoided the acquisitive tendencies of would-be rulers from both the British/Indian giant to the south and the Tibetan/Chinese colossus to the north. This has been achieved partly because the nation was so poor and living in a desperately hostile landscape that, truth be told, no one really wanted her. The other deterrent was that those who had tried in the past had been dealt a severe bloody nose by its funny, fierce and fearless hill men (average height five feet four/1.62 metres) who lived in shacks falling off the sides of the mountain ranges around the skirt of the Himalayas up to 10,000 feet (3,050 metres). They became noted for being exceedingly proficient at slicing off an enemy's head with one swish of a kukri blade (as in the old Gurkha story of a one to one with a Japanese officer armed with a fine samurai sword and swearing that no stumpy kukri knife could match his glistening weapon as he winged the Gurkha in the arm and then cut off his hand. 'Ah,' replied the Gurkha, 'I may be wounded, but you, sahib . . . I suggest that you do not nod your head!')

When Britain sent out her call for help in 1914, there was no holding back: the Nepali rulers gave their blessing and, among a nation that then numbered fewer than 5 million people, 200,000 Gurkhas came forward to fight in British and Indian army regiments – virtually the entire Gurkha male population of eligible age. They suffered more than 20,000 casualties, and their now legendary bravery was rewarded with almost 2,000 awards for gallantry. They repeated the favour in the Second World War with similar consequences, this time with almost 250,000 men serving in 42 infantry battalions and various other elements of the British and Indian armies. They suffered heavily: 8,985 killed or missing and 23,655 wounded. They also garnered 2,734 bravery awards. Gurkhas have fought on the side of the British in almost every campaign in which she has engaged herself from 1816 to the present day, famously including the Indian Mutiny and, latterly, the Falklands, the first Gulf War and Bosnia. Although difficult to ascertain exactly, Gurkha casualty figures for the two world wars and other conflicts before and since are conservatively put at 150,000 wounded and 45,000 killed in action. They have received in all more than 6,500 decorations for bravery, mentions in dispatches or certificates for outstanding gallantry. These include thirteen Victoria Cross awards (plus another thirteen awarded to British officers serving in Gurkha regiments) and two George Cross medals.

More than two million campaign medals have been distributed among Gurkha soldiers. Among the many glowing tributes to their fighting prowess is this from Field Marshal Lord Slim, who was both a regimental officer and a general commanding them: 'An ideal infantry-man, an ideal rifleman . . . he is brave, tough, patient, adaptable, skilled in fieldcraft, intensely proud of his military record and unswerving in his loyalty. Add to this his honesty, parade perfection and unquenchable cheerfulness, and service with the Gurkha is, for any soldier, an immense satisfaction.' And from the mid-nineteenth century to the present, there has been an unbroken annual recruitment of Gurkhas into the British army.

Statistic number two . . .

It is September 1998 . . . and Britain is trawling those Himalayan hillsides for fighting men, just as she has done every year, year in, year out, down the decades – and this author, incidentally, was on hand to tour the British Army's Gurkha Recruitment Centre at Pokhara, 130 miles (210 kilometres) from Kathmandu. Men they call the galla wallahs come around each autumn and the hill boys are lined up, waiting, hoping, longing for the moment they will be selected and marked up with a number traditionally painted on their chests in indelible ink. And this year was no exception. There were almost 60,000 young men aged between 15 (they lie about their age!) and 20 pouring into the villages to be visited by the galla wallah for what is termed Hill Selection. This year, fewer than 200 youngsters were to be finally accepted; that was the miserable quota set by the Ministry of Defence.

The British army has drastically curtailed its intake of Gurkhas in recent times, although 46 Gurkha battalions remain in the Indian army, which has its own recruiting procedures and today employs 120,000 men of Gurkha origin. The Gurkhas all know the British have been taking fewer and fewer, yet 300 young men scramble among themselves for every single vacancy. To some, rejection will be such a dent to their pride and regarded as such a shame on their families that they will throw themselves into one of the fast-flowing rivers or off one of the precarious rope bridges in a steep gorge to their deaths on the way home.

It is the hardship of life in the most difficult of the hill regions that has traditionally produced the stout-hearted, sure-footed and tough men now universally known as 'The Gurkhas' and it is the galla wallahs who are their first line of contact. They are agents of the British Crown who have for decades made their sorties into the hills to find suitable young men. The response is always overwhelming and unprecedented in any other military organisation anywhere in the world, demonstrating a dedication to Britain which is no better revealed than by scanning the 161 Battle Honours of the British

Gurkha Regiments, the thousands of medals won and the bald casualty statistics of those killed on active service and whose names are listed on war memorials and cemeteries in some of the greatest battlefields across the world. Only lately has money become a contentious and controversial issue as inflation grips what is one of the poorest countries in the world, with a per capita income in 1994 of less than £150 per year.

The expeditions by the galla wallahs are an annual ritual to fill a quota of new recruits, who will pass through a meticulous selection programme. The 'lucky' ones can be counted in their hundreds of thousands since Gurkhas first became a fighting force within the British army, lucky because they have achieved what became the burning ambition of virtually every hill boy – which is to be whisked away to be educated, trained, shown the world and provided with enough money for a decent life and to help support the families they leave behind. For Nepal itself, the exportation of Gurkhas is big business – and vital. In 1997 incoming foreign currency sent home by Gurkha soldiers working abroad or to retired ex-servicemen by way of pensions amounted to £41 million – the country's third-biggest earner of foreign currency behind tourism, foreign aid grants and industry.

As Britain shaved its requirement, there was and is a good deal of sympathy to be found among the Gurkhas' many fans in Britain and the Commonwealth, particularly among officers who have served alongside them. Some despondent supporters believe that in all probability these young warriors from afar are heading for the last roundup.

Can they survive as a unit of the British army? Or is it time indeed to cut the umbilical cord and let this well-maintained killing machine popularly known as the Gurkhas drift away once and for all?

PART ONE

Now and Then . . .

To discover the origins of the most curious social phenomenon in recent military history and what remains of the last British army link with traditional native soldiering that began with Clive of India in the mid-eighteenth century, the author joined a trekking expedition to Nepal in the autumn of 1998, visiting both ancient and modern sites with Gurkha connections. Through these links to the past, their history emerges. The party, led by Major Gordon Corrigan, late of the Royal Gurkha Rifles, included ex-military men, a British family with Gurkha ties, a long-serving ex-SAS man, a Ministry of Agriculture official who as a national service soldier was alongside the Gurkhas in Malaya, and Gurkha fans who included a London stipendiary magistrate and the mysterious Beryl. Additional commentary on this journey, italicised in the text, is provided by Maureen Silver, second in command of the expedition, who maintained a communal log.

CHAPTER ONE

Forbidden Kingdom

Our Royal Nepalese Airline 757 came in to land over the massive mountains laced with low-lying cloud and touched down after a fourteen-hour, two-stop flight from London. As it drew us in towards the pandemonium of Kathmandu's recently built and barn-like terminal building, the galla wallahs were already heading for the hills. The monsoon rains were over and this year had left no great damage to the route, and so they began their trek into the Himalayan heartland of Gurkha tradition for the annual search for new recruits. Even so, my own journey across the world was far easier than the one confronting them. Gordon Corrigan, a long-standing friend of Nepal, knows the story well. Until 1997 he was Officer Commanding the Gurkha Training Wing, based in the hutted wartime barracks at Church Crookham, in the heart of Hampshire, England.

It is to that establishment that the young men recruited that autumn would, as always, eventually be transported for their 42 weeks of basic training before being assigned to their battalions in the Royal Gurkha Rifles or their squadrons of engineers, signals and transport. The comparatively small distances to be covered by the galla wallahs as they march into the hills will be far more arduous than the flight to Nepal, and the journey time would be counted in days rather than hours along a route far away from the cacophony of noise and smells that has overtaken Kathmandu, one of the most romantic cities on earth and now, sadly, also one of the most polluted, steaming, overcrowded but still a 'must see'. The galla wallahs will begin their selection programme as they reach the fresher, cleaner air up to around 7,500 feet (2,286 metres).

7

It is there, too, from the base of the Annapurna range above the western town of Pokhara that Gordon Corrigan will lead the trek to meet old friends and familiar faces from the British armed forces who have been shown the world and are retired now, returned to their tiny villages of terracotta and white houses that cling to the spectacular but incredibly harsh landscape that no roads can reach and where the only way in for man and supplies is shanks's pony. There is barely a house among them that has not had some tie with the Gurkha regiments; most have either a past or present serving soldier among their relatives and quite often several.

Once in the hills, these villages are to be reached only by way of a network of interconnecting footpaths through treacherous passes, across deep gorges slung with perilous rope and bamboo bridges (don't look down!) and onwards to some near-vertical climbs. And if the terrain itself is not inhospitable enough, mother nature may throw in some of her worst extremes, including torrential rain, blizzards, earthquakes, landslides, floods and fire. The monsoon rains can turn normally placid, easily crossable rivers into raging white water, landslides occurring everywhere dump hundreds of tonnes of rocks and boulders in the only way ahead, making long detours necessary, bridges collapse, ferries are suspended and leeches attack walkers.

Getting supplies is difficult at the best of times, making it necessary for people literally to turn to the land for every one of their needs, from herbs for medicine, fuel for their fires, fodder for their animals and food for themselves, which is in itself difficult when one considers that farming generally is possible only in terraced strips turned by single-furrow buffalo-drawn ploughs. The simple commodity of drinkable water may be two or three hours' walk away. As we enter the new millennium, life has barely changed in these remote parts of Nepal since the beginning of the last one, which is hardly surprising since the country was closed to the outside world until 1951. And to recap for those whose geography lessons are, like mine, a touch misty, it is not a large country in land area but huge in its height, which one tends to mention in conjunction with distance. It is approximately 530 miles (853 kilometres) long and 140 miles (225 kilometres) at its widest breadth, though averaging around 100 miles (160 kilometres). It is landlocked by Tibet, under the rule of the Chinese invaders, to the north-west and on all other borders by India. Within those boundaries, the contours will draw from the traveller every possible adjective of description that amounts, really, to one very modern word: awesome. Eventually, the vistas are beyond the power of the English dictionary, and one is bound to stand gazing, open-mouthed, speechless.

From the mosquito-infested plateaux watered by tributaries of the Ganges at around 300 feet (91 metres) above sea-level where Nepal abuts India, the land rises in ridges, hills and mountains, slowly and then urgently until reaching the rooftop of our world. Virtually the whole of its northern border is breathtakingly marked by the majestic Himalaya ('abode of the snow') mountains that rise from between 16,000 to 29,141 feet (4,877 to 8,882 metres). Nepal possesses nine of the fourteen peaks in the world over 26,000 feet (7,925 metres), including, of course, Mount Everest and Annapurna. Flattened out, someone once calculated, the country would be at least the size of France.

Below the shrouded, ghostly shapes of the mountains, the foothills run virtually the length of the country, and it is specifically from this territory, the Pahar or Hill Region, covering around 64 per cent of the total land of Nepal, that the Gurkhas have traditionally been recruited. They are divided incidentally as 'easterners' and 'westerners', which in terms of their distinctive tribal, religious and social patterns also reflects on their personalities – an important factor for young British officers assigned to the Gurkhas to remember.

The Nepal Headquarters Brigade of Gurkhas is in Kathmandu, and we dined there on our second night in the city, meeting many veterans of British service including some who had served in the Falklands. The Gurkha recruitment centre itself is closer to the western hills at the foot of Annapurna near Pokhara, with its population of around 80,000. It will take six or seven hair-raising hours to reach it by bus along Nepal's modest main road. In eastern Nepal, the other main area of Gurkha recruitment was traditionally around Dharan and the more southerly Biratnagar. Both still have many British army pensioners resident in the region.

Between the two flanks of east and west is the Kathmandu valley, the heart of Nepal. Because of its fertile and less demanding land-scape, it has attracted the main areas of concentrated population, although still less than a third of the country's rapidly expanding population (currently estimated at 22 million) live what might loosely

9

be termed an urban life. The remainder scratch a living from agriculture. Less than a third of the land area is suitable for cultivation: hence the latest threat of deforestation. Nepal lost more than half its forest in two decades, while Kathmandu is attracting increasing numbers of people – both from its own peasant communities seeking a better life and from the booming tourist trade, the backpackers, trekkers and mountaineers now arriving by the planeload every day. The debris and pressures of tourism are also becoming a dangerous and unsightly addition to local problems even on Mount Everest, which has, to use Brian Blessed's angry description, become a tip. It is also big business for outsiders selling expeditions for ordinary people on the Nepal side of Everest for up to $65,000 a head, occasionally with catastrophic results. By and large, the bodies remain where they fall.

Kathmandu has a burgeoning population of around 1.2 million and in spite of massive problems is for the time being not as bad as some cities and unmissable for the traveller, demonstrating the speed at which the country has dragged itself across two centuries and into the twenty-first in the space of just forty years. Outside influences are a recent phenomenon. Nepal was a medieval feudal kingdom until the oppressive Rana government was ousted in 1951. Until then, tourists and all other non-approved travellers were simply not admitted. The Nepali rulers maintained a total ban on both people and technology to enforce cruel and rigid controls on its diverse and ill-educated people. It was, in every sense of the word, the forbidden kingdom, and its image as the world's most inaccessible society merely enhanced the mystique and mystery that had surrounded it for centuries, and made it all the more enticing when the restrictions were finally lifted. In a country where the extremes are outstandingly apparent in its statistics as well as its landscape, there were only 130 recorded and official European visitors to Nepal between 1796 and 1950, and they were generally from the British diplomatic corps. Midway through the twentieth century it was the largest inhabited country in the world which remained unexplored by Westerners. Many areas were still uncharted.

The first recorded tourists were booked through Thomas Cook, ten Americans and two Brazilians arriving in 1955. They were allowed visas for travel only into the Kathmandu valley; they were barred from going outside that region. Early visitors who followed were dumb-founded by the discovery of this most beautiful, magical city, which had no traffic, no billboards, no concrete and glass, no skyscrapers or tall buildings, no noise or chemical pollution and a city landscape hugely dominated by the most fantastic array of unspoiled temples and pagodas, intricately carved and surrounded by religious and regal sculptures and statues carved in stone and wood. It was, remarked one who came on Kathmandu in the late 1950s, like walking through the doors of an antique shop that had been closed for 200 years.

If the larger towns and cities had one foot in the nineteenth century, life in the outer regions was still anchored to medieval society and trundled slowly on just as it always had, unhurried and totally unaffected by attempts at modernisation in the cities. At that time, Nepal boasted just 124 miles (200 kilometres) of made-up roads, the equivalent of the journey from London to Bristol, serving the entire country. The harsh-ness of that existence was demonstrated by the mortality rate among children. It was among the worst in the world even in the 1960s, when one in three children did not survive and the life expectancy of adults was a mere twenty-nine; today it is around fifty-six. Ox carts were modern technology, but mostly the beast of burden in the hills was man himself and life continued at the pace at which he could walk.

Visitors began to increase, especially after the international publicity and acclaim achieved by Sir Edmund Hillary and Sherpa Tenzing after they had climbed Everest in 1953. But most surprisingly and unexpect-edly for the Nepalis, another extraordinary situation arose in the 1960s when the hippie trail opened up to the East and soon the sandal-clad, marijuana-smoking dropouts from society were arriving literally in their hundreds from around the world when they discovered the pace of life and the fact that drugs were free. They set up a tented enclave near the aptly named Freak Street on one of the three interlinked sections of the ancient and magnificent Durbar (government) Square in front of the temples and palaces that encircle it. From time to time they would go trekking off into the hills to get fresh supplies of the freely growing smokable plants that allowed them to float off into their drug-induced haze. Kathmandu was totally unprepared for the influx of both them and the modernisation programme that followed. Basic aids to modern living mushroomed with an alarming swiftness in the urban areas, although, as in India and elsewhere in the Far East, life goes on virtually unchanged in the more remote parts.

As one of the oldest cities in the world – and completely inexperienced in dealing with even 1960s pressures – Kathmandu is now tragically descending into a crisis, with its human population increasing across the country at the rate of around 600,000 people a year, which is expected to take the population to an estimated 34 million by 2020. To this must be added the onslaught of tourism, which in 1998 reached 280,000 visitors a year, not counting those coming across from India. It is impossible to predict how the environment, already stretched to the limit, will cope. There is simply no infrastructure and money to cope with this explosion of albeit very basic modernity. And even the basics are poor in Nepal.

The fifth of its population who receive electricity suffer regular power cuts. The country has few and erratic public services and transport, has no universal welfare or medical system, endures serious disruption from any extremes of weather and is regularly laid low by a seriously contaminated mains water system resulting from effluent pollution, waste, artificial fertilisers and poisonous lye and sewage from carpet factories. (Visitors beware! The water in Kathmandu and its surrounds is undrinkable: no ice, salads or cold foods or drinks made with or washed in unboiled water; put a shower cap over your face to avoid contact with eyes and mouth; clean your teeth in whisky from the mini-bar if it becomes the only safe bottled liquid available.)

Meanwhile, the populace chokes on the smog from waste gases from cement factories built in the Kathmandu valley by the Germans and which discharge seven tonnes of dust over the area every day of every year to join the dust from marble quarries and fumes from cheap petrol and diesel imported from India. The inhabitants of Kathmandu put up with the deafening noise of traffic and the droppings of scores of religiously protected cattle that wander the streets, and they cover their faces when passing mounds of rotting garbage in a country that has no tradition of garbage disposal. They also face a myriad of clashing odours (not all unpleasant), from sandalwood incense to heavily spiced cooking (lately including that from pizza parlours), all mingling with the combination of the refuse heaps and the aroma of burning human flesh and wood pyres wafting from the cremation ghats at the edge of the holy River Baghmati for the do-it-yourself disposal of the dearly departed, whose ashes are then swept into the river for onward transmission to heaven.

All that was missing in 1998 was the sickly sweet cloud of cannabis smoke that once hung over the vast hippie encampments on Durbar Square. They who turned local youngsters on to harder drugs were booted out of the country, and incoming visitors are controlled by the issue of visas and trekking or mountaineering passes to ensure that the hippies do not return and that the government continues to vet its visitors. In place of the hippie tents, a community of street traders populate the area around Freak Street selling their jade and silver and tin ware, and a vast array of touristy goods has arrived in Durbar Square. The area was for a while as pristine and spectacular as the pigeons and the pollution would allow.

The magnificent temples, sculptures and erotic sixteenth-century images were cleaned and surrounded by paving to accommodate the more culturally sensitive visitors who are these days attracted to Kathmandu. The temples, slightly tatty compared with those in Thailand, follow one after another in a hazy lesson in Nepalese history. The quickening pace of life and all the troubles that that has incurred are a serious disruption and were for a while dismissed by travel writers as part of the Kathmandu experience. It is true that in spite of the city's problems, the sights and sounds – even the smells – of Kathmandu and its neighbouring architectural attractions in Patan and Bkaktapur, now pedestrianised and clean, remain compelling. But Nepal is sliding inexorably towards an environmental catastrophe. International action will, for sure, be needed to rescue it, although some believe it is already too late.

Fortunately, the old city, though crowded, is excitingly walkable except during periods of torrential rains, as occurred on this author's first day in Kathmandu, when the streets turn to mini-rivers filled with unmentionable floating garbage that could seriously damage your health. The narrow streets are packed with shops and traders, and the city is fast becoming attuned to the fast buck of the future: the tourist trade in a backward, half-hearted sort of way:

'... *on to the rackety coach and I really don't know quite how to describe today. It was a shock. Not always pleasant. Parts of Kathmandu we drove through ... were gruesome but benign. It smells, but not often horribly. The coach parked and we walked along an earth track into a total cultural shock. Hawkers (and everyone audibly hawks and spits), exotic, tatty magnificent old buildings, a turgid river which looks totally life-threatening to our eyes but is a blessing to theirs . . . lepers, monkeys, skinny dogs, dozy cows secure in their holy status waiting at bus stops, saddhus with their legs wrapped round their necks, diminutive trainee saddhus with skinny legs wrapped round tiny necks, snakes, beggars, blossoms, strange smells and noises. We viewed funeral ghats, feeling voyeuristic but compelled, watched sons having their heads shaved in their mourning status; saw a young woman in some sort of emotional crisis fling herself into this filthy river for a ritualistic cleansing.*

Doe-eyed children tried to persuade us to buy their wares. A woman begging by the door of the coach with a snotty-nosed kid under her arm stepped back to pick up a dropped camera case and hand it back before she went back into her begging routine. Temples followed in a haze. We solemnly walked clockwise round a stupa. But we were doubly blessed today: in the Temple of the Living Goddess we glimpsed the living goddess herself, a mere child, and nearby we saw a lucky three-legged cow. The living goddess waved shyly before disappearing. The living goddess (Kumari) is in a no-win situation, since when she hits puberty she'll be out of a job and considered a bad bet for marriage . . .'

There is very little crime, yet, and beggars are neither in profusion nor persistent. Indeed tourist hassle is minute in Kathmandu compared with many cities around the world, such as Cairo or Rio de Janeiro, and the population is renowned for its traditional politeness. Visitors may, however, witness the random slaughter of buffaloes or goats on festivals in any one of the temple courtyards, which will be awash with blood and severed heads after the animals' ritual decapitation that must be performed with one blow from a purified blade. Until recently, the rituals were very much part of Gurkha tradition within the British army, and indeed are still conducted in certain places abroad, though not in Britain.

Religion permeates every facet of life in Nepal, with regular festivals of significance and daily rituals, family celebrations and religious observances, all of which must be upheld. Most were respected by the British as they began to take Gurkhas into their ranks, and this respect has been maintained to the present day, although not always understood. Although Nepal is famous as the world's only

Hindu kingdom, its complex and intricate religious tapestry is woven from Hinduism, Buddhism and other faiths dating back to the Middle Ages. The population itself is a mixture of ethnic groups and tribes, each from its own region of the country. The Gurkhas are largely from Mongolian stock, and because they adopt their tribal names as their surnames confusion reigned when they joined the British army. There were literally dozens with the same surname; when inexperienced officers demanded that a certain Rifleman Gurung stepped one pace forward, a quarter of the company would so. Their names also signify the region of Nepal from which they were recruited. The Gurungs, Thakurs, Puns, Tamangs and Magars from the west – who would be assigned to 'western' battalions – and the Rais, Limbus, Tamangs and Sunwars from the east, along with some Sherpas.

These are the names that have traditionally populated the record books of the British army – and a fact not always appreciated by even fans of the Gurkhas is that they originate from what J.P. Cross described as the 'martial classes' of Nepal. They could be recruited only from specific regions of the country. They are largely for export only: to India, the United Kingdom, Brunei and Singapore. The passion for recruitment into military service is confined to the hill men themselves. To those young men for whom life remains harsh and hard, joining the British army may be viewed as their greatest possible achievement, that they may be able to make something of themselves, see the world, earn enough money to educate their families and perhaps ultimately save enough to buy a house in a place where there may be electricity and running water.

The dream materialises for only a few . . .

CHAPTER TWO

Only 57,000 This Year

As we left Kathmandu and journeyed towards the Royal Gurkha Rifles Recruitment Centre at the foot of Annapurna, word that the galla wallahs were approaching had brought excitement to the hill villages. There was excitement, too, on our journey across country towards that destination. It was an unforgettable experience for anyone who has never previously sampled the somewhat experimental manner of roadmanship in Nepal. It may best be compared with, say, the scenario of a large number of Turkish taxi drivers learning to drive fully laden, heavy goods trucks on the Amalfi Coast in Italy, except that here the sheer drops over which only the brave will peer are much steeper and are approached at a pace verging on the ridiculous. There was no point in reducing speed, it was explained in clear Nepali logic, 'because there is a bend around every corner, and we would be slowing down all the time'.

The route took us on a scenic ride through the Kathmandu valley and on towards Pokhara, the westerly town of some note through its Gurkha connections and tourist-attracting surrounds. Cars *en route* were few, but the road was packed with gaily decorated lorries carrying every kind of merchandise, some performing the dual role of passenger vehicles, with large numbers of travellers either perched precariously on top or in any remaining space in the loaded area. Buses, some very ancient indeed, are the only form of public transport and, as in neighbouring India and Pakistan, were always overloaded, passengers hanging on for dear life for the sake of both themselves and their luggage, piled even higher, from the top and sides as they proceed

17

at breakneck speed along a road where the tarmac occasionally runs out, is interrupted by landslides (often), is temporarily blocked by a slow-moving goatherd and his charges or by wandering cattle, for which everything stops. The drivers show no fear and seem to have worked out some form of coded signalling system with their hooters, operated by both the man at the wheel and his assistant, who hangs out of the passenger door. As far as I could make out, three quick blasts from the assistant was meant to signal to the oncoming vehicle that if he moved over about an inch and a quarter (32 millimetres), we would both be able to get through without reducing our speed. One long blast from the driver indicated that we were coming through anyhow, all of which was conducted with the two vehicles approaching each other at a combined speed of around 100 miles (160 kilometres) an hour and, more often than not, on a hairpin bend.

Gordon Corrigan assured us that we were quite safe because we were being driven by an ex-Gurkha soldier who could be trusted entirely to bring us to our destination. However, readers of one of the Gurkha regimental magazines published not many weeks earlier may well have remembered his own descriptions of experience with Gurkha drivers:

> More senior readers of this journal will recall the days when we considered that Gurkha Service Pay – now abolished – was to compensate for the wear and tear on nerves due to being driven by Gurkhas. We all recall the story of the Gurkha driver in Singapore who was told by a staff officer untutored in Mongolian ways to go straight on at the next roundabout. He did exactly that, and for the rest of the day sightseers marvelled at the Land Rover perched on top of the flowerbed which graced the centre of the said roundabout.

When reminded of this story, Gordon Corrigan assured the enquirer that things had changed enormously and that the 28th Squadron, the Gurkha Transport Regiment, had the best traffic record of any unit in Bosnia in 1996! He himself, conditioned by years of 'sheer terror when being driven by an ever-smiling but suicidal Gurkha driver', eventually accepted they were much improved, as evidenced by the fact that many Gurkhas could be seen learning to drive civilian cars on the roads around Church Crookham, impeccably dressed in regimental mufti, gripping the wheel as if it were a Chinese illegal immigrant liable to escape at any moment. 'It did, however, force a number of British officers to take the cross-country route when travelling from office to home as a Gurkha learner driver trying to sit to attention when passing an officer is not necessarily conducive to safety on the Queen's highway,' Corrigan confessed.

We made it in one piece to the recruitment centre at Pokhara; it was vacant, waiting for the galla wallahs to lead the new recruits in from the hills. Lieutenant Colonel R.H. Coleman, formerly in Hong Kong until the long-standing Gurkha base there closed on the handover to China, was in charge of this military oasis built at the time when the country began to open up and formal recruitment of hill men from British posts inside the country became the norm.

Two key centres were built, one in Pakhlihawa and the other in the far east of the country at Dharan. The western centre was moved to Pokhara in the late 1970s, selected for its location at the base of the foothills of the Jomsom and Annapurna ranges and thus the nearest assembly point to the hill men in that region. Butting on the Lake Phewa, Pokhara has noticeably cleaner air than Kathmandu and a generally pleasant climate, although the monsoon rains are much heavier here. The town itself is in a valley set against the stunning backdrop of peaks ranging between 23,000 and 26,000 feet (7,010 and 7,925 metres) whose appearance from behind the clouds at dawn is a photographer's dream. Among the peaks visible from Pokhara are Dhaulagiri, Mansalu and Himalchuli as well as the 35-mile-long (56-kilometre-long) Annapurna massif with its 16 summits over 19,600 feet (5,974 metres). Pokhara is also easily accessible in comparison with other parts of Nepal, lying on the old trade route between India and Tibet, a route that remained open until the Chinese invasion of Tibet in 1959.

In the three years that followed the invasion, 30,000 refugees crossed the border into Nepal, and a refugee camp set up at Pokhara subsequently spawned three Tibetan settlements that were quite different from traditional Nepali villages. Today, the refugee population is fully integrated into the community and has formed its own industry in carpet-weaving and general trade. Meanwhile, the opening up of the trade route to tourism in 1962 began an ever-increasing invasion of

19

visitors to the area which has brought prosperity and rampant commercialisation to what was once a sleepy valley. Building went on apace without any semblance of planning. The building of an airport, a bus terminus and a lakeside complex specifically aimed at tourism followed. The magnificent Lake Phewa, once crystal clear, is becoming stale and polluted. A recent study showed that it may be totally silted up within the lifetime of some of the present residents around it.

The British Gurkha post at Pokhara, with all its excellent accommodation, sports facilities and proximity to excellent trekking terrain, became a popular centre for visitors from the British army in general. Today it receives potential recruits from both eastern and western Nepal, forwarded on by the galla wallahs during their autumn tour of the hills. The galla wallahs are a throwback to the system of recruiting that existed prior to 1951. Until that time, no member of the British army was officially allowed on Nepali soil for the purpose of recruitment, and since 1816 the rounding up of volunteers had been in the hands of local recruiters, who gathered them together, put them through their paces, made an initial selection from among them and marched the successful ones down from the hills, across country and over the border into India.

Outside wartime, Britain had been selecting, at its peak, up to 2,000 or more men every year. By the late 1990s this had been drastically reduced, but the system that was set up so many years earlier had barely changed. The Brigade of Gurkhas makes its search for soldiers just once a year, in one fell swoop. In 1995 the intake was quite low because those selected would become operational only a few months prior to the closure of the long-standing Gurkha base in the New Territories, Hong Kong, which would result in a further contraction of Gurkha manpower and a large number of redundancies.

As a result, a mere 153 recruits were to be enlisted that year and 160 the following year. Even so, this did not stop the hill boys from pressing forth in their thousands to attempt to get in or anxious fathers and grandfathers using all kinds of ploys to ensure that their boys were seen and viewed favourably. The selection process passes through three distinct phases to whittle down the numbers to the Ministry of Defence quota. Each stage is set up as a kind of quality control filter so that only the very best of those who apply are actually brought to the next stage. The first filter is performed by the galla wallahs themselves. They carry out an initial inspection of volunteers in the immediate area in which they work, each seeing around 3,000 young men. Many of the volunteers will have walked for two or three days to meet the galla wallahs, usually with no money or food and only the clothes they stand up in.

Others are seen on the galla wallahs' tour programme, which is known well in advance. For the 1995 intake, the local recruiters saw 57,000 candidates. Of those, a mere 7,000 passed through to the next filter, called 'hill selection', in which predetermined procedures are set up to provide fairly cursory tests for medical condition, general levels of fitness, physical ability, education and IQ. They are given a number, which is marked in indelible pen on their chest so that they cannot be switched with another less able candidate.

Marks are awarded for the hill selection tests, and the top ten per cent are finally sent forward for the final phase of the filtering system. To use the 1995 figures as an example, there remained 700 in with a chance from the original 57,000 applicants, and these would now be marched down from the hills to the road and transported to the Brigade of Gurkhas' post in Pokhara to begin the central selection procedure – the final filter that will provide the 153 new recruits.

There, they begin an intensive pre-selection programme that includes for each of them a nerve-racking one-to-one interview with a British officer at the post, at which one of the first tasks is to establish the true age of the applicant; it is widely known from past experience that many young recruits have provided false evidence of their age and thus joined the British army well before the minimum age. It was an ever-present problem and has been since the Gurkhas began, as Gordon Corrigan explained:

One lad last year [1997] got in on his fifth attempt. I reckon he was 18 when he came to me, so you can judge that he was about 13 when he first tried. I reckon, overall, at least 20 per cent of our potential recruits were under age, some of them seriously, and quite a few got in. You can tell if a lad is under age by one or two physical signs, such as sticking-out ears. I would ask them their age, and naturally they would say 18. I would immediately ask what was their date of birth, and they would quote a date in the English calendar, obviously rehearsed. Then I would ask what was the date in the Nepali calendar, and you could see the little mind working furiously. No one had told him that I might ask that. The youngest I ever came across had already passed the selection and I had serious doubts about his age, but he had apparently produced documents. That, of course, was not difficult. When they turn up at the local office for the identity forms, they never had to produce anything that showed their true age; most of them could not anyhow. I saw him later but then he knew he could trust me; I asked him to be honest and tell me his true age. It turned out he was a month short of 15 when he was accepted, so in real terms was 14. I suppose I ought to have owned up to the regiment, but I took the view that he had passed selection, he had done well and, regardless of his age, had done everything we had asked of him. The fact is, there is no such thing as an immature Gurkha. When they are 10 years old, younger even, they are sent off up to the high lands at about 13,000 feet [3,962 kilometres] with all the sheep and the cattle and they will be up there for months on their own. They've always done it, and fending for themselves like that is a great tutor of independence of mind and spirit.

Vigorous physical tests follow which, if applied with such precision and determination in the recruitment of soldiers throughout the rest of the British army, would undoubtedly cut recruitment levels even more than they are already. For example, the minimum physical standards for Gurkha recruits is:

- 13 heaves to the bar, compared with 2–8, depending on choice of arm for British soldiers;
- 25 sit-ups in 1 minute and continue until unable to complete any more; one Gurkha completed 420. The British requirement is 25 in 1 minute;
- run 1½ miles (2.4 kilometres) in 14 minutes, followed immediately by a further 1½ miles (2.4 kilometres) in under 10 minutes. No equivalent test elsewhere in the British army;
- run up and down an 1800-foot (549-metre) steep hill carrying 75 pounds (34 kilogrammes) on the back, 1½ miles (2.4 kilometres) in distance in under 35 minutes. No British equivalent.

Candidates must also complete an obstacle course and carry out individual and team command tasks. The brigade's policy has remained unchanged for years and is designed to ensure that it gets the very best men who possess the traditional martial qualities. The final selection is not made lightly. The recruits who had performed best through the aptitude, stamina and mental tests invariably stood out and there was little doubt that among them would be Gurkha officer material. The last places to be filled were usually the most difficult, since they were generally those at the lower end of the results table who might never make more than lance corporal. They were an equally important bunch. Although thousands have already been disappointed by rejection, the moment of true heartbreak arrives for those who had reached this far but were now to be discarded. It was perhaps the hardest part of the British officers' job at Pokhara. None was to be told reasons for rejection, other than on medical grounds, and all would be given the hope that they may apply again the following year. In fact, some were already on their second or third rejection. Others clearly had the potential but had failed simply because they were, as yet, underdeveloped or underweight. It was always more difficult, however, to have to explain other flaws that the interviewing officer had noticed or had relied on some gut feeling that this lad wouldn't do. And so, as a general rule, reasons were never given.

When the decisions were announced, most accepted rejection with a brave face. Some could not help the tears; others – whose family may well have been relying on his acceptance for a variety of reasons, such as tradition, good face or their own wellbeing – may have been so disappointed and ashamed that they felt they could not return to their homes. Many have been known to commit suicide on the way back, and a couple of bridges that became popular locations for such drastic recourse were eventually harnessed with a wire-netting safety frame.

The rest, having beaten odds of around 300 to 1 to get accepted, are deliriously happy. As their friends who did not make it prepare to leave and return home with the modest allowance they receive for their trouble, those who stay divest themselves of most of their personal possessions and hand them to the unsuccessful youngsters as some sort of consolation. The new recruits are then enlisted and formally begin their 42-week training course, for which they will now be flown to the United Kingdom – an adventure in itself, with most of these men never having been in a motor vehicle, let alone an aircraft. The greatest adventure of all, and their chief ambition, is to be sent to the United Kingdom.

Although the core 22-week training syllabus was virtually the same as for regular British army recruits, the add-on packages were designed specifically for the Gurkhas and, apart from the fairly basic administrative and linguistic differences, the psyche and ethos of British and Gurkha soldiers could be – at that stage at least – miles apart. As Gordon Corrigan explained:

> The average British recruit usually hails from urban, welfare-orientated society where there is natural distrust of authority. He will often come from what British society would consider to be a deprived background – single-parent families, unemployment, experimentation with drugs and a casual attitude towards property. He will see the army as one option among many and not necessarily as a lifetime career. Leaving the army, or the premature termination of service in it, does not spell disaster or disgrace. Concepts such as honour, family name and reputation are not primary motivating factors. The Gurkha, on the other hand, comes from a society where family and clan ties are close and very strong. Most Gurkhas have a background that engenders natural independence of mind. His basic animist and shamanist religious beliefs breed a natural fatalism and an acceptance of hardship which is far stronger than any Western concept of individual rights. While he could probably not describe himself as such, the Gurkha sees himself as a freeborn volunteer, beholden to no one, to whom a military career is a way of life which he wishes to pursue as successfully and for as long as he possibly can. The British army aims to take this free spirit and mould him into a soldier – without breaking that spirit.

In November 1994 Prince Charles took the salute at the final recruits' passing-out parade in Hong Kong. The following month the depot was closed and moved *en masse* to Queen Elizabeth Barracks, Church Crookham, where it became known as the Gurkha Training Wing. The 1995 intake of recruits became the first to be trained in the UK, leaving Kathmandu in four parties in February on Royal Nepal Airlines charter flights to London Gatwick. Its training regime has always been tougher than that of British regiments, and the theme was continued with the move to the UK. Apart from the general aspects of preparing for military life, Gurkha recruit training will include instruction in aspects of everyday life in England which are totally alien to many of the Gurkhas who have been taken off the hills for the first time in their lives and have never experienced the wonders of modern living – let alone in an English town. To date, they will have been brought from their villages to the Gurkha post at Pokhara, driven to Kathmandu airport, flown to Gatwick and delivered to Queen Elizabeth Barracks. Outside barrack life, the adventure now began to take on a whole new set of learnings – all drawn up in exercise form with military precision in such basics as crossing the road and understanding that he can place a letter in a little red box and expect to have it delivered the following day, a magical happening!

Their introduction to British life is tenuously begun walking the streets of towns and countryside around the barracks – a sight now familiar to those who live in the area. Their first excursion into this brave new world is in groups led by a section commander to the towns of Fleet, Farnham, Farnborough and Aldershot. Over a period of several days, they discover the complications of zebra crossings, traffic lights, public transport, public telephones, the post office and so on. The next stage will be a tour of larger towns in groups of four without a leader from the permanent staff. When these manoeuvres have been completed successfully without mishap, an 'urban orienteering exercise' is begun. The trainee Gurkhas now set off in pairs to visit London, negotiate trains and the Underground, which has been known to put the fear of God into even some of the toughest recruits. Misunderstandings are not uncommon. One recruit from a particularly remote part of the Himalayas was confronted by a middle-aged lady dressed in twinset and pearls waving a tin emblazoned with the letters RSPCA. He duly put a coin in the tin and later reported back to his platoon commander that in England the beggars are most respectable and very well dressed.

In most other aspects, the removal of the young Gurkhas from their natural habitat halfway up the Himalayas into hi-tech society is achieved with rather less aggravation for the recruits than in the days when they were trained in Hong Kong, where their natural politeness tended to be viewed as a form of weakness by the Chinese. With their training now complete, the Gurkha soldiers will make their preferences for the future pattern of their career known. Some quite often want to follow in the footsteps of their fathers, even if it means a career as a clerk. The Officer Commanding GTW will make the final decision as to where each man is to go, a decision taken late in the course when aptitude, education and newly learned skills can be properly assessed. And now their career begins . . . a minimum of 15 years for a private, and often 25 years or more for officers, at the end of which they must be taken back to the spot exactly from where they came in Nepal.

CHAPTER THREE

In the Place Where It All Began

The small town of Gorkha is an important stopover on the journey into Gurkha military history and is to be found 12 miles (19 kilometres) north of the Kathmandu to Pokhara road. It is in a high place, and the drive up to the Gorkha Hill Resort, a small hotel surrounded by Annapurna vistas, was challenging and at times worrying. The passengers applauded when the coach finally quivered to a halt. Gorkha is historical in both its location and origins, reaching as it does towards the clouds with a collection of architecture that befits its status as the former seat of the Shah dynasty, creators of modern Nepal and of the Gurkha tradition.

It is one of the last townships approachable by this road (thereafter the journey to the hill villages must be on foot) and the Brigade of Gurkhas has built one of its Area Welfare Centres there, a club-like building for ex-Gurkhas to meet and where they may collect their British army pensions. Among those on hand to greet the arrival of the travellers was Havildar Bhanbhagta Gurung, holder of the Victoria Cross awarded for his outstanding acts of bravery against the Japanese in Burma in 1945 (about which more will be told later). He lives close by; others face a long trek down from the hills to collect their money. Transferring it through banks is not yet the solution. Few possess bank accounts, and anyhow Gorkha is hardly equipped for the age of electronic monetary transfers. When I stopped off to change currency the teller had to send out for a local newspaper (two days old) to discover the current rate of exchange.

The importance of this town, however, cannot be understated. It possesses a great monument to Nepali and Gurkha heritage: the Gorkha Durbar, a palace and fort which is a shrine of shrines in the context of this story. From the base of it, the hill astride which the fortress is perched like a giant eagle's nest does not look much of a climb. It was built with strategic genius in the late seventeenth century as the kings and the generals of the House of Gorkha planned their expansion across the country and beyond. We set off towards it at a pace that proved to be far too rapid for the unfit and inexperienced like myself, quickly overtaking a moving giant haystack which I'd espied ahead and which in fact hides a wizened little man who is carrying a huge pile of animal fodder, probably weighing a hundredweight (50 kilogrammes) or so on his back. His daughter is at his side, a delicate-looking child aged about six or seven. She has a canvas strap around her forehead attached, on her back, to a wicker basket in which she carries a very large and very heavy metal pitcher filled with water from the tap in the village below. Such sights are not uncommon.

The way up this hill, which after an initial gentle slope becomes steeper and steeper at each step, is by a well-maintained footpath of steps, initially in concrete and then hewn out of the rock. At various stages it leads off to settlements built on ridges on its side. It may look an easy climb, but it isn't: only later I learned that these steps are, in total, the equivalent of climbing to the top of the Eiffel Tower *twice*. Eventually, I am overtaken by the giant haystack and the girl with the pitcher of water, who have continued climbing at one pace throughout and made it to their destination far quicker than I. When finally I reached the top, a mere 4,800 feet (1,463 metres) above sea-level, breathless and steaming, Major Corrigan was already there, leaning against the battlements casually smoking a cigarette, taking in the magnificent view, dressed in check shirt with sleeves rolled to the elbows, well-pressed cavalry twill trousers and brown suede shoes, and preparing a short discourse on the history of this place. The view merely adds to the breathlessness. It is easy to see why the Gorkha kings selected the site for their fortress. Apart from the impenetrable security of it, there directly to the north are the peaks of the High Himalayas, with the superb sight of the Manaslu at 26,768 feet (8,159 metres) flanked by Ganesh Himal in the east and Dhauligiri in the west. Thus, the Gorkha Durbar fortress was pretty well unassailable when it was built, although today it is more easily reached by helicopter, and the King of Nepal had his own helipad built on the side of the hill for his visits to the palace for the festivals, religious celebrations and sacrificial offerings held there.

It is to this day a substantial and beautiful collection of interlinked buildings surrounded by high walls that enclose both temple and residential quarters. The entrance is patrolled by two stern-looking guards who are on hand to ensure total observation of the rules concerning this most holy of places – that there may be no photographs taken and all items of leather (shoes, belts, camera cases, etc.) must be left outside the perimeter walls. They also steadfastly refuse entry to one part of the building, a temple, which remains completely off limits to visitors.

This temple is maintained by members of a particular Brahmin caste and only they and the ruling monarch are allowed inside. It is said that ordinary mortals will die a horrible death if they set eyes on the religious symbol inside the temple. The Brahmins sacrifice animals at the entrance to the temple, and there had been a major sacrificial event not long before we arrived, as was very evident from the bloodstains. It was for the Dasain festival in September, the most important in Nepal's calendar of celebrations, marking the victory of the goddess Durga over the Wicked One. The festival lasts for between 10 and 15 days, and altars are erected in every house. For this festival, attended by the king, 108 buffalo and 84 goats are driven up the hillside each year (spares are included because invariably some of the animals fall over the side) for a ritual slaughter which begins at midnight on the eighth day.

Each animal must be killed with a single blow from a purified kukri knife, or ceremonial blade. The higher the blood spurts, the more blessings the sacrifice is thought to produce; flagstones are awash with blood, and the stench of it fills the air still. The sacrificial offerings are widely performed in ceremonies across Nepal.

The most famous of kings in the House of Gorkha, Prithvi Narayan Shah, was born in this fortress, and this is where the Gurkha and all its historical connections with the British army truly began, high in that eyrie. Prithvi Narayan was to become an outstanding figure in the history of Nepal, the man who joined all the pieces of diverse kingdoms together. The Gorkha expansion had been proceeding slowly but surely under his father's reign, but at an early age Prithvi Narayan apparently dedicated himself to planning a swift conquest of the Kathmandu valley and beyond to create a single state under his control. He travelled widely to seek a personal view of the world and to buy weapons to further his ambitions when the time came. He bought modern weapons in India and studied the positions of the British Honourable East India Company whose troops he may yet have to engage.

On his return to Gorkha, he built a number of arsenals in the hills and recruited and trained his troops to use modern weapons. He spent a full 26 years planning his military strategy before he succeeded his father in 1742 and finally launched his savage and barbarous campaigns, using the fortress as his base. He conquered many regions of Nepal, capturing the trade routes running between India and Tibet, and in doing so unified the nation.

There remains, however, a curiosity in the history of the land of Nepal that has not yet entirely been resolved as we enter the twenty-first century – that of its name. Nepal existed as a small kingdom for more than 1,500 years, yet modern-day Nepal began its evolution as a nation only with the rise of the House of Gorkha. Nepali historian Chandra Bahadur Gurung tells us in his 1998 book *British Medals and Gurkhas*: 'Even today, many hill people do not realise that Nepal is the name of their country . . . Their perception is that it is a small valley somewhere in the central part of the Gorkha Raj where the king resides.'

Those hill people who have had the benefit of modern history books which bring the story up to date may be excused this confusion because in a way they are not far off the mark. Nepal was a tiny kingdom in the Kathmandu valley until it was swallowed up by the Gorkhas led by Prithvi Narayan, a modestly built but ferocious fighter in silk pants who recruited his warriors – the equivalent of modern-day Gurkha soldiers – from the surrounding hills. He quickly took possession of most of the other kingdoms in sight, including the three principal royal houses located in the valley of Kathmandu. His army of Gorkhas – or Gurkhas, as they were later known – became notorious, feared throughout the country and renowned for their military prowess, their courage, their brutality and their religious fervour. Many regions just gave up in the face of their onslaught; others stood and fought – and usually ended up much the worse for it.

It took Prithvi Narayan three attempts to coerce the King of Patan into an alliance, by laying siege to the town of Kirtipur. During the fighting, Prithvi Narayan Shah's brother was killed, and when his troops failed to take the town he withdrew and set up a blockade of the entire valley, closing off all trade routes and executing blockade runners. The second siege of Kirtipur was again unsuccessful, and the Gorkha army went away to attack another region, only to reappear at Kirtipur a few months later. After another siege lasting six months, Prithvi Narayan sent in a message guaranteeing the safety of the town if they surrendered peacefully. When they did so, he ordered his Gurkhas to slice off the noses and lips of all males over the age of 12 – a punishment normally reserved for adulterous women – in revenge for the killing of his brother. A total of 865 noses were severed and, put together, they weighed more than 80 pounds (36 kilogrammes). Only the players of wind instruments were spared mutilation so that they could provide welcoming music for the march past of his victorious army.

The Gorkhas moved on to Patan in 1767, but their attention was diverted by the arrival of a 2,400-man expeditionary force sent by the British East India Company to aid the kings of the Kathmandu valley, their clients. *En route*, however, the British column was badly hit by malaria after its journey through the swamps of the lowlands, called the 'terai', and had to withdraw, leaving the Gorkhas to complete their mission. On 29 September 1768 Gorkha troops crept into Kathmandu while the population was celebrating a religious festival and took the town without a fight. Prithvi Narayan Shah was crowned king and for the first time, a hill ruler, the Rajah of Gorkha, had become sole ruler in the Kathmandu valley. His first act in 1769 was to expel all foreigners from the territory he held, including traders, agents for the East India Company, Roman Catholic missionaries and even musicians or artists influenced by northern India's style.

The conquest of the three kingdoms was the start of the expansion of Gorkha control that eventually spread throughout the Himalayan region. The death of Prithvi Narayan Shah in 1775 stalled the Gorkha expansion, but it was soon resumed by his successors, and by 1790 their army had moved east, west and northwards towards Tibet. The Chinese, alarmed at the Gorkhas' progression and their possession of vital trading routes, dispatched a very large army from Beijing and forced the invaders out of Tibet, pursuing them to within 28 miles (45 kilometres) of Kathmandu. The Nepalese were humiliated and forced to sign a treaty with the Chinese, surrender their trading routes and pay tributes to the Beijing government which continued until 1908.

Subdued by the Chinese, the Gorkha generals now cast their eyes north-westwards towards princely states on the outer rim of India, laying siege to Kangra until 1809, only to be rebuffed by the army of the Sikh state in the Punjab. It was a move that brought them into direct conflict with the British East India Company. The most important of the various East India companies established by European nations, the original charter was granted by Queen Elizabeth I on 31 December 1600. In 1657 Cromwell ordered it to be reorganised as the sole joint-stock company with rights to the Indian trade. Charles II granted the company sovereign rights in addition to its trading privileges. Thereafter, the charter was renewed several times in the eighteenth century, each time with financial concessions to the Crown. The victories of Robert Clive, a company official, over the French at Arcot in 1751 and at Plassey in 1757 made the company the dominant power in India.

The company's annexation of territories had pushed its influence all the way to the Punjab; the East India Company and the Gorkhas were on a collision course. The largely uncharted boundaries of company territory in the region had long been a cause for concern in London. Gorkha generals, aware of this lack of definition, snatched towns and villages in regions that might be disputed. In spite of some frenzied diplomatic activity between the company and the Nepalese troops, confrontation eventually became inevitable as the aggressive Gorkhas upset the company's clients in the hills and sent troops to help police the area. An attack by the Gorkha army on 22 April 1814 killed 18 police officers at an outpost in Butawal, and thus the minuscule state of Nepal was at war with Britain.

The Court of Directors in London, made up of East India Company and Crown representatives, called for a report and an assessment of the situation. Their intelligence sources in Nepal had noted that the Gorkhas had built a substantial munitions industry in the hills and had established exceedingly efficient supply columns using forced labour. Their soldiers, the company was informed, were well known for their speed of movement and their willingness to fight to the death under the most extreme conditions. They also had an intricate knowledge of the terrain, far better than that of British troops who had never been called into service in that area. The company's military advisers estimated that the Gorkhas could field an army of around 15,000 troops but had a very large reservoir of additional men who could be called up in support.

The company was reluctant to take on such a skilful and clearly successful army, which had required the might of a vast force of Chinese to chase it out of Tibet. However, the Gorkha generals refused to be turned by diplomatic threats, and on 16 November 1814 Lord Moira (later the Marquess of Hastings), Governor-General of Bengal, was authorised to declare that the British Empire was at war with the aggressive little state of Nepal, by then under the command of its fire-eating Prime Minister Maharajah Bhim Sen Thapa. Unlike Prithvi Narayan, he did not fully appreciate the power of the East India Company or the might of its armies. He believed that the British would never penetrate Nepal's hills, which 'are formed by the hand of God and are impregnable'. He was not far off the mark, at least in the early stages of the campaign. The British generals, moving towards what was the first ever campaign in the hill regions, planned to make their attack on the Gorkhas on two fronts so as to force their enemy into a wide spread of manpower. Four columns totalling 22,000 men were sent into the attack, two on the east and two on the west for the first of a series of invasions into the hills of northern India, with the intention of moving on into Nepal and eventually marching on Kathmandu itself. The eastern force, confronted by very difficult terrain and run by two generals inexperienced in hill warfare, failed in every one of its objectives, and the first campaign all but collapsed. A third British general, the ageing but gallant Rollo Gillespie, left his encampment at Meerut, 70 miles (112 kilometres) from Delhi, and headed towards the Nepali border with 4,000 men and 20 guns.

His force captured Dehra Dun but was then halted for almost six weeks by Gorkha resistance run from a small, isolated fort at Kalunga. It was a typical Gorkha garrison, built on a hill 500 feet (152 metres) high and surrounded by dense undergrowth and a palisade of rough-hewn logs and rocks piled 12 feet (3.6 metres) high. It held a mere 600 men and women, mostly Magars and Gurungs, who stood on its walls watching Gillespie's men approaching. Gillespie had them surrounded and was sure that because they were so heavily outnumbered they would come to terms and give up. He sent a message to that effect and expected a positive reply. Instead, his opposite number in the fortress tore up his letter and in the next few days threw back repeated attacks by the British, which moved one of Gillespie's officers, James Baillie Fraser, to record: 'They fought us in fair conflict like men, and in the intervals of actual combat, showed us a courtesy worthy of a more enlightened people.' Another, John Ship, who was at the time an ensign in the 87th Foot, wrote in his memoirs: 'I never saw more steadiness or bravery exhibited in my life. Run they would not and of death they seemed to have no fear, though their comrades were falling thick around them, for we were so near that every shot told.' In the middle of the battle a curious sight brought the British bombardment to a halt. A Gorkha soldier clambered over the ramparts and, waving his arms, approached the British lines.

The British, expecting a surrender, ordered an immediate cease-fire to allow the soldier to approach. As he neared them, he pointed to his face; his jaw had been shattered by a musket ball and he was clearly pleading for medical assistance. A surgeon was summoned and gave him immediate treatment. And now a surrender? No, no, said the soldier. He intended to return to the fort. The British laughed at his gall and let him go back. Once safely over the side, the British resumed their pounding of the fort.

Impatient for success and angered that he had been held up by such a tiny force, ill-equipped and with few supplies, General Gillespie decided to lead a full-frontal attack at the head of his own regiment, the Royal Irish Dragoons. He was shot down 30 yards (27 metres) from the palisade and died in the arms of his aide, Lieutenant Frederick Young. The standoff remained for a month or more. Every British attack on the fort was repulsed. When a breach in the palisade was achieved, the Gorkhas and their women assailed the British with every kind of missile available, until, out of food, water and ammunition, the fort finally gave way to British attacks.

There was never a surrender, though. As the Gorkha position became desperate, the 85 able-bodied men still standing escaped under cover of darkness. When the British finally entered, they found incredible sights of wounded men and a few women and children. The battle of the Kalunga fort had been ferocious and, in spite of the

Gorkha defeat, it was the British who suffered the heaviest casualties, losing 31 officers and 732 other ranks against the Gorkha losses of 520. Although the fort was won, it could hardly be called a victory; more of a draw, as was demonstrated a few years later: two white obelisks were eventually erected side by side on a hill at Kalunga, now to be called Nalapini; one was a memorial to General Gillespie and those of the British regiments who fell with him, and the other was in memory of the 'gallant adversary'.

General David Ochterlony, a highly efficient commander who knew the landscape and the tenacity of his enemy, fared rather better. His column outflanked the Nepalese in the west and sent the army of General Amar Sing Thapa, of around 3,000 troops, into retreat. This one major victory did nothing to dampen the Nepalese spirit, and the British made another concerted campaign later in the year which met with similar inconclusive results. Clearly, they needed more firepower if they were to dislodge the Gorkhas. This time, the Court of Directors gave approval for the movement of 35,000 men and 120 artillery pieces under General Ochterlony for a thrust towards Makwanpur in the Nepalese lowlands and then on to take possession of the Kathmandu valley. Meanwhile, the King of Sikkim, whose country had been overrun by the Gorkha armies four years earlier, used the opportunity to hit back in the east.

Ochterlony had 14,000 regulars and 83 guns under his direct control. He defeated the Gurkha General Amar Sing Thapa at Jaithak, but such was the British admiration for their adversary that after his surrender Amar Sing was permitted to march out with all his arms and all his personal property. Overstretched and once again heavily outnumbered, the Nepalese forces were heading for defeat across the board and were forced to seek a settlement before being totally overrun. Diplomats agreed a peace treaty that reached Ochterlony on 5 March 1816 signalling a cessation of hostilities. Nepal was forced to withdraw from Sikkim, and from the territories west of the Kali River and most of its lands in the terai. The British East India Company was to pay 200,000 rupees annually to Nepal to make up for the loss of revenues from the terai. Kathmandu was also forced to accept a British resident of the East India Company, which its government hated.

The expansion of the House of Gorkha was at an end, and, worse, it was confined to new boundaries that still exist today. For the Gorkhas, it was merely a new beginning. The British were so impressed by their fighting prowess that even before the Anglo-Nepali War was brought to a formal conclusion, a number of officers – including General Ochterlony himself – had suggested that the Gorkha hill men should be recruited for new battalions made up entirely from their numbers. One of them wrote in 1815: 'They are hardy, cheerful and endure privations and are very obedient, have not much of the distinction of caste, and are a neutral kind of Hindoo, eating in messes almost everything they meet with, except beef. Under our government they would make excellent soldiers.' And so an important and highly unusual clause was included in the peace agreement, known as the Treaty of Segauli after the place in which it was signed. The clause gave the British army the right to recruit Nepalese subjects.

Even before the significance of the clause became generally known, the British army was already recruiting men from the defeated Gorkha troops. Among those most seriously promoting this proposition was 30-year-old Lieutenant Frederick Young of the 13th Native Infantry, and if there were any man deserving of the title of founding father of the fighting force within the British army that would become universally known as the Gurkhas, it is he. Young had been at the battle of Kalunga as aide-de-camp to General Gillespie, who died in the young lieutenant's arms after taking a shot to the chest. Later, Young was allowed to form his own original corps from irregular levies, hill men recruited from Garhwal, Kumaon and elsewhere in India. But they were not Gorkha hill men, and they ran away on their first confrontation with the Nepalese army. Young himself refused to run and was taken prisoner. His captors surrounded him and, grinning, wanted to know exactly why he had not taken flight with the rest.

Young told them that he was a British officer, commissioned by the Honourable East India Company in 1800 when he was just 15, and he did not come all this way simply to run off at the first sight of the enemy. The Gorkhas liked his style. Although a prisoner, Lieutenant Young became friends with his captors, and he, too, noted their cheerfulness and made a study, as best he could, of their customs. Young was eventually freed at the time of the peace treaty, unharmed, well fed and with a number of new friends. He also pressed to be allowed to recruit his former enemy into the British army, and a month later, on 24 April 1816, he received authorisation to form the first battalion of Gorkha recruits taken from prisoner-of-war camps.

He rode to the site and put the word about that he was seeking volunteers to join the British army; 3,000 men came forward. Young made his selection and formed what was to become the first battalion of Gurkhas at Sirmoor, near Dehra Dun, which also became a famous regimental centre for later Gurkha battalions. Lieutenant Young became the first commandant of what was first called the Sirmoor Battalion, later the Sirmoor Rifles and finally the 2nd King Edward VII's Own Gurkha Rifles, which was to remain in service for the next 165 years – until 'Options for Change' forced its closure.

Other battalions followed, each with eight companies each of about a hundred and twenty men commanded by British officers: two, called the Nasiri (meaning 'friendly') Battalions, were raised at Subathu and were later amalgamated to form what became the 1st Gurkha Rifles (later the 1st King George V's Own Gurkha Rifles). Another, the Kumaon Battalion, raised at Almora, became the 3rd Gurkha Rifles (and later the 3rd Queen Alexandra's Own Gurkha Rifles). Seldom, if ever, in the history of warfare have two sides been so impressed by the other's performance that they could not wait to merge. As for Lieutenant Young, he remained with his Gurkhas for the next 28 years of his life, as commandant of the Sirmoor Rifles. This recognition of the fighting qualities of the Gurkhas and the regard in which they were held by the British officers in general was soon to be firmly cemented in the annals of British military history in India which for so long dominated the progression of the British Empire, its wealth and trading fortunes . . . all emanating originally from this little town named Gorkha and its former rulers.

CHAPTER FOUR

The Pact

As the army of the Honourable East India Company introduced a recruitment campaign, the trek of hill men from the Himalayan foothills of Nepal, across country into India, began in earnest to fill five single-battalion Gurkha regiments. From these beginnings a Gurkha brigade was formed which, only later, would history come to view as being part of the blunt instrument of suppression in the subcontinent by the British colonialists. Although the company now had official permission to recruit volunteers, doing so was not easily achieved. No British representative of the East India Company or any officer of the British army was allowed to enter Nepal for the purpose of recruitment, or for any other reason for that matter without invitation. King Prithvi Narayan's view of the British held sway for years on end: 'First the Bible, then the trading station, then the cannon.' Missionaries, traders and soldiers were all kept beyond the frontiers. News that the British were recruiting travelled by word of mouth, and then through the teams of recruiters sent to the Indian border towns. Each battalion was responsible for finding and training its own recruits and handed the task to the Gurkhas themselves – the forerunners of modern-day galla wallahs. They would be sent on long expeditions into the hills to gather up young men to serve in the British army in India. The battalions also dispatched teams of men to roam the Indian border towns to entice the young hill men who came to the plains of India as porters. Usually drink was offered, although many of the young men needed no such persuasion.

Our own 1998 expedition into those same hills would find that surprisingly little had changed. Civilisation had arrived in modest form, and even in the late twentieth century the party of travellers from Britain, surrounded by their minders and porters, was viewed with astonishment by youngsters and some female villagers who had never been down from the hills to the major towns. Maureen Silver's log records the first days in the rising hill country as we travelled towards the places that have for generations supplied the boys for the British military service, where customs and traditions are still firmly anchored in the nineteenth century:

'This trek has, for the 16 of us, 25 porters, 10 kitchen staff, 4 helpers, 5 servers. And they set out loos for us . . . a decent frame with a seat over a decent hole within a tent which has a zip and a pocket for damp loo paper. The knack is to remember the lethal little guy rope out front that holds the whole thing together, and to pay visits before it gets too lively in there. Lieutenant Lal has a pair of bright yellow socks and a wonderful smile and we left in good spirits, although I'm not sure when trekking what kind of expression to adopt. Should it be grim determination or joy at communing with nature? The lead porters who dismantled camp briskly floated off carrying from straps around their heads things like half a dining-room table and 16 sets of cutlery.

We had a long leisurely lunch – all sorts of delicious things plus a dollop of pilchards – and then Gordon Corrigan threatened us with another two hours' walking. It turned out to be much less than that. Obediently, we did not straggle in any direction. It is hard to explain what happened over the next few hours but it was a most remarkable experience. Looking up the hillside, all the inhabitants of [the Gurkha village of] Ghachok were waiting for us . . . elders, kids, women holding garlands of flowers, musicians with drums and long curved horns. The welcome was overwhelming. Gordon Corrigan was greeted with evident affection. We were all garlanded and covered in tikka. People wished us 'Namaste' and then fell in beside us and we marched on. The music blared. From time to time we stopped to let everyone catch up. The children peered up at us curiously, and we did look bizarre, streaked with sweat and red dust. We were led majestically to our campsite, which had a far more important significance than we realised. We were seated in a semicircle in front of some kind of flimsy structure draped in yellow flowers. The whole village gathered behind us expectantly. Musicians sat at the front and continued playing.

A man danced with the air of a court jester. The village priest traced symbols on the ground and burned incense.

A little goat was led in, looking jaunty and cute, with flowers hanging between his horns. Then arrived the main attraction, a spanking-clean, beautiful young buffalo with large sad eyes, looking calm enough. The music went up in tempo. A handsome young man, tall for a Gurung, and dressed in modern black Levi's and a black shirt, stood holding a kukri, which looked impossibly small for the task now apparently at hand. A few drops of rain fell. There was a fair amount of discussion among the various officials. The worried look is the same all over. The buffalo was tethered, his head tied low but still seemed calm. His keeper scratched his quarters and backside. It started to rain more heavily. We looked so strange, us Westerners, smeared with red and covered with garlands.

The young Gurung cut a melon or pumpkin in half as a trial and then dispatched the little goat swiftly by decapitation. Someone picked up the body and ran round with it so that people could dip their fingers in the blood at the neck. Everything built up, music, rain, tension. And the young Gurung looked pale and tense. He had the buffalo moved to his satisfaction, pushed this way and then that. By now the animal was anxious, and it took several men to hold him still. The blow was swift and for a second I thought he'd muffed it, because the blade seemed to stick. But the body went down and the sweet head stayed tethered. Gordon Corrigan, I think, said, 'By God, he's done it . . .' The young man's head was swathed in a long white scarf by one of the officials and then we added ours. There seemed yards and yards of fabric. He seemed shocked in some distant way, almost in a trance. It was pouring hard by now, a real deluge. 'A good omen,' Gordon said. Everyone scattered apart from the guys methodically butchering the carcass. We made for our tents . . .

After dinner (fresh buffalo sent up from the village and prepared by our cooks) the Nautch (dance) group came, not quite the 'mothers' group' we had expected. This is not the WI. Women work hard in Nepal, although they are by no means subservient. The mothers' group is in charge of roads, general maintenance, hospitality. They also carry massive loads of crops on straps around their heads. This was evidently going to be a serious dance, and we were all going to participate. No campfire because they are careful about burning wood *up here; it is a luxury. We use lanterns, and people sat in a semicircle on the ground and the musicians played. It was the same tune over and over again. We all got pulled in to dance while the court jester performed. We looked so clumsy beside these graceful, delicate people. But it was so happy and sweet tempered. There were speeches afterwards. Whatever Gordon says in Gurkhali cracks them up. We went back to our tents and the crowd dispersed, some wobbly on millet wine. One chap seemed reluctant to return to his village. He sat curiously immobile all night in the middle of the campsite. It turned out he was an ex-Gurkha and he was guarding us. All in all there had been around 50 ex-servicemen present, coming from this village and the surrounding area to welcome Gordon and his odd followers.*

Next morning there was a long day's walk ahead, through largely farming areas and round the edges of terraced paddy fields. We watched a chap adroitly managing his brace of handsome oxen plough a tiny strip of field. We could easily be in the last century. Perhaps we are . . .'

And now back in that last century . . .

By the 1820s, Gurkhas were piling across the border for the chance of small but regular income from the British who – from accounts reaching Nepal – thought highly of their soldiers and their courage. The British relied on its military power to which the heavy hand of colonialism resorted when all else, such as bribery, extortion and political manipulation of chieftains, failed. Local disagreements among Indian principalities also aided the British move towards its creeping control of the entire subcontinent and other regions that fell within the description of 'East Indies', such as Burma. Just as the French, a few years later, began recruiting soldiers from across Europe into its force of mercenaries which was to become known as the French Foreign Legion, the British almost immediately began to appreciate the benefits of Gurkhas as some Indian states staged fierce but vain opposition to the onward march of the East India Company.

It was not entirely due to British admiration of the Gurkhas' military prowess that prompted their recruitment by the East India Company, either. The battalions of good indigenous soldiers experienced in hill warfare saved British soldiers from bloody and vicious battles – and they were much cheaper. Secondly, the Gurkhas were infinitely more trustworthy, loyal and – above all – obedient than the Sepoys, the native troops in British service whose growing resentment of the white masters was fermenting to the point where the cork could blow at any moment. From a British point of view, the qualities of the Gurkha were considerable, especially as the Sepoys grew increasingly resentful of the East India Company's relentless march across the subcontinent abusing and ignoring the great customs and religious ceremony vital to Indian life.

The Gurkhas were poised precariously between the two, and when the time came they remained loyal to their employees, the British, and not their near religious neighbours. They would distinguish themselves again in 1845 when the Khalsa army of Sikhs, also strong fighters, crossed from the Punjab following the death of Ranjit Singh and attacked British positions. It was the start of a war that was to last almost two years and prove costly to both sides and whose wounds remained a bleeding mess for the British administration for the next 100 years. Both the Nasiri and Sirmoor Battalions of Gurkhas were in constant action, and General Sir Hugh Gough wrote in his report of battle action that he was compelled to pause in his narrative 'to notice the determined hardihood and bravery with which our two battalions of Goorkhas . . . met the Sikhs whenever they were opposed to them. Soldiers of small stature and indomitable spirit, they vied in ardent courage in the charge with the Grenadiers of our own nation and armed with the short weapon of the mountains were a terror to the Sikhs throughout the great combat . . .'

Annexation of the Punjab by the East India Company followed, and over the next six years James Andrew Broun Ramsay, tenth Earl of Dalhousie, then governor-general of the company in India, annexed five more states. Another, Oudh, in north-west India and independent for more than a century, was annexed in 1856, causing considerable unrest, especially in its largest town of Lucknow.

By then, India was divided into three presidencies, Madras, Bombay and Bengal; Bengal was the largest, taking in the Punjab. In 1857 around 180,000 troops were positioned across the vast Bengali landscape, which covered 82,000 square miles (212,380 square kilometres). The majority of the troops, around 150,000, were Indian, some 24,000 were European, and there were fewer than 1,500 Gurkhas in the region. The dilution of British forces, however, was clearly a major setback when the Indian Mutiny flared in the spring of 1857, centred first among Indian Sepoys at Meerut, a town near Delhi, and sweeping through northern India across a 1,000-mile (1,609-kilometre) tract towards Calcutta. The British could muster fewer than 5,000 European troops against some 55,000 Sepoys, most of whom were to join the revolt; many of their British officers, who were convinced their men would remain loyal, were hacked to pieces in the melee that followed.

The Gurkhas actually tried to head off the mutiny, the cause of which is often overlooked. Discontent moved to open dissent when the East India Company issued new Enfield rifles to their native troops. To load the rifles, the Sepoys had to bite off the ends of greased cartridges. Rumours that the cartridges were greased with the fat of cows and pigs outraged both Hindus, who regard cows as sacred, and Muslims, who regard pigs as unclean. Although there was no love lost between the Gurkhas and the Sepoys, the Gurkhas had attempted to reassure them by demonstrating on a musketry course that they should have no problem in using the greased cartridges. The Sepoys were not convinced and, when the cartridges were forced on them, rose against their British officers. Eighty-five soldiers were chained for refusing to use the new cartridges and became the focal point of the mutiny. They were freed by their comrades and all went on the rampage, killing many of their officers, and set out for nearby Delhi, where they were joined in revolt by colleagues at the local garrison.

Regiments mutinied at Cawnpore and Lucknow. With British soldiers vastly outnumbered, the Gurkhas were pulled in from all quarters as the rebellion quickly spread over northern India. The troubles stretched along the Indian lands close to the border with Nepal from where the British received an immediate offer of help. Jangbahadur Rana, the despotic dictator of Nepal since 1846 and one of a long line of hereditary Prime Ministers who remained in control of the country until 1951, was in fact a committed Anglophile. Although he would not tolerate the British in his own country, he had offered his nation's friendship when he visited Britain in 1850, staying for a whole year. Overcome with pride during an audience with Queen Victoria, he gave the British his pledge of faith. When the troubles arose in India, Jangbahadur Rana honoured his promise and gave immediate clearance for the East India Company to raise more Gurkha regiments, the first of which would later become known as the 4th Prince of Wales' Own Gurkha Rifles.

The Gurkhas already in the company's service were playing a vital role in defence of the British position in Delhi. Three days after the mutiny began, orders reached the garrison at Dehra Dun that the Sirmoor Battalion was to move in great haste to Meerut, where the British were barely holding out. To achieve the deadline given, the Gurkhas had to march 30 miles (48 kilometres) a day in the blazing heat of an Indian summer until they reached the Ganges Canal, where they were embarked in 45 canal boats. *En route* they were attacked by a large band of rebels but sent them scattering. Eighteen were captured and tried on the spot; thirteen were found guilty and shot. The battalion resumed its journey along the canal, then with great haste disembarked when Major Reid learned that they were needed to reinforce a British column under General Archdale Wilson under attack near Delhi, 27 miles (43 kilometres) away. They marched through the night, arriving at dawn, and found the regiment they were to support, the 60th Rifles, suffering badly from heat and exhaustion. The 60th thought they were enemy and opened fire. When they realised they were Gurkhas, they gave them a rousing reception but, Major Reid noted in his diary, 'my poor little fellows were so dead beat that they could not return the hearty cheers with which they were welcomed'.

In spite of the warm welcome, confidence in native regiments had been totally undermined and there was still a suspicion among some officers about the loyalty of the Gurkhas, that they, too might go to the other side. The Gurkhas' encampment was therefore placed close to the artillery, whose officers were given secret orders to turn the guns on them at the slightest sign of their joining the mutiny. None came. As the two elements dug in for what was to become a four-month siege, their mutual admiration grew into a regimental friendship that endured for decades to come, when the 60th had been renamed the 2nd Green Jackets. If proof were still needed, the Gurkhas pretended to take up one of the many calls the rebels made to them for them to join their cause. They kept shouting out, 'Come on, come on, Gurkhas. We expect you to join us.'

One morning the Gurkhas called back, 'We are coming.'

A group of them darted out from the cover of the British positions and into the rebel stronghold. When they were less than 30 yards (27 metres) from the centre of the mutineers, they opened fire, killing some 30 or 40 of the 'scoundrels', according to Major Reid's log for that day.

Thereafter, Reid's Gurkhas met numerous attacks, often by as many as 8,000 rebels at a time, eventually in hand-to-hand combat with kukris drawn. On 15 June Reid logged his order of battle:

I gave the word forward; our little fellows were up like a shot and advanced in beautiful order to the top of the hill. By way of bringing the enemy on, I sounded the retreat having previously warned my men what we were going to do. It had the desired effect; on came the mutineers. We met just as I got over the brow of the hill. I gave them one well-directed volley and then ordered my guns to open. This sent them to a round-about and about 50 were killed and a great number wounded.

Twenty-five Indian Order of Merit awards were given to men of the Sirmoor Rifles during the Siege of Delhi, twelve won by line boys, the sons of serving soldiers who ran supplies and ammunition, most born in India. Unable to get back to Nepal, many of the Gurkhas had married local women and thus raised doubts about the abilities of their offspring, whose genetic characteristics, which were so apparently exclusive to the true Gurkha breed, might be affected. Major Reid took issue with that possibility:

So much for doubts about their physique or courage . . . I saw a boy squatting behind a rock with a rifle in his hands . . . He got up and saluted me, and said, 'I came here with the recruits. I have disobeyed orders, sahib, but I could not help it. My father was on duty and I went there to assist him in getting out his cartridges. He was killed, and I then went to one of the 60th Rifles to help him in loading quickly. He was shortly afterwards wounded. He gave me his rifle . . . and then went at it myself. After firing a few shots a bullet struck me which made four holes in my legs, but I am not much hurt.

Reid enlisted the boy, although he was only 14, and sent him to hospital for treatment. The Sirmoor Rifles stood their ground in 26 attacks between the first week of June to 14 September, as well as joining British battalions in their attacks on mutineers. Reid was becoming alarmed at the number of his 'little fellows' who had been killed or wounded, especially after the King of Delhi had promised ten rupees for every Gurkha's head brought to his war office. Their losses are on record in the regimental log with the comment: 'The poor little Gurkhas have somewhat less than half the number of effective men that they had on the day of their arrival here, and yet they are always jolly and cheerful, anxious to go to the front when there is an attack.'

The struggle had been ebbing and flowing in various parts of India, and Gurkha contingents had been deployed in all the areas of severe fighting. In the Kumaon hills the 66th Goorkhas were key members of a British force at Haldwani holding out against two rebel forces, each of about 1,000 men with supporting guns. A force of about 500 men from the 66th Goorkhas with two six-pounder guns marched all night through the forest and took the rebel army by surprise at the village of Charpura. Heavily outnumbered, the small force of Gurkhas advanced, firing rapidly, and put their enemy to flight. They then took themselves back to Haldwani, a distance of 34 miles (54 kilometres), arriving soon after midday – the whole operation completed in under 13 hours.

By early August 1857 the British commanders were preparing a major assault on Delhi following the long-awaited arrival of British reinforcements. They believed they could bring the Indian Mutiny closer to collapse, but there was still no certainty that they would do so, in spite of the firepower of the regiments now assembled. Brigadier General John Nicholson, known as the Lion of the Punjab, personally led the assault on Delhi at the head of the Kumaon Gurkha Regiment; around 8,000 soldiers of other units, including the main column provided by the 52nd Foot, followed them in. Bitter and vicious fighting ensued, with Nicholson himself among the casualties and Major Reid, commanding a column of 2,500 men, wounded. Throughout Delhi, the terrible vengeance taken by both sides was evident in a bloody struggle that claimed many hundreds of lives. The British, as victors, dealt a heavy punishment against both rebels and the innocents caught up in the struggle. Nor did it end the mutiny. Fighting continued across the affected regions, often developing into tedious guerrilla warfare.

As the mutiny moved into its second year of fighting, the pockets of heavy resistance were gradually being overcome, and in one such outbreak the first of the Gurkhas' 26 Victoria Cross awards was won. The date of the action was 10 February 1858. The recipient was Lieutenant John Adam Tytler, aged 33, the third son of Dr John Tytler, a surgeon with the East India Company, and his wife Anne. He joined the Bengal Infantry in 1844 and was soon afterwards posted to the 66th Native Infantry, which later became the 66th Goorkha Regiment of Native Infantry, and later still renamed as the 1st King George V's Own Gurkha Rifles. Tytler was appointed adjutant in October 1853 and was with the 66th Goorkhas during their significant defeat of rebels at Haldwani in September 1857. In February 1858 the 66th returned to action at Haldwani. Lieutenant Tytler was with 500 men of the 66th commanded by Captain Ross and supported by 210 other infantry, 200 cavalry and two six-pounder guns when they came upon two large rebel contingents of around 5,000 infantry and 1,000 cavalry. The next day, 10 February, two companies of the 66th moved against the rebels in the face of heavy fire from the enemy guns. Lieutenant Tytler made an outstanding contribution, as recorded in the citation for his VC:

> . . . under a heavy fire of round shot, grape and musketry, Lieutenant Tytler dashed on horseback ahead of all, and alone, up to the enemy's guns, where he engaged hand to hand, until they were carried by us; and where he was shot through the left arm, had a spear wound in his chest and a ball through the right sleeve of his coat.

Lieutenant Tytler thus became the first officer of a Gurkha regiment to be so honoured. (At that time, only British officers and not native Gurkhas were eligible for the award, a situation that remained until 1911.) Tytler was eventually given command of the 4th Goorkha Regiment, raised in 1857, and remained in command for 17 years. He was twice Mentioned in Dispatches and was appointed a CB (Companion of the Most Honourable Order of the Bath) in 1872, which, in that year, took precedence even over his VC. In 1878 he commanded a brigade on the North-West Frontier with the rank of brigadier general. He died from pneumonia, aged 54, on 14 February 1880 while on active service in the Punjab.

Lieutenant Tytler's award of the VC was the first of two milestones recorded in the early accounts of the Gurkhas in British service. The second was described by the late Brigadier E.D. 'Birdie' Smith, prolific writer on Gurkha affairs, as 'the most significant moment in the long history of friendship between Britain and Nepal'. It came a month or so after Tytler's action, as the Indian Mutiny entered its final throes. Nepali Prime Minister Jangbahadur Rana, whose offer of his own troops had been rejected earlier by the British commanders, was now asked to participate. He gladly obliged and arrived ready for action across the border at the head of his own small army of six regiments, numbering around 5,800 men mustered over the previous four months in Kathmandu.

The Nepalese army moved on the besieged Lucknow, where they joined forces with General Sir Colin Campbell's troops to end the rebels' long occupation of the town. The great Indian Mutiny was on the way out and was finally defeated that summer. The most important result of the rebellion was the abolition in 1858 of the East India Company and the transfer of the administration of India to the British government. The Nepalese did not return empty-handed. They piled their spoils of war plundered from Lucknow and the surrounding countryside of Oudh – wealthy and rich compared with their homeland – and began a snail's-pace trek back to the hills with a heavily laden wagon train of 3,000 or more bullock carts bursting with their booty. The British also formally handed back to Nepal the terai they had commandeered after the 1816 battles. Jangbahadur Rana received a personal honour from Queen Victoria, the Order and Jewels of the Knight Grand Cross of the Order of the Bath. And the Nepalese leader gave his promise that if ever the British needed his help in the future, they only had to ask.

Jangbahadur Rana remained in power for a further 19 years, until his death in 1877. His body was burned beside the sacred River Baghmati, and the three senior Maharanis committed suttee on the pyre. Although a tough, ruthless ruler of his country, he forged links with the British royal family that would survive generations. Politically, Nepal and the United Kingdom established a friendship that would be called on – largely to Britain's advantage – again and again on crucial occasions in the twentieth century – and consistently in its supply of Gurkhas.

CHAPTER FIVE

Onwards and Upwards

It has always remained a fascination among British officers confronted by newly recruited Gurkhas to discover that, to begin with, many of them walked quite gawkily on level ground, such as a parade ground, could never run well in a straight line, yet were always quite at ease going uphill whatever burden they might be carrying and that no one, man or beast, could go faster than a Gurkha leaping and crashing down a steep, rocky hillside. Since they had spent most of their formative years walking upwards, downwards or sideways with their feet hardly ever pointing straight in front, the vagaries of marching in a straight line or the precision of drill instruction were met with considerable unease among all new recruits – so much so that it became a common sight, and still is, to see new young Gurkhas actually practising the art of drill in off-duty hours. Learning the 'little peculiarities' that came with working alongside Gurkhas was one of the specialities of officers interested in making a career in the Gurkha regiments from the very earliest days of their formation.

The diaries and memoirs of officers who served with the Gurkhas are full of stories that demonstrate the necessity to get to know their foibles and their character traits as well as their particular skills. In fact, they had to learn them twice – because those recruited from western Nepal were quite different to those brought from the east of the country. In the early days of medical inspections of recruits, for example, several MOs unused to seeing men with such strong muscular development of the neck (for carrying), lower torso, thighs and calves would mention the possibility of deformity.

51

But this was a natural phenomenon among young men who'd spent their lives running up and down mountainsides almost from the time they could walk often on goat tracks and usually carrying some heavy load humped on the back and secured with a strap around the forehead. It was regularly noted that hill men – unlike Indians or any other recruits who were not specifically from typical Gurkha regions – were capable of enduring great discomfort and fatigue, as if they were in a permanent state of yoga-inspired resistance to pain.

Remaining with that theme for a few more paragraphs before continuing our journey through Gurkha history, it is interesting to compare their performance on the side of a mountain with the 1998 trekking group to the Gurkha homelands. Accepting that the group was made up largely of people approaching a certain age, the observations in Maureen Silver's log are none the less revealing on that stage of the journey, which we will pick up at around 6,500 feet (1,981 metres):

'Lunch was to be taken beside a river on our walk up to the camp close to a village called Luang also filled, we are told, with families with deep Gurkha heritage.

Ahead, the residents of the little village waited to greet us. We sent a polite message on ahead saying flowers OK, but could you please hold back on the tikka. All our clothes are saturated from the rain and doused in red dust and we don't want to be rude, but enough is enough. We are starting to fester. So they simply garlanded us to death. I couldn't actually get my chin over the flowers around my neck. This is a beautiful little village, apparently relatively affluent because there are a lot of ex-Gurkhas here. And they have gathered their rice harvest early so that our tents could be pitched on their paddy fields. At our next stop, our camp commandant, the ex-Gurkha Major Dal, offered us gin and tonic. I thought he was joking . . . but no. It was duly produced from their very large backpacks. Perhaps they thought this village would be an anticlimax after the buffalo sacrifice. Drinking G and T in this environment? Only the English . . .

It rained hard again, but we are now experienced campers and we awoke next morning to clear skies and the mountains glistening in the sun. Glorious breakfast in unparalleled surroundings about which descriptive powers are now totally exhausted. The garlands withering on the tents still smell pungent. Kids from this village come by, out on a training run. They hope to be Gurkhas. There's no bottled mineral water left, so we stocked up on boiled (still warm: the plastic bottles wilted, but we are really tough now) and Gordon C gave a short talk about leeches. Leeches?

What to wear today? It's not a question of fashion; everything is soaking wet and starting to smell and it is a long climb ahead. The next stop is the Annapurna Conservation Area Project (garlanded again) for a briefing by an admirable young man, smartly dressed and very serious about his task. The population of Nepal is increasing by 600,000 p.a. and they have to make their land progressively more productive. But their fastest-growing industry is tourism, which necessitates a workable compromise between farmers and local people and visitors. Inevitably, we will spoil this country and these people, us tourists. Outside we met a line of ex-servicemen who had waited so patiently that it seemed unkind to miss any one of them. They all have a story to tell about how they joined the British army, and the line seemed to grow no shorter and nor do their accounts. Then we proceed up steps (this whole country is built on steps) to meet the champion lady millet wine maker of the region whose little house was immaculate. And then we unsheathed our walking-sticks and hitched up our rucksacks and set off.

This was a long day's trekking. Too long. We climbed steadily, then steeply and had to cross lots of mountain streams, none of which was a hazard and each of which was refreshing, but they mounted up. We went up, then down and finally seriously up . . . and into leech country. The leeches are here . . . little skinny innocuous-looking caterpillars, inchworms, craning their heads for the next best opportunity – which we were, in lieu of cattle or dogs. Like the rain, the leeches shouldn't have been around. The leech season was supposed to have ended weeks ago.

Once we had got over the novelty of identifying them, we discovered that they were silent and painless and crafty and surprisingly swift. Michael S. had one in his hair; Beryl early on got one embedded in her ankle, which Gordon Corrigan removed in time-honoured style with his cigarette. Gordon took advantage of this crisis to inform us we should not stop walking at the brisk pace which he would determine in this leech-infested area. No one stopped walking.

Except Andrew P., that is. Andrew, who was game, fit and no weakling, not by any stretch of the imagination, had none the less been undermined by stomach trouble, eventually more seriously than the rest of us who had suffered. He hadn't made much fuss about it, but finally wilted and started to feel faint. He evidently could walk no further. We tried to coax him on 'just to the next tree'. The Gurkhas fanned him and urged him to keep moving.

Gordon Corrigan said, 'Andrew, you are going to be carried now.' Andrew winced and shook his head. The embarrassment of it all! Big chap, carried by little Gurkhas.

Gordon insisted. 'You must understand, Andrew, this is not a request; it is an order.'

Andrew must have felt both mortified and relieved. Porters were produced for the job, plus one of the Gadsby boys. They made us feel being carried was a good option. They ran past us, as we toiled on with our boots and sticks. They were shorter than most of us, the porters, and probably two-thirds Andrew's body weight and wearing tatty flip-flops. They were stunning.

The mist came down and out of it, like a mirage, appeared this establishment called Austrian Camp. It was both comforting and disconcerting: 'Hot showers, solar heating, cold beer.' We toiled on to our campsite, which was further than I hoped, and there were the blessed tents, all set out, and a sort of lodge and a wooden construction, where the cooks were already well at work, and what passed as a standpipe with running water, no less. This was also, we now discovered, the leech country everyone had been dreading. Leeches love water, and this campsite was infested. Everyone got attacked. Sam H. went to rinse off at the standpipe, sensed some sort of alien damp under his armpit and took his shirt off to reveal streaming blood. But being ex-SAS he didn't flinch. Tom S. stood up to be served his second gin and tonic since our recent arrival and discovered a crafty leech weaving around on his folding stool, so he'd just escaped one in the bum! We all discovered quiet aliens disappearing through our clothing into our tender flesh. But I must say, Gordon Corrigan was right. The fear is psychological rather than physically threatening. I came home with two lumps, the result of half-satiated leeches, and those lumps simply faded. Anyway, I decided the standpipe was bad news and asked for a bowl of water, which was swiftly provided and which I took into my tent and used to wash my very sweaty and, for the first time, cold body. Bliss is simply achieved.

We gave Andrew soup and rice to restore him, and lots of fluids. Gordon asked me to check him every ten minutes and indicate if I thought he was dying. He patently was not and must have been irritated by all the other people following the same instruction. He probably just needed to sleep but was civil about all the enquiries of 'How'ya feeling now?' and, like the phoenix, emerged in the morning from his own ashes. Great meal again, but we were tired and this was the last night going up, so the cooks and porters wanted to sing and dance for us. Some of us pitched up and danced.

Michael S. took three big bull leeches into the tent on the bottom of his tracksuit trousers. In the morning I said to Clement in the next tent, 'We had leeches in the tent last night.'

'Yes,' he said sarcastically. 'I heard them.'

The Himalayas were smiling at us, close enough to touch. There was a nervous air about. Today we must be going down. And down is a nightmare, and probably worse than up, and I was right to be jumpy. First half wasn't too bad. We stopped for lunch (passing en route *a group of French-Canadian trekkers who observed audibly that we were not young, zut alors!) and moved into more obviously touristy areas. The altogether wonderful cook had had carried down some enormous chocolate decorated cake for Gordon B.'s birthday which he had mixed and steamed that morning and there was a cake-cutting ceremony.*

Going down was dire. Treacherous steps, slippery rocks, gazing into cloud-strewn bottomless valleys and sheer drops; mountain goats, we ain't! An angelic young man, son of the cook, floated at my elbow with offers of assistance. Steps down just went on and on for hours and there were poor optimistic souls toiling up the other way. We made encouraging noises but no one had the heart to tell them the truth about how far they had to go.'

In these villages visited on the trek described above, the lifestyle of generations of Gurkhas before and after their service could be seen, for it has barely changed. Almost from the onset of widespread recruitment of Gurkhas by the British, it became a family tradition of service: fathers and sons, brothers and cousins. Many ex-Gurkhas have family connections with the British and Indian Gurkha regiments that could be traced back to the late eighteenth century. One of the most remarkable Gurkha family trees was that of Jabbar Sing Thapa, who enlisted as a youth in the Indian army in 1790. His son, Ballea, joined the Nasiri Gurkha Battalion in the 1830s, later transferring to the 4th Gurkhas, and served in that battalion through six campaigns, rising to the rank of today's equivalent of Gurkha major in 1861. He was Orderly Officer to King Edward VII, when as Prince of Wales, he visited India in 1875 and was presented with a hunting knife by the prince. A statuette of him, with knife, was cast and placed in the officers' mess along with a portrait by W. Simpson of the *Illustrated London News*. Ballea's son, Nathu, also served in the 4th Gurkhas and rose to become second in command of his company. He died in 1885 after serving in five campaigns. Two of his three sons also joined the 4th Gurkhas while the youngest went into 10th Gurkhas. The second son, Sheru, died of cholera shortly after his return from the Manipur Campaign of 1891. The eldest son, Rannu, served in major campaigns of the late nineteenth century, and his portrait, painted by Major C.G. Borrow, hung in the officers' mess for many years until 1947.

Rannu's eldest son, Lachman, was recruited in 1905 and was killed in France in 1914 leading a brave counterattack at Givenchy. Rannu's second son also joined the 4th, was captured at Kut-el-Amara in the First World War and spent the rest of the war in a Turkish prison. On his release, he was commissioned in the 1/4th* Gurkhas and served in Waziristan. He became Gurkha major – the third generation of his family to hold that distinguished rank in the same battalion. By the beginning of the Second World War, eight grandsons of Rannu Thapa were serving in the two battalions of the 4th Gurkhas, and as the family tree spread there were Thapas from his family serving in the British army continuously from then to the present day, all eventually returning to their villages once their service contracts had run their course, and usually bringing home a collection of medals. One other remarkable statistic showed that in 1978 there were 46 sets of brothers serving in the 6th Queen Elizabeth's Own Gurkha Rifles at the same time. One of the retired Gurkha majors, interviewed in 1998 during research for this book, was one of four brothers who all joined Gurkha regiments – following the footsteps of father, grandfather and great-grandfather. Such cases are by no means unusual and, to a lesser

---

* 1/4th refers to the 1st Battalion of the 4th Gurkha Rifles. As in all future references, the style denotes battalion and regiments.

degree, the same is to be found among the family histories of many British officers.

The loyalty and obedience of the Gurkhas became the subject of several studies and official reports after the collapse of the Indian Mutiny. It was noticed, for example, that although desertion was commonplace in the armies of Europe, and that mercenary forces like the French Foreign Legion suffered dramatically from it, it was virtually unknown in Gurkha regiments. Those other little foibles, mentioned at the beginning of this chapter, were being recorded. Theft and dishonesty were virtually unknown, and to be wrongly accused of them caused great consternation. The Gurkhas also showed none of the anguish usually evident among new young soldiers confronted for the first time with the blood and guts of battle. Nor with the hardships of forced marches, rough terrain and the necessity to kill your own food if you wanted to eat. They were all good hunters but could never see the point of doing it as a sport; if you fished, you ate. Their good humour was a general quality and tended to verge towards the black and macabre in certain situations – such as the time reported by John Masters when the body of a sentry in the 4th Gurkhas was being cremated and it kept sitting up in the blazing fire. The Gurkhas laughed uproariously and still were laughing as they hacked the body to pieces to make it lie down in the flames.

Something similar was recalled by wartime Gurkha officer Anthony Harvey, who tells the story of one of his initial Gurkha encounters with the Germans, probably at Atessa, when the kukris were drawn and the Germans were petrified. At the end of the battle, the British occupied a house in which there were eight German corpses in the cellar. A British regimental sergeant major ordered a Gurkha company to bury them. A large pit was dug and the Gurkhas duly placed the eight bodies into it and were beginning to shovel earth on top of them when one of the bodies moved. He was quite clearly still alive. One of the Gurkhas pulled out his gun and was about to shoot him when a British officer saw what was happening and said, 'What are you doing?'

The Gurkha replied, 'The major sahib said we were to bury eight bodies. You wouldn't expect us to bury him alive, would you?' The German was duly rescued from the pit and survived the ordeal, protesting loudly.

Such stories abound, as will be seen as these pages progress, and became as much a part of Gurkha legend as the men themselves. The fact that officers were fond of recalling them – and continued to do so down the ages – aided the Gurkha cause, and officer-level enthusiasm for them not just as courageous fighters but for their character and characteristics persuaded the British that the policy of dedicated Gurkha regiments must continue. Furthermore, after the ending of the Indian Mutiny there were plenty of trouble spots along virtually the whole of both the north-east and north-west rim of Britain's Indian Empire that were ideal for Gurkha deployment.

The infamous North-West Frontier was the most northerly province of British India, covering a vast, tribal territory of the most inhospitable landscape and the terrifying cruel and heavily armed warring groups, who fought among themselves or joined together to fight the British, depending on how the mood took them. The history of that era later spawned dozens of adventure stories and many stiff-upper-lip British films and arose from the experiences as the conquering British swept diagonally north-westwards across India from their original trading posts in Surat, Calcutta and Madras.

Eventually, they reached the mountains that separate the subcontinent from Afghanistan, extending 400 miles (644 kilometres) from north to south, populated on both sides of the border by a proud, independent and raw population divided into many tribes, with no central ruler or authority. The British would find themselves brought to a halt against them, with intermittent action against violent tribal leaders who became famous in the newspapers of the day: Shere Ali Khan, the Faqir of Ipi, the Red Shirts of Peshawar, the Mad Faqir of Swat, the Khan of Amb and the Islamic fire-eater Haji Shaib Turangzai, nicknamed by the British as the 'Hot Gospeller'. Battle locations became equally famous through newspapers and movies, including the Black Mountains and the Khyber Pass.

The Pathans, a murderous breed of fanatical Muslims, well known for their fearless fighting, their treachery, their blood feuds and their vendettas, would give them most trouble – and continued to do so well into the twentieth century. In a way they were similar to the Gurkhas in their natural ability as fighters. They were the exact opposites in appearance and manner, tall, lean guerrillas who enjoyed torturing their captives, gouging out their eyes, slicing up their flesh or cutting off their testicles and stuffing them into their mouths before killing them, dreaming up the slowest of deaths if time allowed. They never took prisoners, and British soldiers were warned in advance that if they ever fell into the hands of the Pathans they should make every effort to kill themselves as soon as possible. The region became a nightmare, and if the Indians had had their way they would have left the Afghans and the Pathans to their own devices and withdrawn to the settled agricultural line of the River Indus. But since Britain controlled the government of India, and did so until 1947, a blurred compromise was introduced, supposedly on the fear of a possible invasion of India by the Russians.

A belt from 10 to 100 miles (16 to 160 kilometres) wide was drawn on the maps, to be known as the administrative border. The British condescended to allow the Pathans to rule themselves if they stayed on their side of that line and allowed access to the strategic passes. They also agreed to pay tribal leaders handsome allowances in return for good behaviour. To enable prompt action in the event of the rules being broken, the British built forts and stationed soldiers on the border. Incoming administrators overseen by bright young chaps from the heart of England could not avoid their natural instincts to suggest that Pathan children should attend school, be steered away from their bloodthirsty ways and perhaps even embrace Christianity. It didn't work, and eventually there appeared out of nowhere the unnatural towns, surrounded by barbed wire and guns and housing thousands of men and mules of the British/Indian armies.

It was one of the worst postings in British India – or best if you were a young soldier anxious to hear the sound of guns being fired in anger. The days were few indeed when the resident troops were not called into action, and those who saw it most regularly were the Gurkhas, part of the British force that fought two of the three Afghan Wars. Most Gurkha regiments saw service on the North-West Frontier, but it was the 5th Gurkhas, originally raised as the Hazara Goorkha Battalion during the latter stages of the mutiny in 1858, which came to regard this godforsaken place as a permanent posting. They stayed for the next 90 years.

The most decorated of all the Gurkha regiments, whose soldiers won seven Victoria Crosses, the 5th was the only one to be given a 'Royal' prefix and officially designated as the 'Frontier Force'. Its full title from 1923 was the 5th Royal Gurkha Rifles (Frontier Force), and many brave actions and five battle honours are in its record books. The first of its VCs was Edinburgh-born Captain John Cook, who had joined the 5th on 27 March 1873 and was appointed a wing officer. At the start of the second Afghan War in November 1878, the 5th became part of three columns under the command of Major General Frederick Roberts that were moving on Afghanistan via the Kurram Valley. There Roberts discovered that the Afghans had 18,000 men with 11 guns lying in wait for his invasion force at Peiwar Kotal, a mountain 9,400 feet (2,865 metres) above sea-level. In the battles that followed, Captain Cook led repeated charges against enemy barricades with a joint force of Gurkhas and men from the 72nd Highlanders. At dawn, as the Afghans fled their positions, Captain Cook collected a few men and charged and killed a large number of enemy who were trying to rescue one of their guns. During this operation, Captain Cook saved the life of Major Galbraith, assistant adjutant general, by wrestling to the ground an Afghan about to shoot him. His citation for the Victoria Cross read:

> ...during very heavy fire, Captain Cook charged out of the entrenchments with such impetuosity that the enemy broke and fled, when perceiving at the close of the melee, the danger of Major Galbraith who was in personal conflict with an Afghan soldier, Captain Cook distracted this attention to himself and aiming a sword cut which the Douranee avoided, sprang upon him and, grasping his throat, grappled with him. They both fell to the ground. The Douranee, a most powerful man, still endeavouring to use his rifle, seized Captain Cook's arm in his teeth until the struggle was ended by the man being shot through the head.

Captain Cook's luck ran out four months later. In December 1879, then a major, he was seriously wounded leading two companies of the 5th Goorkhas in the advance on Kabul. He died a week later.

It was during the Afghan campaign that the 5th Gurkhas formed a close working relationship with the 72nd Highlanders (later the 1st Seaforth Highlanders). When Major General Roberts received a peerage, he chose as supporters for his arms a 72nd Highlander and a rifleman of the 5th Gurkhas. Roberts's elevation to the peerage also had a side-effect that was to establish beyond doubt the place of the

Gurkhas in British military history. It was he who persuaded the War Ministry to undertake a dramatic expansion of Gurkha regiments, initially doubling their size with an additional battalion for each of the five regiments, which in turn meant the launch of a substantial recruitment campaign.

Maharajah Sir Bir Shamsher Rana Bahadur, Prime Minister of Nepal at the time, and his brother, General Chandra Shamsher, commander-in-chief of the Nepalese army, agreed to cooperate on a limited basis. Their biggest concession was to allow British officers into Nepal to supervise a permanent system of recruitment. They established a recruiting depot at Gorakhpur, close to the Nepalese border, and this depot was to become the base for all recruiting parties looking for Gurung and Magar recruits in west-central Nepal. There, they formulated a recruiting 'season' – consisting of recruitment and training – which set the pattern for the future. The first season was in 1886, when 854 young men were brought into the post and 788 were accepted and assigned to battalions for training. Gorakhpur was close to the main station of Bengal North-Western Railway, so recruits could be dispatched quickly to their respective units. Around the same time, the British government purchased land close to the railway station to set up a 'Goorkha village' to house up to 600 recruits at a time, until they could be processed and sent on to their battalions. Until then, they had been put in privately run places that, it had been noted, were full of disease and temptation. The whole area was sealed off and, once the recruits were inside, only they, the recruiting parties and small shop-keepers were 'on any account allowed to reside within the limits of the village'.

When the British began to recruit from the eastern regions specifically for the 7th and 10th Gurkhas, further recruiting stations were opened in Darjeeling. From these centres, recruitment of Gurkhas increased dramatically, and by the turn of the century the Brigade of Gurkhas, as it had then become known, had quadrupled to 20 battalions in 10 regiments. To keep the battalions at full strength, an annual intake of around 1,800 to 2,000 men was required.

Then, as now, finding enough candidates for the available places was never a problem. Recruiters could afford to be increasingly selective, and it was then decreed that only Gurkhas could enlist in Gurkha regiments, all under the control of British officers and honorary Gurkha officers. The Gurkhas themselves were very happy with that situation and with the army's own preference for what might be termed tribal recruitment. Among the various studies on the type and location of recruits, Captain H. Bingley wrote three handbooks for the Indian army and concluded that fighting ability depended not just on race but also on the hereditary instinct and social status of the men enlisted. He wrote: '. . . it is essential that every effort should be made to obtain the very best men of that class which a regiment may enlist. Men of good class will not enlist unless their own class is well represented in the regiment.'

His point was that more and more recruits should be sought not merely from the same tribes but the same clans and even the same families. It was obviously taken up. It also, in a curious, unimagined way, helped the future of those families by keeping the male lines generally fit and healthy to produce more children who would become Gurkhas. Well into the twentieth century, Gurkha recruits hoping to be enlisted arrived for their medicals with all manner of ailments and diseases. Leprosy, tuberculosis, smallpox, cholera and diphtheria remained all too common in Nepal, along with less life-threatening but uncomfortable problems such as worms and other parasitical infestations. Army doctors discovered in these young men diseases they themselves did not know they had, and in that respect those who passed through the rigid selection procedures were actually not typical Nepalese hill men; they were the best. It was that system, developed from 1886 onwards, that brought the Gurkhas up to the style and strength that mattered when the time came for even greater calls from the British on their abilities and particular skills.

CHAPTER SIX

Distance No Object

History has well-recorded incredible, lumbering, death-prone marches that faced armies across the globe striving to complete their government's bidding. Colonising forces stormed through the lush plains of Africa, across the deserts of North Africa and the Middle East, through the jungles and swamps of the Far East, and in many cases losses through untreatable and unknown diseases picked up *en route* were far, far greater than casualties in action. India was, like the curate's egg, good in parts, and certainly better placed than many other parts of the world. The rail systems begun by the East India Company and pursued by the British administration of the late nineteenth century eased the movement of troops and population and eventually provided some of the great railway journeys of the world, but for the most part there was no substitute for the march.

When the British military's prestige was at its lowest ebb in the Indian adventure following the loss of the Khyber Pass in August 1895, for example, the largest force ever raised in the subcontinent was assembled to regain the pass and secure future control of it. The Gurkha battalions were to be part of that force and, once again, proved an invaluable asset. The Khyber Pass was the most important route connecting Afghanistan and India. It winds north-west about 30 miles (48 kilometres), varying in width from 15 to 450 feet (4.5 to 137 metres). The mountains on either side could be climbed only in a few places, and the precipitous walls vary in height from about 1,400 to 3,500 feet (427 to 1,067 metres). For centuries the pass was used by invaders to enter India, and it naturally became the scene of many skirmishes during the Afghan Wars between Anglo-Indian-Gurkha soldiers and the Afghans, including the most famous battle of all, the battle in January 1842 in which about 16,000 British and Indian troops were killed. When control of the pass once again slipped from British hands in 1895, an army of 44,000 was raised for what became known as the Tirah Campaign, to invade the largely unexplored area of the Peshawar Valley and make punitive strikes against the massed tribal forces of the region. The British force was to be supported on its march by a massive supply column of 60,000 transport animals – pack elephants, camels, mules, donkeys and bullocks. In spite of the huge preparations, the Tirah Campaign became something of a forgotten colossus. It lasted almost 18 months and because of the refusal of the tribal armies to meet for a head-on battle – preferring instead to snipe from the hills – there were few spectacular clashes of arms.

Perhaps the most notable of the few major flare-ups was a combined assault by the 2/2nd Gurkhas and the Gordon Highlanders against a substantial Pathan assembly on the heights of Dargai. It was the beginning of a long friendship between the Gurkhas and the Gordons, the latter demonstrating their affection for the former by volunteering to carry their dead and wounded down from the hills. The running battles with tribal warriors provided some heated moments, but at the end of the day the region was calmer than it had been for 50 years and remained so for a dozen years afterwards.

When the campaign was over and the Gurkhas were returning to the base at Dehra Dun, they found to their surprise a reception party awaiting them when their train stopped at Rawalpindi. The Gordon Highlanders were lining the station to cheer them on their way. At a brief reception for officers gifts were exchanged – the Gordons presenting the Gurkhas with a silver shield and statuette, the Gurkhas returning the compliment with the presentation of two specially made kukris, one for the officers' mess and one for the sergeants' mess. Thereafter, the battle-weary Gurkhas faced a very long walk home for their leave. The railway system of India barely touched Nepal, and with no other transport available the journey back could take weeks. British government officials overcame some of the problems by allowing married quarters for wives and children of Gurkhas where possible or even feasible, but the situation was far from conducive for a married life that depended so deeply on the tradition of an arranged marriage.

British officers faced an even longer journey if a visit to England was on the cards, and a system of long leaves evolved whereby they took six months every three years. For the Gurkhas, this suited the parents of new recruits who, on returning home after their first three years, would find their bride waiting for them for a prompt marriage and hopefully, before the leave was over, the bride would be pregnant, and the child would be three the next time he or she saw the father – if indeed he came back.

While the North-West Frontier acquired a certain romanticism in fictional and true accounts of British stoicism, real dramas were also taking place at the opposite end of the Indian border territories, on the North-East Frontier. The whole of that region of vast and difficult lands was to become a place of much Gurkha activity from the end of the Indian Mutiny right through to the end of the Second World War. This often impenetrable theatre of operations, bounded by the borders with Tibet, China and Burma, was the scene of events that resulted in the award of 11 of the VCs won by officers and men of the numerous Gurkha battalions who fought there over several decades, culminating with their outstanding contribution of men and brave deeds in Field Marshal Slim's 14th Army victory over the Japanese in Burma in 1944–5.

Gurkhas had been posted to Assam and north-east Bengal intermittently for many years. The terrain was tough, even for the hill men. They also met the primitive aggression of tribes such as the Abors, Nagas and Lushais who, even in the late nineteenth century, still fought with spears. Though warlike, these tribes were not quite so bent on bloodletting as the Pathans on the North-West Frontier. The hills were covered with dense jungle, which Colonel Leslie W. Shakespeare of the 2nd Gurkhas described as 'no level ground beyond small stretches of a few hundred yards; the rivers are mountain torrents, the lower hills covered with the bamboo jungle which in the higher ranges gives place to green trees, oak and pine, and the only communications are along narrow goat trails leading from village to village'.

As British traders and settlers pushed further into the state of Assam to develop the tea industry, local tribes became restless and a trifle unruly when confronted by alien administrators and a mass of whites ordering them about. The Nagas and the Lushais, who were stout defenders of their territory, carried out regular raids on the tea gardens. They put the fear of God into the European settlers and were not averse to the occasional massacre of families and coolies. In one such raid, a British couple named Winchester from Elgin, Scotland, were among the victims. Their daughter Mary, then aged five, was abducted by the leaders of the raiding party. It was known she was alive when kidnapped, and that she was still alive in captivity was confirmed by local Indian government representatives. Months of attempted negotiations led by the lieutenant governor and even offers of a reward all failed to get Mary released. British government officials approved 'the immediate dispatch of a punitive expedition' to locate and rescue the child and punish the Lushai tribesmen at the same time. Two battalions were taken from the 2nd and 4th Gurkhas to join a large force mounted under Brigadier General C.H. Brownlow, called the First Looshai Expedition, in late autumn of 1871.

The Lushai hills proved difficult terrain, and there were a number of lively skirmishes. A major battle erupted at a village called Lal Gnoora on 3 January 1872. It had been surrounded and placed under attack by a battalion of the 2nd Gurkhas commanded by Colonel Macpherson, with Major Donald Macintyre as second in command. Macintyre, then 40 years old, had been commissioned in 1850 and posted immediately to India to join the 66th Regiment of Native Infantry (Goorkas). He had fought in numerous campaigns, including the Kurram Expedition to Afghanistan, with various Gurkha battalions. Now, he was second in command at the gates of the village of Lal Gnoora, where enter-at-your-peril signs were clearly evident. The Lushais had evacuated their families and surrounded the village with lines of nine-foot-high (2.7-metre-high) bamboo spikes. They also created a smoke screen, burning their own property within the village. As the battalion launched its attacks, Colonel Macpherson and his number two contemplated the situation. Macintyre, with Gurkha rifleman Inderjit Thapa, selected a spot under clouds of smoke, clambered over the stockade and began attacking the Lushais from within, cutting a way through for the battalion.

For his efforts, Macintyre was awarded the Victoria Cross. He was

also Mentioned in Dispatches, promoted to the brevet rank of lieuten-
ant colonel and received the thanks of the Governor-General in India.
Rifleman Inderjit Thapa received the Indian Order of Merit, Third
Class.

As for Mary Winchester, she was found alive, still with the Lushais
who had abducted her, unharmed and apparently doted on by them.
When she was handed over to the Gurkhas, she was, beneath the grime
and rags she was wearing, discovered to be a beautiful child approaching seven years of age, with hazel eyes, delicate features and showing
no signs of malnutrition. By this time she had adopted the ways of the
Lushais with whom she lived, spoke their language and smoked a pipe.
She cowered not a bit from them, nor the troops who took custody of
her, and if there was confusion it was only when she was ushered into
the presence of the brittle Brigadier General Brownlow. The Lushais
obviously idolised the child and the general noted that she appeared to
be ordering them about 'somewhat majestically'. Before they finally
and reluctantly gave her up, the Lushais had cut her long hair and
distributed it among themselves as a memento of the little British child
who had temporarily come into their midst.

Although the mission to rescue her had been well planned, the army
clearly had doubts that she would ever be found, and little thought had
been given as to what was to be done with her if indeed she was rescued.
Her parents were now dead, and there was no one to care for her in India.
Eventually, she was transported, under careful military escort, to
Calcutta, where she was taken aboard a ship bound for England. There,
she was delivered to the grandparents she had never met in Elgin,
Scotland, there to be anonymously readjusted into Western life.

Lieutenant Colonel Macintyre resumed his duties with the much-
coveted VC behind his name. He was appointed commanding officer
in April 1876 and promoted to colonel in September of that year. He
was present with the battalion at Delhi during the Prince of Wales's
visit on 11 January 1876 and took the battalion on one of the Gurkhas'
first overseas tours of duty to Malta and Cyprus in 1879. Macintyre's
distinguished career ended on 24 December 1880 when he had the
rank of honorary major general. One of his three sons, Donald junior,
also went into the Gurkhas, serving in the 2nd King Edward's Own
Gurkha Rifles from 1905 to 1919; his second son, Frank, served in the
Royal Naval Air Service in the First World War, and his third son, Ian,

became a captain in the Royal Navy and was awarded the CB, CBE and DSO in the Second World War, which he ended as captain of the aircraft carrier HMS *Indefatigable* in the Pacific.

Gurkha operations through the remaining years of the nineteenth century were largely concentrated on these two very busy frontiers, the North-West and the North-East Frontiers, and provided sufficient action for a permanency of three regiments at various locations. The 42nd Regiment, for example, remained in eastern India until 1899 – after a tour of duty there lasting exactly 77 years. The regiment, which was to become the 6th Gurkha Rifles in 1903, remained in existence until 1994 and, as we will see, attracted many accolades and battle honours in years to come.

The majority of severe fighting was experienced in the North-West Frontier, although there were noteworthy incidents in the east which again resulted in the addition of another VC to the Gurkha honours list and a collection of medals for the Gurkha soldiers themselves. One of the most dramatic occurred towards the end of March 1891, when the independent state of Manipur on the North-East Frontier rose in rebellion, removed the ruler acknowledged by the government of India and set up another in his place. As Manipur was a protected state, slightly larger than Wales, in south-eastern Assam, the British decided they would prefer that Manipur remain in the fold and proposed to send a force to remove the rebellious Senapati, the local army commander behind the coup.

Frank St Clair Grimwood was the British political agent at Manipur, but in view of the relative calm of recent times his own force at the British residency was a mere 100 men of the 43rd (Goorkha) Regiment of Bengal (Light) Infantry (later the 2/8th Gurkhas) – of whom 33 were based at the outpost of Lang Hobal, four miles (six kilometres) away. It was quite insufficient to undertake the arrest of the Senapati. Grimwood appealed to Mr James Wallace Quinton, the British commissioner in Assam, who decided to go there himself with four civil officers and an escort of seven British officers and 454 Gurkhas under Lieutenant Colonel Charles Skene from Kohima to arrest the rebel leaders and restore the situation.

The Manipuris were waiting and put up hefty resistance for two days. They then sounded the cease-fire and suggested a truce. Commissioner Quinton foolishly agreed and took Frank Grimwood and

Lieutenant Colonel Skene, with three other officers – all unarmed – to a meeting with the Senapati to discuss terms. They were all promptly captured by rebels armed to the teeth and hacked to pieces. The 454 Gurkha troops, meanwhile, resting in the residency grounds and unaware of what had happened, were then attacked without warning by overwhelming numbers in the darkness and, having used most of their ammunition, could barely put up a fight. When shelling began, the senior British officers remaining, Major Louis Boileau and Captain George Butcher, took the now widowed Ethel Grimwood and escaped from the residency with the intention of trying to reach Cachar, 100 miles (160 kilometres) to the west.

Major Boileau gave no orders other than passing word that his men should withdraw as best they could and then took off with Mrs Grimwood, leaving behind the remaining 270 Gurkhas, all of whom were eventually captured or killed. The young and very beautiful Ethel Grimwood, dressed in a white silk blouse, patent-leather shoes and a long blue skirt, guided the group of escaping officers because she knew the territory better than they did. They travelled by night, resting mostly during the day, climbing 3,000 feet (914 metres) above the plain until they were exhausted and without food. Hostile Nagas tribesmen with spears had begun to stalk them when Mrs Grimwood fell and twisted her ankle. At their most desperate moment, they came on 200 Gurkhas who, unaware of events in Manipur, were marching their way forward to take up a normal tour of duty at Imphal. Ethel Grimwood cried with relief and threw her arms around the Gurkha officer at the head of the column.

Meanwhile, the rebels seemed to have control of Imphal and were at that moment advancing on the Lang Thobal post. Fortunately, a runner who escaped from the residency arrived ahead of them to warn the Gurkha officer commanding the 33 men at the post, Jemadar Birbal Nagarkoti, who decided to withdraw immediately. He planned to make his way to the post at Tamu, commanded by Lieutenant Charles Grant, about 50 miles (80 kilometres) away across very rough country. Charles Grant, a brave and resourceful officer from Bourtie, Aberdeenshire, Scotland, had been at Sandhurst before being commissioned into the Suffolk Regiment on 10 May 1882. At the beginning of 1891 he was in command of the small garrison in Tamu, on the Assam–Burma border. Having heard the news from Jemadar Birbal Nagarkoti,

Lieutenant Grant immediately telegraphed for permission to go immediately to the garrison at Manipur. Permission was granted, and he left on the morning of 28 March for Manipur with 80 men of the 43rd Gurkha Rifles and 3 pack elephants carrying ammunition and supplies. Progress was slow, but they reached Kongaung early on 29 March and drove 200 men of the Manipur army out of Palel early on the thirtieth.

They reached Lang Thobal later that day and found it had been occupied by a very large force of Manipuris. Lieutenant Grant's own small unit crept to within shouting distance of their enemy and then made a bayonet charge, with the Gurkhas emitting their bloodthirsty war cry. Lieutenant Grant was wounded during the heavy fighting. The Manipuris pulled back but rallied for a renewed attack a few hundred yards back before finally running in full retreat to take refuge a mile away in the hills. It was later learned that there were over 800 Manipuris manning the position at Lang Thobal – ten times the number Grant had with him.

Lieutenant Grant was now low on ammunition and knew he could not withstand another scrap and so resolved to hang on to Lang Thobal until he was relieved. Unfortunately, the Manipuris counterattacked the next morning, and only a strict policy of fire only when you see the whites of their eyes saved the day. Further attacks followed, supported by two field guns, but these were also repulsed. The following day the Manipur leaders sent a message together with a bribe of rations in an attempt to get Lieutenant Grant to withdraw. Although short of supplies, he sent them back saying he would do so only if he could have a member of the royal family as hostage. The Manipuris refused and brought in extra troops until they had built up a force of 2,000 men and began a continuous bombardment of Grant's position. Grant's Gurkhas held on until 9 April when, out of food and with virtually no ammunition left, Lieutenant Grant received orders under the white flag to withdraw to Tamu.

Lieutenant Grant was promoted to captain on 10 May and to brevet major on 11 May and was awarded the Victoria Cross on 26 May. The citation in the *London Gazette* read:

For the conspicuous bravery and devotion to his country displayed by him in having, upon hearing on 27 March, 1891, of the disaster at Manipur, at once volunteered to attempt the relief of the British captives, with 80 Native Soldiers and having advanced with the greatest intrepidity, captured Thobal, near Manipur, and held it against a large force of the enemy. Lieutenant Grant inspired his men with equal heroism, by an ever-present example of personal daring and resource.

In his own report of the Manipur incident, Grant recommended that every man in the party should receive the Indian Order of Merit, which was duly accepted. All received six months' pay and allowances. Ethel Grimwood, saved from possible death by the Gurkhas, was herself awarded the Royal Red Cross – a new decoration commissioned by Queen Victoria in 1883 – and a pension for life. The two officers who deserted the residency and left their Gurkhas leaderless, Major Louis Boileau and Captain George Butcher, were court-martialled and cashiered. Lieutenant Grant went on to become a full colonel, eventually commanding the 89th Punjabs before he retired in 1910 and returned to live in Sidmouth, Devon, where he died at the age of 71.

Coincidentally, another Lieutenant Grant, though of no relation to Charles but also with the 8th Gurkhas, serving in the 1st Battalion, won a VC a few years later. John Duncan Grant, the son of a British army colonel, S. Grant RE, was educated in England and attended the Royal Military College at Sandhurst. He was a member of an expedition force drawn from the 8th Gurkhas and Royal Fusiliers ordered to march on Tibet by the government of British India. The dispute had been rumbling for a decade, and when the Tibetans failed to arrive as promised at the negotiating table Sir Francis Younghusband was dispatched to Tibet with six companies of Gurkhas. They were, on this occasion, to become Gurkha cavalry, although they were not well versed in the equestrian arts and kept falling off their horses. They were given small packhorses rather than proper cavalry mounts so that they did not have so far to fall. The bridles did not fit and the girths were too long. Eventually, some decent tackle was acquired, and even a batch of more suitable horses was delivered, and they had a long cold winter to practise while hanging around to see if the Tibetans were coming to talk. By the time they moved off, horse and rider were pretty well as one. They set off on what was supposed to be a peaceful march, the Gurkha cavalry described in regimental records as a 'jolly, swashbuckling crew', although they were soon laid low by bitterly cold

71

weather in the Himalayan uplands, so cold that rifle bolts froze in the breeches.

In March a blizzard struck a supply column. There were 70 cases of snow blindness and the Gurkhas went 36 hours without food. The column moved on and by the early summer the peaceful march had become an invasion. The Gurkhas were fired on, and one action recorded by 1/8th Gurkhas was fought out at 18,000 feet (5,486 metres), which Maurice Biggs reckoned must be a record height for an infantry battalion at that time. A key element in the progression of the expedition was the overpowering of a Tibetan fortress at Gyantse, built at the top of a sheer rock face rising around 600 feet (183 metres). It was held by about 6,000 Tibetans. The order to attack the fort was given on 6 July 1904 and was to be done in two phases, first with a softening up by artillery and then a storming of the rock face.

Lieutenant John Grant and Havildar Karbir Pun led the storming party that charged the Gyantse fort. The citation in the *London Gazette* gave a full account of what happened and for which Grant was awarded his VC and the havildar won the IOM:

> ... on emerging from the cover of the village [they] had to advance up a bare, almost precipitous rock face with little or no cover and under heavy fire. Showers of rocks and stones were at the time being hurled down the hillside by the enemy. Lt Grant followed by Havildar Karbir Pun at once attempted to scale it but on reaching the top he was wounded and hurled back as was the havildar who fell down the rock some 30 feet [9 metres]. Regardless of their injuries, they again attempted to scale the breach and covered by the fire of men below were successful...the havildar shooting one Tibetan on gaining the top.

The Gurkhas quickly followed them, and the fort was taken. The Tibetans did not again attempt to contest the advance of the invaders, and they marched unopposed into Lhasa on 3 August 1904. Sir Francis Younghusband and his party entered the city to become the first Europeans, apart from a few missionaries and pilgrims, to visit the Tibetan capital. Unlike the Chinese who invaded in 1951, they did not stay.

John Grant lived on for 60 years after winning his Victoria Cross in Tibet, retiring in 1921 as a full colonel and with a CB. After he died in 1967 just before his ninetieth birthday, his widow donated the £25 honorarium given annually to the widows of holders of the Victoria Cross to the Walter Walker Scholarship Fund for Gurkha Children.

PART TWO

Ayo Gurkhali!

France, 25 September 1915. 'The beginning of the great battle of Loos in which the regiment was to win undying fame by its dash and steadfastness and in which casualties were so high . . . no battle at which the regiment had previously been present compared in any way to this nor probably will any in which they are likely in the future to be engaged.' So wrote Lieutenant Colonel C.D. Roe, Commandant, 2nd Battalion, 8th Gurkha Rifles, on the events in which the Gurkhas' famous battle cry became a familiar sound in the world theatres of war. The bloodcurdling scream of 'Ayo Gurkhali' would put the fear of God into the Germans and the Japanese in two world wars.

CHAPTER SEVEN

Slaughter of the Innocents

In 1928 Lieutenant Colonel C.D. Roe, Commandant of the 2nd Battalion, 8th Gurkha Rifles, published a short history of the battalion, now at the Gurkha Museum in Winchester, Hampshire, largely in diary form, from which the extract on the preceding page is taken. He promised that all ranks would receive a copy of the book so that they may 'read and know what fine deeds have been done by their forebears . . . the honours gained and sacrifices made on the battle-field'. He also made the point that his book, detailing the battalion's exploits, should be 'the most cherished possession of every officer and soldier' in the unit.

There was, however, at the time of Roe's publication an additional reason to reinforce and retell the highlights of recent Gurkha exploits. Historians and military analysts were, in the bitter aftermath of the First World War, taking the policies of the war managers apart and attempting to make some sort of sense out of the carnage. They couldn't, of course. So many millions had been slaughtered, their ghosts wandering through the mist and the mud of the battlefields that were still an unholy mess a decade after the war had ended. A generation of young men had been lost to every nation who partici-pated, and while military explanations to this day remain controversial the popular view prevailed that it was a slaughter of innocents.

They were all, in their way, innocents, but as this book focuses on the Gurkhas we will look at the particular poignancy, verging on the criminal, which surrounded the transportation of these young warriors in their tens of thousands half across the world to do battle in a place and a war for which they were at that time totally unsuited, completely unprepared, badly equipped, wearing the wrong clothes and with arms that were barely adequate to fight rebels on the North-West Frontier in nineteenth-century India, let alone the guns and gas of the German war machine in the world's first mechanical war.

Lieutenant Colonel Roe would make no such implication in an era so close to those events, and his book was rightly full of the gung-ho pride typical of the day recorded in comments in the newspapers and in letters home: '... the 2/8th with splendid dash went bang through the whole lot of the German trenches and captured their third line, though with appalling losses ... ' Another admitted that 'the regiment has acquired a magnificent reputation amongst those who know at the expense, really, of its existence'. On that particular day, 25 September 1915, the 2/8th battalion went out to do battle at Loos with words of encouragement from Lord Kitchener himself, who had inspected them 24 hours earlier. They had already been cut to ribbons several times in the recent past and had been reinforced with new arrivals; although originally almost 800 strong, they went out on that morning with 10 British officers, 8 Gurkha officers and 502 other ranks. In the evening, at the end of a day of incessant activity, they could muster only 1 British officer and 49 other ranks. The battalion won huge acclaim from all around it that day, but it virtually went out of business in the process. It was, without doubt, a price too high, and one that was shared by the remaining Gurkha battalions, shipped into this terrible conflict.

So let us return to the beginning of the war and the Gurkhas' enthusiasm to get going on their Great Adventure, their first real entry on the world stage that would take them to the battlefields of France and Flanders, Gallipoli, Mesopotamia, Salonika, Egypt and Palestine, never appreciating for one second what would confront them. While virtually every Gurkha battalion was involved in the Great War, it is worth staying with the 2/8th as an introduction to this section of their history to discover how they prepared for battle. It was, by no means, an orderly call to arms.

The battalion had experienced a fairly peaceful period in the preceding two or three years, when the most taxing times came from divisional and brigade manoeuvres and the pomp of grand reviews. On 7 August 1914 the battalion commandant received orders for mobilisation from their base at Lansdowne, 150 miles (241 kilometres) north-east of

Delhi. They were to be packed up and ready to move within 10 days. The mad scramble to prepare for battle in a far-off country under conditions for which Gurkha training and aptitude had never been tested, meant in fact no preparation at all. They basically just packed up and left, marching out of Lansdowne on 21 August with a strength of 9 British officers, 14 Gurkha officers and 606 other ranks. A draft of men from the 1/3rd Gurkha Rifles was hurriedly sent over to account for the men currently on leave.

The Gurkhas were filled with a mixture of apprehension and the excitement of, firstly, going over the ocean and, secondly, the prospect of fighting directly in the British army in a major war. This was viewed by most of the Gurkhas as an adventure, and no warnings from British officers could convince them of the horrors that might lie ahead; not that their superiors had much idea, either, at the beginning of their journey. It was also virtually impossible for their officers to explain to their men the causes of the war or what, exactly, they would be fighting for. The men had no concept of this so-called democracy and in their innocence would be hard put to understand that so many nations could enter into conflict sparked by the murder in Sarajevo of a member of the Austrian royal family and his wife.

There were a few teething problems to be ironed out, quite incidental to the fact of going to war. The Gurkha soldiers were uneasy about travelling over water because Hindus were forbidden to cross the 'kala pani' or black water unless given special dispensation, and a special purification ceremony, the pani patiya, was required when a Hindu returned from overseas. The hill men were very poor sailors, and many of them became violently seasick before they even left the harbour. They could not understand where the water came from or where it went; rivers always had a beginning and an end. One Gurkha famously enquired if the ship ran on rails at the bottom of the sea; otherwise how would it get to where it was going? Nor did many of them have any clue about their geographic location, and that famous phrase 'Are we there yet?' may well have been invented especially for them; they were asking it even before they reached the coast of India to board their ship.

The battalion arrived at Karachi on 3 September and embarked on the SS *Erinpura* bound for France, calling *en route* at Port Said, where three British officers who had been on leave joined the ship.

They arrived at Marseilles on 13 October and left immediately for Orléans, which they reached on 21 October. The hostilities were already well under way. In spite of the pressures of the long journey by foot, rail and sea, they had only four days to unload their gear and prepare for the final stage of their journey, arriving at Gorre, via Thiennes and Robecq, on 29 October, exhausted and filled with every emotion imaginable. After just three hours' rest they were marched to the frontline trenches near Festubert, coming under shellfire as they went and thus became the first Gurkhas to fight on British lines in the Great War in conditions that, in every respect imaginable, were totally alien to them.

By 1 a.m. on 30 October, they took possession of the trenches vacated by the Manchesters and spent the night improving defences and rectifying a problem that was to confront all Gurkhas in trench warfare: the trenches were too deep for them to see over the top to fire. It happened time and time again. If the Gurkhas took possession of trenches from a vacating unit, they were too deep; if they themselves had dug them, they were too shallow for the next goup of soldiers to possess them.

At dawn, their baptism of fire began when German shellfire rained down relentlessly on them in the cold, miserable and mud-filled, stinking dugouts, followed by an infantry attack in the late morning against the right flank of the 2/8th position. Three double companies took severe losses and had to withdraw. In their first 24 hours at the front, the losses were horrific: 6 British officers, 4 Gurkha officers and 146 rank and file killed; 3 British officers and 61 other ranks wounded. At dusk, they were relieved by the Leicesters and went into bivouac at Gorre, where they merged companies, some of which had only one or two still standing, and remained at rest until dawn on 3 November, when they returned to battle and remained in continuous combat for 19 days, losing another quarter of their men in the process.

From then until 21 December, 2/8th battalion was alternately resting at billets at Essars or in frontline trenches at Le Plantin, ten days at a time. Their losses were comparatively light: 3 killed and 11 wounded up until the last day of that period of their engagement. Then, as they prepared once more to return to their billet, they were involved in heavy fighting near Festubert. In that one action, they lost 1 Gurkha officer and 22 men; a further 5 British officers, 1 Gurkha officer and 22 men were wounded. For his gallantry in this attack, Subadar Shamsher Gurung, who was severely wounded and spent three days and nights crawling back to Allied lines, was awarded the Order of British India.

The battalion was now so badly reduced that it was temporarily taken out of action and into billets. Only 293 men remained fit for operations, and many of those, like most in the battlefields, were severely affected by frostbite and trench foot. They were ordered to remain in their billets until 2 March to await the arrival of reinforcements from India, when their strength would be raised to 11 British officers, 14 Gurkha officers and 710 rank and file.

The same story was being repeated along the line. The 2/8th battalion was just one small contingent of the Gurkha presence in France. Their much-acclaimed fighting prowess proved beyond doubt that, though mercenaries they may have been, there was no question that they were giving their utmost. Nepal was proving to be a most valuable ally. Apart from the continuous supply of its hill men, she donated a million rupees to the war effort and on King George's birthday in 1915 presented him with 31 machine guns.

By the end of November 1914 Gurkhas were being poured into France, and all units were soon heavily engaged: the 1st Battalions of the 1st, 4th and 9th, and the 2nd Battalions of the 2nd and 3rd Gurkhas saw rapid action. The 1/4th Gurkhas, called from their depot at Bakloh, would have been there earlier, but they were unfortunate enough to have sailed in the SS *Baroda*, whose engines seized up several times, leaving the ship floundering in the monsoon. The Gurkhas, desperately seasick, truly believed that the black water was about to devour them. They arrived at the front in early November, having marched out with 736 officers and men. After one single week in the trenches at Givenchy, they were down to 423. In spite of their losses, the regimental history records that 1/4th Gurkhas were 'given the honour of cutting the enemy's wire and guiding the attacking companies to the gaps'.

The company commander leading the operation was killed at the first attempt with a volley of riflefire to his head as he crawled forwards towards the German wire. Two of his men were also shot dead. Two others actually made it to the wire but were shot as they attempted to cut it, and yet two more were shot still gripping the guiding wire. Only four of the company made it back to safety. They were all awarded the Indian Order of Merit.

The 2/2nd Gurkhas had an abysmal introduction to the war in Europe – their fighting strength of 529 was cut to 382 within a matter of 2 days, a toll that included all 8 British officers. There were moments of elation, as when Rifleman Gane Gurung of the 2/3rd Gurkhas noticed small-arms fire coming from a battered house in Neuve Chapelle and proceeded to make a lone attack on the building. Standing only five feet two inches (1.57 metres), Gane Gurung emerged with eight very tall Germans marching in front of him; the men of the 2nd Rifle Brigade, moving into position as he came by, spontaneously gave him three cheers. He was awarded the Indian Order of Merit.

The Indian army fielded a corps consisting of two divisions: the Meerut Division and the Lahore Division, both of which included Gurkha battalions. Each division had three infantry brigades, although one was disembarked to guard the Suez Canal. Unused to the insidious, bitter cold, damp and blizzards, Indians and Gurkhas alike suffered badly in that atrocious winter in northern France and Belgium. Another immediate problem became evident as the losses mounted: replacements were slow in coming because they had to travel so far. Secondly, officers in the Indian Corps regiments were difficult to replace. Few were available outside India who could speak Gurkhali or Hindustani and who understood the particular ways of the Indian army soldier.

In March 1915 the British had an initial success in an attack at Neuve Chapelle but soon began to suffer setbacks. The 2/8th, so badly mutilated on their arrival, had been out of action since the end of December and by March had replenished its fighting strength to 735 with new drafts from Nepal. For the first two weeks of March, during the battle of Neuve Chapelle, they were used as divisional reserve and employed in the front line as ammunition and ration parties. Even they were clearly frustrated by the poor line management. As Lieutenant Colonel Roe made clear in his battalion history, confusion reigned and 'only after many contradictory orders did we move on to Rue Delannoy'. The Indian Corps, similarly at odds with the war planners, suffered 4,000 casualties around Neuve Chapelle mostly in three days of the battle, on 10, 11 and 12 March.

As the British generals tried to bring order to the disarray, they drew up plans for a new offensive, only to have them ruined by a totally unexpected and devastating development of the war. It began outside the little town of Ypres, in Belgium – the town that died twice as Germans and Allies fought ferocious battles in the early months of the Great War. It lay in a small pocket on the Flanders plains three miles (4.8 kilometres) inside German lines and became a citadel of courageous resistance, known to all as 'Wipers'. Its strategic location as the gateway to the channel ports meant that Ypres was under constant attack. What followed was, in the words of Sir John French, commander of the British Expeditionary Force, 'practically indescribable'. Thursday 22 April was a glorious spring day; the hedgerows of northern France were beginning to glisten with the white of bloom, and in the fields wild flowers blossomed around the crater scars. The day had passed relatively quietly, but just before 5 p.m. the Germans began their bombardment again. Heavy mortarfire pummelled Ypres and the villages in front of it. Then Allied troops on the northern shoulder of the salient heard that they would describe as a 'loud hissing sound' coming from the German lines. A cloud of whitish vapour appeared along the German front. It was, as Beatrix Potter wrote in *The Battle Book of Ypres*, an uncanny vision which gathered to the height of three men and rolled along the ground towards them, propelled on a gentle breeze. The cloud increased in intensity until it was estimated to be at least five miles (eight kilometres) wide and half a mile (0.8 kilometres) in depth, a massive man-made fog of poisonous fumes, heading inexorably towards the unsuspecting troops.

In the first-ever use of poisonous gas in warfare, the Germans had placed 5,730 cylinders containing 160 tonnes of chlorine along a four-mile (six-kilometre) stretch of the front. It was a devastating chemical that attacked the lungs of its victims, producing an instant accumulation of liquid in the windpipe, frothing into the mouth and blocking the lungs so that the casualties actually drowned in their own fluids. As the gas cloud began to knock down the enemy, German infantry, their faces masked with moist gauze tied across their mouths and noses, advanced firing at will, but even they were shocked by the scenes of sheer horror that would confront them. Bodies littered the battlefield. Men with faces of tortured agony had collapsed gasping for air. Those who were still alive were heaving up the terrible yellow fluid from their lungs. Their weapons, the metal buttons on their uniforms and even their watches had turned green.

In his account of the resultant battlefield mayhem, Colonel E.D. Swinton wrote:

Behind the wall of poisonous vapour which had swept across fields, through woods, came the German firing line . . . Allowing sufficient time for the fumes to take full effect, the Germans charged forward over a practically unresisting enemy and, penetrating the gap thus created, pressed on silently and swiftly south and west . . . and then when their infantry had reached well behind the enemy lines, the Germans opened hot artillery fire with a bombardment of high-explosive shell and shrapnel of various calibres and also with projectile containing more asphyxiating gas.

It was many hours before the Allied commanders were able to assess the scale of the disaster that had overwhelmed them. In fact, the gas scorched a four-mile (six-kilometre) hole in the Allied lines. Sir John French wrote: 'It was impossible to realise what had actually happened. Fumes and smoke obscured everything and within an hour of it being launched the whole position had to be abandoned along with 50 guns.'

All the men could do was hold moistened cloth over their faces during a gas attack. In the trenches, soldiers had to urinate on socks, handkerchiefs or any other pieces of material they could rip from their battledress to tie around their faces. The gas attacks continued on 1, 6, 10 and 24 May. Yet five more weeks of fighting around Ypres secured no breakthrough. A stalemate had been reached, and the Germans brought the battle to an end. German losses totalled 35,000 officers and men; Allied casualties were about 70,000. In those five weeks around Ypres, the Germans had released 500 tonnes of chlorine from 20,000 canisters. As the Second Battle of Ypres was being left for historians to record and assess, the first chapter in the history of chemical warfare had been written.

There were moments of light relief in all of this carnage. When gas masks were finally delivered to the British troops, there were gales of laughter provided by the black humour of the Gurkha ranks. Each time a man put on his mask, his colleagues thought it was a huge joke.

Kipling wrote of the devotion of the Gurkhas to the British Crown, demonstrated at the Lying in State of Edward VII in 1910, when only British Guardsmen and two Gurkhas were selected to guard the body.

Major Dal Bahadur Gurung, formerly a Queen's Gurkha Orderly Officer and a Member of the Victorian Order after service at Buckingham Palace, is a fourth-generation soldier whose maternal great-grandfather was one of the two Gurkhas selected to guard Edward VII's coffin, shown above. (*John Parker*)

Where the Gurkha tradition began – the mountain-top fortress near the town of Gorkha, Nepal, where King Prithvi Narayan Shah enlisted men from the Himalaya foothills to conquer all in his path. It is today a must-see for visitors to Gurkha homelands.

Side by side, two white obelisks erected in the memory of the fallen at the battle of Kalunga in 1815. British officers were so impressed by their cheerful and courageous foe they erected memorials to them as well as to their own men killed in action – and promptly began recruiting Gurkhas into their own ranks.

And so came into being the British Gurkha Rifles – as here, with the 4th Goorkhas as they were then known, photographed in 1880.

Gurkhas fought famous battles for the British against the Indian army sepoys during the Indian Mutiny of 1857. They also had skirmishes with the Sikhs, although all were later united in the Tirah campaigns on the North-West frontier which continued well into the 1940s.

Line Boys – sons of Gurkhas living in married quarters were recruited as line boys, running supplies to battle fronts from an early age.

As far as the eye can see, a column of the 5th Gurkha Rifles stretches back into the distance on route to battle with ruthless, bloodthirsty tribesmen on the North-West frontier which occupied Gurkha regiments intermittently for more than sixty years.

In the trenches: men of the 9th Gurkha Rifles in France in 1914. Their height – average 5ft 3in – posed a problem. Trenches dug for British soldiers were too deep while theirs were too shallow for the Brits. Tall British officers were banned from Gurkha units, because of the high mortality rate.

A historic moment in the First World War – the first-ever air drop. Supplies, slung below the pilot's seat, were thrown out to besieged British regiments at Kut-el Amara, in Mesopotamia. The heroic effort in 1915 was hopelessly inadequate for the 2,600 British and 10,486 Indian and Gurkha troops and their commanders had to surrender them into the custody of the Turks. Almost 5,000 were never seen again.

Battle honours abounded in the Second World War, most notably marching to further notoriety with Field Marshal William Slim's 14th 'Forgotten Army' in Burma and defeat of the Japanese.

Two of the Japanese tanks destroyed single-handedly by Rifleman Ganju Lama of the 7th Gurkha Rifles (*pictured right*), using a PIAT anti-tank weapon in June 1944 for which he was awarded the Victoria Cross.

Home leave and communications with their native Nepal remained a problem for Gurkhas well into the twentieth century. Nepal was closed to the outside world until 1951 at which time the nation possessed just 124 miles of motorable roads. The first car was not seen in Kathmandu until the mid-1930s. With no link to India, it took 120 porters eight days to carry the vehicle to the nearest point where it could be driven. Similarly the bridges and connections across a hostile landscape, regularly hit by earthquakes and landslides, were precariously navigated. In the latter, little had changed by the end of the century.

Traditions remain pretty well unchanged. The Gurkhas were given every opportunity to recognise their religious ceremonies and festivals, although these were never performed in Britain. The most important of these ceremonies involved the swift and clean sacrificial beheading of a buffalo; the ceremony remains a common sight in Nepal and the temples of Kathmandu today.

Gurkha women in the married lines, permitted in India and other Asian postings but not in Britain until 1996.

From the Malayan Emergency of the 1950s through to the Borneo Confrontation of the 1960s, virtually all Gurkha regiments took a hand against Communist terrorists and Indonesian incursions into British protectorates. In both, demonstrated here with their first use of helicopters (*above*) and later rounding up terrorists in Sarawak in 1968, they made a highly successful partnership with the SAS.

With a standoff in the German offensive, the British counter-attacked, but they were brought to a halt once again in mid-May at Festubert, the scene of earlier costly action for the Gurkhas. The 2/2nd lost five British officers within five minutes of their appearance at the front. The 1/4th lost 243 men out of 603 engaged. Among them was No. 4817 Rifleman Motilal Thapa, whom Captain J.R. Hartwell discovered as he slid for cover, wounded, into a crater. He found Motilal Thapa badly wounded with one arm totally shattered. Both men had been blown up in the first advance. They lay back to await the stretcher-bearers, but none came. Captain Hartwell slipped into uncon-sciousness and awoke to find Motilal lying by his side with his one good arm holding his field service cap over the captain's face to keep the sun from his eyes. Clearly in terrible pain, he was saying to himself out loud: 'I must not cry out. I am a Gurkha.' Motilal had lost too much blood, and when aid finally came, he was beyond saving. He died before they reached the medical station.

The 2/8th, meanwhile, which had acted as the supplies party until new recruits arrived from Nepal, was thrust back into the frontline trenches by the Rue de Bois in April and throughout the summer of 1915. The pattern – and that of all Gurkha units – was now a familiar one of heavy duty at the front, heavy shelling, heavy casualties, followed by a brief respite in the billets and back again to the front. It was clear, however, that some great effort was under way as both sides took advantage of the fine weather to re-equip and replenish ammuni-tion and supplies. The expected 'big one' arrived in September – the great battle of Loos. Lord Kitchener came to inspect the Gurkha (and other) soldiers and give them words of encouragement, fighting for the honour of the regiment and so on. His arrival, like an unwanted spirit, was always a bad sign. If recent history was to be relied on, it meant that during the massive onslaught that now lay ahead, a very large proportion of the chaps would perish. So let us defer to the events chronicled by Lieutenant Colonel Roe in his history of the 2/8th:

On 25 September began the great battle of Loos in which the regiment was to win undying fame by its dash and steadfast-ness . . . No battle in which the regiment had previously been present compared in any way with this nor probably will any in which they are likely to be engaged in the future. It was certainly the battle on the greatest scale ever attempted by the forces of our Empire . . . certainly the annals of war up to September 1915 had no parallel. Such was the field when the 2/8th formed for the attack at dawn, being the left battalion of the assaulting British Garhwal Brigade of the 7th Meerut Division of the Indian Corps, the other two being the 2/3rd Gurkhas on the right and the 2nd Leicestershire Regiment in the centre; on our left was the 4th Black Watch.

The Gurkhas and the Leicestershires in the event went in behind smoke grenades, some wearing gas masks, and although the attack looked to have been successful, as the troops came into view through the smoke the Germans opened fire with their machine guns and picked them off as if at a duck shoot. Lieutenant Colonel Roe's account continued:

With great dash the battalion assaulted and seized the German lines. Lieutenant Inglis (in the front line) was killed immediately but 50 men of his C Company pushed on to the 3rd German line and a position occupied beyond it. Now ensued desperate fighting with the battalion practically isolated, units on the left and right could not be located. Finally A Company, heavily shelled and fired at from a flank, came and linked up with C Company. Gradually others came up and the commanding officer, Colonel Morris, was wounded when bringing up a party of D Company. The position was obscure but 2/8th were hanging on to what they had won but men were falling fast.

Several efforts were made to clear up the situation and Captain Buckland on two occasions endeavoured to link up with other units. A gallant but ineffectual counterattack was organised and, led by Subadar Sarabjit Gurung, was directed against very strong enemy forces who were coming in from the right but the odds were too great and our attack was killed to a man. The strength of the battalion was by now reduced to about 100. Finally after much fighting in holding to the position won our strength was reduced to around 30. The battalion (or what was left of it) was forced to retire as troops on the flanks had fallen back.

At the end of the day the casualties were: 9 British officers, 8 Gurkha officers, 453 rank and file; 166 taken prisoner, many of them wounded and who subsequently died. Lieutenant Colonel Roe quoted the reactions of General Sir James Willcocks, commanding the Indian Corps:

> And what of the 8th Gurkhas who had begun the war on that bleak day, 30 October 1914? The old battalion had practically disappeared . . . they suffered so terribly in the early days . . . it was determined to leave its mark deep cut on the soil of Flanders. Colonel Morris, who had been severely wounded a year earlier, paid with his life, as did many of his officers . . . and we may pronounce that the 8th Gurkhas indeed did their duty and found their Valhalla.

It was with some hint of disdain and a good deal of emotion that Lieutenant Colonel Roe concluded his account of the 2/8th in France:

> This in a few cold words gives some idea of what our comrades did on that day, a day which became honoured as the battalion annual day and long may it continue so as to remind those of us who come after how the old corps bore itself on these distant battlefields. Our depleted battalion now moved to billets to be rested and to be gradually made up to strength again . . . [thereafter] returning to the arduous and dangerous duty in the front trenches, with attendant loss of comrades until 10 November 1915 when the battalion left for Marseilles bound for Egypt after 18 months' service in the fiercest portion of the greatest war in history under conditions difficult and strange enough to try sorely any troops. That our battalions came through this ordeal with honour will always be our pride.

Meanwhile, the 2/3rd battalion, part of the Meerut Division's holding attack at Loos, was given a pivotal task in the later stages of the operation. It was discovered that the British artillery had not cut the German wires as planned, hoped and expected. As a result, German machine guns mowed down the men of the 2/3rd as they came forward, hampered as they were in the attack by having to wear gas masks because of the chlorine escaping from their own damaged canisters. The battalion was being cut to pieces, and it was decided that a party of 38 men led by an officer should fight their way through a German trench and attempt to cut the German wires, thus providing a route through.

The party was gunned down to a man, the sole survivor, Rifleman Kulbir Thapa, though badly wounded, suddenly found himself alone. He began to crawl back towards the British lines, travelling just a few feet at a time. He had not gone far when he came upon a wounded soldier from the 2nd Leicestershire Regiment who was also badly shot up, had lost a lot of blood and was unable to move. Kulbir made him as comfortable as possible and stayed with him throughout the rest of that day and all night – in spite of the British soldier's urgings that he should go on and save himself.

As dawn broke and a heavy mist lay over the battlefield, Kulbir Thapa decided it was time to move out; the mist would give him at least some cover. He hoisted the British soldier across his back and set off in the direction of the Allied lines. It was a tortuous journey often within spitting distant of German positions, when he had to drag and pull the wounded man across the ground, and then through barbed wire. Further along in this nerve-racking journey, Kulbir Thapa came across two more wounded men, both Gurkhas and both unable to walk. He explained he had to get the British soldier to a place of safety and once he had done that he would come back for them. He carried on until he located a deep shell crater where he could hide the Leicestershire soldier, and then he returned for the Gurkhas. He carried them both safely, one after the other, into the Allied lines and then returned to the British soldier. As he carried him back, Kulbir was spotted by a German lookout and came under heavy fire; half-running, half-stumbling, he made it back. All three men survived, and Kulbir himself became the first Gurkha to be awarded the Victoria Cross. His citation, published in the *London Gazette* in November 1915, was a glowing tribute to his outstanding courage, an act of singular bravery that came not in the heat of battle but in the cold light of day and over a sustained period of two days. Kulbir, then 26 years old, also survived later fighting with his regiment, was promoted to havildar and went on to Egypt, eventually returning to India to complete his service contract. He eventually retired on a pension and died in his homeland of Nepal in 1956 at the age of 68.

Although focusing on the 2/8th and 2/3rd in the above recollections of Gurkha activity in France and Flanders, similar exploits confronted all battalions, and General Sir James Willcocks was unequivocal in his praise, stating that the Gurkhas were undoubtedly his best soldiers. In the event, the battered Indian Corps, which included the Gurkha battalions, was withdrawn and posted elsewhere in the late autumn of 1915. It had sustained 25,000 casualties up to that point, and 8 of its members won the Victoria Cross. There could be no doubting the Gurkhas' contribution once there, but there was considerable disquiet as to the wisdom of sending them in the first place.

CHAPTER EIGHT

Gallipoli: Chaos and Calamity

The attempted Allied advance on the Gallipoli Peninsula became famous for the damage it caused to the reputations of its principal architects in the British War Cabinet and the horrendous casualty figures: almost half of the one million men eventually committed to the operation on both sides fell victim to sickness or battle wounds. The campaign was more generally associated with the exploits and the heavy losses of the Australian and New Zealand Army Corps (ANZAC). Less well known is the involvement of the Gurkhas, who were shipped to the Dardanelles strait in ever-increasing numbers during the period of high activity at the special request of the commander of land forces, General Sir Ian Hamilton. The Gurkhas were to form an integral part of the land attack by a joint force of British, Australian, New Zealand, French Foreign Legion and Indian Army soldiers in what would prove to be a vain and disastrous attempt to invade Turkey and take her out of the war.

The campaign was devised by British munitions minister David Lloyd George, First Lord of the Admiralty Winston Churchill, General Kitchener and Admiral Sackville H. Carden. Their aim was to open up a further war theatre to distract the Germans from throwing a new offensive into the stalemate in France in the early months of 1915, take Turkish pressure off Russian forces in the Caucasus and provide Russia with a direct link to the Mediterranean via the Black Sea. The plan as originally devised was meant to be a wholly naval operation, but it failed at the first hurdle. In February 1915 a Royal Navy flotilla with assistance from the French shelled the forts guarding the Dardanelles strait. The Turks were in disarray and running until three ageing British battleships sailed into an unnoticed minefield and were sunk. The naval commander ordered an immediate retreat for fear of having more of his vessels sent to the bottom, and the whole episode did no more than alert the Turks and their German allies to the weakness of the strategically important Gallipoli peninsula.

With the naval bombardment halted, the British war planners decided on an invasion by land forces, to be mounted as soon as feasible under the command of General Hamilton. He was a widely experienced soldier but on this occasion somewhat timorous and apparently worried by the suicidal approaches that his forces would have to negotiate; as he rightly predicted, enemy machine gunners could simply mow down invading troops – as they did. The landings of the Allied forces were set for mid-April, for what proved to be a hurried and ill-defined assault. With less than three weeks to go, Hamilton wrote to Kitchener on 25 March 1915: 'I am very anxious, if possible, to get a brigade of Gurkhas, so as to complete the New Zealand Divisional Organisation with a type of man who will, I am most certain, be most valuable on the Gallipoli peninsula. The scrubby hillsides on the south-west faces of the plateau are just the sort of terrain where these little fellows are their brilliant best . . . each little "Gurk" might be worth his full weight in gold at Gallipoli.'

Hamilton had asked for 100,000 men but was given far fewer, at best around 76,000, including, initially, three battalions of Gurkhas – 1/5th, 1/6th and 2/10th – who came together in what was to be known as the 29th Indian Brigade, but they did not arrive in time for the first assault. There were delays for the British troops, too, in that the ships carrying men, supplies and animals from England had not been loaded in combat order (i.e. first needed, first off) and the ships had to tie up in Greece to be off-loaded and repacked. By the time the British, with one French division, arrived, German officers commanding the Turkish defence had amassed 60,000 troops along the coastline to be attacked. On 25 April 1915 the expeditionary force prepared to land on five sites around the key locations of Cape Hellas on the peninsula and at An Burnu, 12 miles (19 kilometres) or so north. The Allies came ashore in cutters towed by steam pinnaces, and cut a dash across the landing beaches. At some locations, opposition was minimal; at most places, however, the Turks had dispersed machine gunners across the surrounding hills. As the Allies came ahead, they were sent diving for cover. At An Burnu, where the Turks were dug in on a hillside known as Chunuk Bair, the ANZAC troops designated to take it were turned back by ferocious fire with a loss of 5,000 men.

The 1/6th Gurkha battalion commanded by the Honourable Charles Bruce was the first of the Gurkhas to arrive at Gallipoli, landing in Cape Hellas. There was no time to settle in; they were put on stand-by almost as soon as they landed and suffered their first casualties only hours later. Within two weeks, the Gurkhas were leading the assault in their first major operation to take out a Turkish high point, alive with machine gunners who were doing untold damage to the invasion attempts. The Royal Marines and the 1 Dublin Fusiliers had already tried but were driven back. The rocks were sheer and 300 feet (91 metres) high. With typical Gurkha sure-footedness, they ran up the side of it, firing as they went, and set the Turks to flight after some sharp hand-to-hand fighting in which 12 enemy troops were decapitated, apart from those shot. Eighteen Gurkhas were killed in the operations and forty-two were wounded. Hamilton signed an order stating that henceforth this hill would be known as Gurkha Bluff.

The 1/6th were not so lucky – if lucky means losing *only* that number of men – when they joined the attempt to dislodge the Turks from their stronghold on another impregnable vantage point, a 700-foot (213-metre) dominant height known as Achi Baba as part of the ongoing battle of Krithia. The attacks and counterattacks, along with others all along the war zone, raged on for days and then weeks, with the Allies making some headway only to be thrown back. In early June, the 1/5th and 2/10th Gurkhas arrived, but they soon discovered the difficulties, if not the impossibilities, of attacking an enemy lodged in well-hidden nests while the only protection to troops below was in the shadow of overhanging rocks. All three Gurkha battalions were now engaged, and they often used their kukris to striking effect. The Turks are said to have lost 10,000 men a week. British casualties were also enormous: around 7,000 men on that one operation. The Gurkha units, invariably at the head of advancing Allied columns, were hit badly. Within a few hours, the 1/5th lost 129 men and 7 British officers. On the same mission the 1/6th took 95 casualties. In their first 35 days at Gallipoli, the 2/10th Gurkhas lost three-quarters of its

British officers and 40 per cent of its other ranks. The Gurkha brigade had been put to every test since its arrival and urgently needed reinforcements and respite. It was withdrawn from Gallipoli and sent to the isle of Imbros for a month.

They returned rested and ready for battle in early August to a place that was hell. The midday sun was now overpoweringly intense, and on the shimmering waves of heat wafted the appalling, acrid stench of rotting human flesh from the dead, lying where they fell in no man's land smothered with millions of flies which switched with alacrity to the men's rations at mealtimes. The Allies made little progress from the eight beachheads they had established, and on 7 August, with the arrival of 20,000 reinforcements, including the return of the 29th Brigade of Gurkhas, whose numbers were increased by the arrival of the 2/10th from France, Hamilton began a new offensive. It was to be his grand effort against Turkish positions. Once again, however, the cautious leadership of the British command offset the increase in firepower while the Turks were inspired by the leadership of Kemal Atatürk, later president of Turkey, and the skill of German commander Otto Liman von Sanders. The advancing force faced steep and difficult terrain, rocky outcrops, sheer cliffs or dense scrub. So-called guides turned out to be useless because there had been no time for a recce of the lie of the land. The joint force of Gurkhas led the advance in darkness to capture the first objective while the 1/6th Gurkhas went with the Australians attacking the second nearby peak. In his field report, General Hamilton would record:

> The first step in the real push – the step which above all others was meant to count – was the night attack on the summits of the Sari Bair ridge. The crest line of this lofty mountain range runs parallel to the sea, dominating the Anzac position. From the main ridge a series of spurs run down towards the level beach, and are separated from one another by deep, jagged gullies choked up with dense jungle. It was our object to effect a lodgement along the crest of the high main ridge with two columns of troops but, seeing the nature of the ground and the dispositions of the enemy, the effort had to be made by stages. The two assaulting columns, which were to work up three ravines to the storm of the high ridge, were to be preceded by two covering columns. The whole of this big attack

was placed under the command of Major General Sir A.J. Godley, General Officer Commanding New Zealand and Australian Division, assisted by heavy bombardment from HMS *Colne*. The scarped heights were scaled, the plateau was carried by midnight. The grand attack was now in full swing, but the country gave new sensations in cliff climbing even to officers and men who had graduated over the goat tracks. The darkness of the night, the density of the scrub, hands and knees progress up the spurs, sheer physical fatigue, exhaustion of the spirit caused by repeated hairbreadth escapes from the hail of random bullets, all these combined to take the edge of the energies of our troops. Dawn broke, and the crest line was not yet in our hands, although, considering all things, the left assaulting column had made a marvellous advance. With this brilliant feat the task of the right covering force was at an end. Its attacks had been made with the bayonet and bomb only; magazines were empty by order; hardly a rifle shot had been fired. Some 150 prisoners were captured, as well as many rifles and much equipment, ammunition and stores. No words can do justice to the achievement of [these] men. There are exploits which must be seen to be realised . . . At 4.30 a.m. on August 9, the Chunuk Bair ridge and Hill Q were heavily shelled. The naval gun, and the guns on the left flank, and as many as possible from the right flank took part in this cannonade which rose to its climax at 5.15 a.m. when the whole ridge seemed a mass of flame and smoke, whence huge clouds of dust drifted slowly upwards in strange patterns on to the sky. At 5.16 a.m. this tremendous bombardment was to be switched off on to the flanks and reverse slopes of the heights. General A.H. Baldwin's column [a brigade of four battalions] moving up [towards the peak] . . . to launch the battalions in successive lines. In plain English, Baldwin, owing to the darkness and the awful country, lost his way . . . time did not permit detailed reconnaissance of routes which is so essential where operations are to be carried out by night.

And now, under the fine leader, Major C.G.L. Allanson, the Sixth Gurkhas of the 29th Indian Infantry Brigade pressed up the slopes of Sari Bair, crowned the heights between Chunuk Bair and Hill Q, viewed far beneath them the waters of the Hellespont, viewed the Asiatic shores along which motor transport was bringing supplies to the lighters. Not only did this battalion, as well as some of the Sixth South Lancashire Regiment, reach the crest, but they began to attack down the far side of it, firing as they went at the fast-retreating enemy. But the fortune of war was against us. At this supreme moment, Baldwin's column was still a long way from the crest whence they should even now have been sweeping along the whole ridge of the mountain. And instead of Baldwin's support came suddenly a salvo of heavy shell.

Major Allanson of 1/6th Gurkhas fills in the gaps in Hamilton's account with his own description of the assault on the Turkish position at the peak:

I had taken my watch out: 5.15 a.m. I never saw such artillery preparations; the trenches were being torn to pieces; the accuracy was marvellous as we were just below. At 5.18 it had not stopped and I wondered if my watch was wrong. 5.20. Silence. I waited three minutes to be certain, great as the risk was. Then off we dashed, all hand in hand, most perfect and a wonderful sight. At the top we met the Turks; Le Marchant was down, a bayonet through the heart. I got one through the leg, and then for about what appeared to be ten minutes we fought hand to hand, we hit and fisted, and used rifles and pistols as clubs and then the Turks turned and fled, and I felt a very proud man: the key of the whole peninsula was ours, and our losses had not been so very great for such a result. Below I saw the strait, motors and wheeled transport on the road leading to Achi Baba. As I looked round I saw that we were not going to be supported and thought I could help best by going after those who had retreated in front of us. We dashed down toward Maoris but only about 200 feet [61 metres] when suddenly our Navy put six 12-inch (0.3-metre) monitor shells into us and all was terrible confusion. It was a deplorable disaster; we were obviously mistaken for Turks and we had to go back.

The Gurkhas held the peak for 15 minutes and prepared a gap for General Baldwin's column of four battalions to exploit, but they simply failed to turn up. The column became hopelessly lost and by the time the men had found their way again, it was all too late. Some reinforcements did arrive from the South Lancashires and the War-wickshires. For the whole of the following day, the Gurkhas and British troops were marooned on the rocks below the peak, under baking sun with no water and running low on ammunition. The wounded among them were in a desperate plight but could not be reached through gunfire which opened up every time someone tried. General Hamilton's field report gives a vivid account of the final collapse of the operation for which he had such high hopes:

> The Turkish commander saw his chance. Instantly his troops were rallied and brought back in a countercharge, and the Lancashires and Gurkhas, who had seen the promised land and had seemed for a moment to have held victory in their grasp, were forced backwards over the crest, and on to the lower slopes whence they had first started. At daybreak on 10 August, the Turks delivered a grand attack from the line against these two battalions, already weakened in numbers, though not in spirit, by previous fighting. First our men were shelled by every enemy gun and then at 5.30 a.m. were assaulted by a huge column, consisting of no less than a full division plus a regiment of three battalions. The Lancashire men were simply overwhelmed in their shallow trenches by sheer weight of numbers, while the Wilts, who were caught out in the open, were literally almost annihilated. The ponderous masses of the enemy swept over the crest, turned the right flank of our line below, swarmed round the Hampshires and General Baldwin's column, which had to give ground, and were only extricated with great difficulty and very heavy losses.

This one outrageously foolhardy operation cost the British, Australian, New Zealand and Gurkha troops 12,000 casualties and, worse, the losses continued as the British commanders stubbornly stayed put at a place that was all but lost. Apart from the casualties of battle, literally thousands fell with disease from the stinking, fly-blown arena. The troops prayed for the coolness of winter and then wished they hadn't; it brought bitterly cold winds and torrential freezing rain which flooded trenches so that some resembled fast-flowing rivers. Towards the end of November, a south-westerly gale blew in a raging blizzard and for days the Gallipoli peninsula became a white hell. The delivery parties bearing food, water and ammunition could not get through, and many companies were simply cut off, out of touch and starving. And now, to the toll of the wounded and weary was added more appalling statistics: the Allies lost a further 10 per cent of their manpower to the weather: 200 men drowned in the trenches; at least 100 simply froze to death; 58 Gurkhas lost one or both feet from frostbite; and in the 2/10th alone there were 477 cases of frostbite of whom 10 died and 80 were crippled for life.

All the Gurkha battalions had suffered heavily, both in battle and to the conditions. The 2/10th, for example, had arrived at Gallipoli with 13 British officers, 17 Gurkha officers and 734 other ranks. Now, as it prepared to depart six months later, only one British officer and seventy-nine Gurkha other ranks remained from the original battalion. In the two years since the battalion had left India, it had suffered 1,450 casualties and a mere handful of the original members remained active.

The British officers, however, were amazed at the Gurkhas' general resilience even at the most desperate of times, and the spirit of that admiration was no better captured than in the diaries of Captain Watson Smith, B Company Commander, 1/6th Gurkhas, writing at the time of the blizzard and cold:

The 29th [November] was the first time since the 26th evening that I was able to get off the men's boots, and the state of their feet appalled me. In nearly every case they had lumps of ice between their toes; their feet were white as far as the ankle and insensible to touch. Throughout all this time I never heard a single complaint. The men were cheerful and ready to laugh at a joke. No praise could be too high for them. To give one instance, my field orderly, Hastabir Pun, had accompanied me everywhere during the three days; always he was at my heels, and never had been anything but cheerful and yet on the 30th, when I made him show me his feet, to my horror I found them black with gangrene from neglected frostbite. He had never said a word to me and never would have. His case is not an exceptional one, but merely a typical example of the courage these Gurkhas displayed.

The stalemate remained solid. Hamilton was relieved of his post and was replaced by General Sir Charles Monro, who recommended immediate evacuation, and so called to an end the Gallipoli expedition which had been dogged by bad luck and poor leadership but highlighted by outstanding heroism from British, Australian, New Zealand, French and Gurkha troops. The final act of evacuating the remaining 90,000 men, 4,500 animals, 1,700 vehicles and 200 guns turned out to be the most skilful part of the whole operation – carried out under the noses of the Turks at night while by day the Allies appeared to be continuing their daily routine. Expecting a massive bombardment and many thousands of casualties, 30,000 hospital beds had been prepared in Mediterranean hospitals but were not needed. There had been deaths enough: Anglo-ANZAC casualties during the Gallipoli expedition totalled 205,000 out of 410,000 called into service there; the French sustained 47,000 casualties out of 79,000 men, and the Turks between 250,000 and 300,000 out of 500,000. In spite of its overall failure, the Gallipoli campaign weakened the Turks enough to facilitate the British seizure of Palestine in 1917. The action also distracted the Germans from a plan they had in 1915 to begin another offensive in France, but the cost was ridiculously high.

Among the first in at Gallipoli, the Gurkhas were also the last to leave: C Company of the 2/5th Gurkhas tied pieces of blanket around their boots to deaden the sound of their footsteps and crept down the beach to waiting navy boats, thus ending their involvement in this sorry story. There was a postscript to it some time later, when General Hamilton's secretary wrote to the colonel of the 6th Gurkha Rifles: 'It is Sir Ian Hamilton's most cherished conviction that had he been given more Gurkhas in the Dardanelles then he would never have been held up by the Turks.'

Nor was that the end of it, not by a long chalk. The Gurkhas were now destined for even greater challenges east of Suez and especially in the ancient state of Mesopotamia. As one of the earliest centres of urban civilisation, Mesopotamia covered an area which is modern-day Iraq and eastern Syria, between the Tigris and Euphrates rivers as they flow south out of Turkey before they converge and flow into the Persian Gulf. The river valleys and plains of Mesopotamia were always open to attack from the rivers, the northern and eastern hills, and the Arabian desert and Syrian steppe to the west, and Mesopotamia's richness regularly attracted its neighbours. At the start of the Great War, the Ottoman Turkish Empire held Mesopotamia which provided a vital link to the Gulf. Around it on either side were British and French colonial interest in Persia, Arabia and Syria, and beyond to Egypt and Suez.

Here, the 'other war' – overshadowed by events in Europe – exploded, and the Gurkhas were involved almost from day one, when two key objectives were identified for the Allies: to maintain control of Suez and to protect the Persian oilfields.

These objectives became even more crucial when on 14 November 1914 Turkey proclaimed a holy war – Muslims against the Christian British. In a region whose lands had been controlled by rival colonising forces for centuries, the war in Europe was of little consequence. Those communities were confronted by a confusion of political and religious values which cut right across the continents of Asia, Africa and the Middle East, and, of all British possessions and protectorates, India especially followed events with interest. Indian troops would also figure strongly in the attempts to dislodge the Turks, and at various times during the war all ten Gurkha regiments had one or more battalions fighting in Mesopotamia.

When Turkey entered the war on the side of Germany and Austria, Britain moved a large force into southern Mesopotamia, and the names of towns and cities that were to become familiar to later generations in the twentieth century were in the theatre of war. All British operations were to be controlled by the government of India through the Viceroy. They began by capturing Basra, and General Sir John E. Nixon, who commanded the Anglo-Indian troops, was to annex what territories he felt necessary to give British control of Mesopotamia.

In April, after beating off two Turkish attacks, Major General C.V.F. Townshend, commanding the 9th Indian Division, began his advance up the Tigris in a flotilla of boats. Major General George F. Gorringe was sent up to the Euphrates, and he definitely drew the short straw. The summer heat beat on his men, and as they progressed they ran out of navigable water and the boats had to be pulled through swamps. The troops dropped like the flies that surrounded them, from dysentery, malaria and heatstroke. Almost half of 2/7th Gurkhas, part of Gorringe's force, were laid low. Even so, they pressed on and fought several minor battles, one of them in particular becoming part of regimental history. The Gorringe force was held up by a Turkish outpost at Nasiriya, and the Gurkhas, weakened by sickness, looked for a while as if they might lose the scrap. That was until Naik Harkarat Rai of the 2/7th, realising that his colleagues needed a touch of impetus, leaped out from the Gurkhas' position, screamed out the cry 'Ayo Gurkhali!' and made a dash for the Turkish entrenchment followed instantly by his company, all yelling like wild things with kukris swishing and swirling. Thirteen Turks fell dead, several of them decapitated. The date, 24 July, became known as Nasiriya Day in the 7th Gurkha Rifles and was thereafter celebrated annually as their regimental day.

The march through Mesopotamia had gone well. Much ground had been won with relatively few casualties, and General Townshend became aware that those above him had Baghdad in their sights. It would be a marvellous coup, Nixon argued, to take the Mesopotamian capital, with its population of around 150,000. Townshend was against the idea unless his force of 10,000 infantry, including his Gurkha contingents, 1,000 cavalry, 38 guns and 7 aircraft was substantially increased. The issue was being debated back in London when he was ordered to advance on Kut-el-Amara, 200 miles (321 kilometres) from Baghdad and close to where the two rivers converged, where the Turks had put down a force of around 10,000 men. Townshend had little difficulty with them and put the Turkish army to flight after capturing 1,300 prisoners and all their guns.

The Turks drew back to Ctesiphon, the ruined former capital of Mesopotamia, and Townshend moved on in pursuit. The issue of launching an attack on Baghdad once again came up. Lord Kitchener was firmly against; Townshend, he said, had insufficient troops for such an undertaking, and there were not enough reinforcements available. General Nixon remained bullish, and he was supported by the Viceroy of India, who was a man of influence in this war. So Townshend was ordered to push on and advance to Ctesiphon, where the Turks were now spread out and dug in. Unknown to the British, reinforcements had been rushed in. Not only was Townshend out-gunned, but he would face a combined force of regulars and Arab conscripts of close on 21,000 men.

So began the countdown to one more great disaster in the adventures of the Gurkha soldiers who, needless to say, were at the forefront of early attacks on the difficult Turkish position in Ctesiphon. Around 300 men of the 2/7th and about 100 men of the 21st Punjab Regiment had become marooned on high ground surrounded by an entire Turkish division. They held off several thousand Turkish riflemen for many hours until Townshend pulled back. He made several unsuccessful attacks on the Turks over the next eight days, and bitter fighting ensued, with the loss of 4,600 men of the British force. Townshend was forced to withdraw his force back to Kut-el-Amara, a small town on the loop of the river Tigris, with the Turks in hot pursuit.

On 3 December they threw a cordon around the British encampment and called on Townshend to surrender. He refused and remained confident that a relief column would come to their aid and put the Turks to flight. Such a force was even then being prepared to march but would face *en route* constant harassment from the Turks, which slowed it down to a snail's pace. By late January the relief column was nowhere near the siege site and conditions were deteriorating. According to regimental records, the Gurkhas kept their spirits up and were as 'busy as ferrets'. The Indian troops were less happy, however, because, as the food began to run out, the animals were being slaughtered on a daily basis for food, and they adamantly refused to eat horsemeat on religious grounds; they said they would rather starve – and that now seemed a strong possibility. By March, the relief column had still not managed to reach the besieged troops, who were now desperate for supplies. For the first time in history, aircraft were used to drop 16,800 pounds (7,620 kilogrammes) of food, flying low and dangerously over the Turkish cordon and through random firing from the ground.

The air drop was welcome but quite inadequate to keep the thousands of men in rations for more than a few days. Meanwhile, the relief troops were not only unable to break through the Turks' cordon but were now coming under continuous attack themselves from a strong Turkish presence, commanded by German General Kilmer von der Goltz. Over a period of several weeks, the relief force suffered 21,000 casualties; it was bogged down less than 20 miles (32 kilometres) from the now starving garrison, whose last hope of escape from the terrible conditions in which they were forced to exist seemed to have vanished.

In London there were rumours of an important announcement being made about the trapped British force, and on 29 April the War Office released a statement which shocked the whole nation:

After a siege which has lasted for 143 days, Major General Charles Townshend, commanding the 6th (Poona) Division today surrendered unconditionally to the Turkish general Khalil Pasha at Kut-el-Amara in Mesopotamia. Resistance to the Turkish onslaught has been conducted with gallantry and fortitude but failed because of the shortage of supplies.

The news caused great dismay throughout the Empire, especially in India. For a British force of such magnitude to lay down their arms, *The Times* noted, was 'without precedent'. And so it was that 2,600 British and 10,486 Indian and Gurkha troops were volunteered into the custody of the Turks. More than 4,200 were never seen again, most having fallen and died by the wayside on a forced march across 500 miles (804 kilometres) of desert to Aleppo. The British officers were separated from the Indian and Gurkha troops. Colour Havildar Fatehbahadur Limbu took command of the Gurkha prisoners and appointed Colour Havildar Bhotri Khattri to the role of adjutant. He insisted on discipline being maintained and on regimental standing orders being observed to the letter, and in this way the Gurkhas remained fitter and more adaptable to the situation in which they now found themselves. Unlike the Indians, they had decided that their religious constraints did not prevent them from eating horsemeat during the siege and as a result were stronger and less prone to disease. Thus they were able to withstand the march and prison camp life better than both their British and Indian counterparts.

An entirely new 1/7th Gurkha battalion was being rushed into service and into Mesopotamia to join a major offensive against the Turks, planned for the early months of 1917. Major General Frederick Maude was appointed to command a massive force of 166,000 men who were to storm up to Baghdad, marching on both sides of the Tigris. More than 110,000 of them were Indian and Gurkha soldiers, the largest contingent of Gurkhas ever brought into battle together with 1/2nd, 4/4th, 1/7th, 2/9th and 1/10th. A determined enemy continued to snipe Maude's army, but on 11 March 1917 the British entered Baghdad, a dirty, unattractive city of fetid alleys, which disappointed the Gurkhas. They could not see why so many lives had been sacrificed for this horrible place. Maude was one of the victims. He died of cholera just a year after his appointment to lead the Baghdad offensive.

The Gurkhas were quite right in their naive judgement, too. Lives were sacrificed unnecessarily. The cost to British, Indian and Gurkha troops in the Mesopotamian campaign had been extraordinary, staggering even, compared with Europe and Gallipoli, where the circumstances were so completely different. The Anglo-Indian forces lost 4,335 officers and 93,244 other ranks; of these, 29,700 were killed. And they were all in vain. A mere 25 weeks later, the Turks threw in the towel of their own accord and Mesopotamia would have come to the British free, gratis and for nothing had the military hierarchy and the Viceroy of India not been so damned impatient.

CHAPTER NINE

My Gurkha and I

The Gurkhas?

Who were they, these 'little olive-skinned soldiers from the East', as one writer described them, who fought for the British Empire to their last breath, that the newspapers had begun writing about with increasing frequency? The British public, and the world, had suddenly become aware of them. They were not entirely unknown before the Great War, but public perception of them had tended to put them aside, filed away as being part of some native section of the Indian army. Note: the *Indian* army, not the *British* army, and there was more than a touch of snobbery about the titles and the units that fell under those precisely observed headings. The Gurkhas were Indian army and not British army (at least, not until 1947, when it all changed and they could be enlisted into one or the other). The difference between the two, as John Masters pointed out, was 'a fundamental factor in the social and military life of imperial India'. In other words it was a class thing.

They were two distinct bodies of armed soldiers within Britain's Empire jewel. The first consisted of large detachments from the British army, wholly British regiments from top to toe, steeped in long tradition and past glories that frankly its colonels would not wish to see diluted by the influx of ethnic units. The second was the Indian army, a massive establishment run by an officer corps whose senior men were predominantly British. The two organisations were pulled together under the grand title of the British Army in India. Between the two world wars, the British army strength in India levelled off at around 48 battalions of infantry, 4 regiments of cavalry and a veritable host of artillery units. The Indian army was generally between three and four times the size of the British army in India.

The association between the two groups was not always harmonious, and the mutiny could never be forgotten. The received perception of the Gurkhas, both from the military standpoint and from public affection, began to change quite dramatically after the Great War, when their singular courage in epic battles became more widely known and, although part of the Indian army, began to get a life of their own. A pattern of enlistment and service for both officers and ranks emerged which was to endure for the rest of the century.

British officers invariably sought to join the Gurkha regiments because of their reputation as fighting units and the probability that by being among them they would at least see some decent action. For some it was the continuation of family ties – sons and grandsons of former officers in the Gurkha Rifles. As with the Gurkhas themselves, family connections have always been important but did not necessarily provide the aspiring Gurkha officers with an easy route into the regiments.

Until the beginning of the First World War, the commanders-in-chief in India held the patronage of appointments to the Gurkhas and jealously guarded them. Lord Kitchener during his time insisted on giving his personal blessing to appointments and also made it a rule that officers should not be exceptionally tall. This related firstly to the fact that the Gurkha trenches were less deep than usual, and it was believed that many taller officers were killed because of it, and secondly because by tradition Gurkha officers led from the front, and if they were tall they stood out like a sore thumb surrounded by their smaller ranks. The requirement was eventually dropped and there was a rush of young officers – filled with the tales of Gurkha exploits – trying to get in after the Great War.

Among them was one Lieutenant William J. Slim, who fought alongside them at Gallipoli when he was serving with the Warwickshires and witnessed a number of Turks being carved up by kukris. He was so impressed by the valour of the 1/6th Gurkhas that he applied to join the regiment and became one of its most influential figures. Later still, he was raised to the peerage, and with a field marshal's baton led the 14th Army in Burma during the Second World War, in which, as we will see, he was to ensure that the Gurkhas played a substantial role.

Just as the Gurkha soldiers themselves would eventually face a thorough examination and intense competition to get in, it was already the case with officers by the 1920s that the regiments could afford to introduce a vetting procedure to ensure that they got the right men, who were not just top-quality military professionals but who had, or would learn, understanding and compassion for the troops they were to command. That, in the Gurkhas, was as important as any other consideration.

Likely candidates from the list of probables and possibles would be invited to spend a week or ten days of their leave with the regiment to which they had applied. Likable chaps were later voted on by the officers who were to accept him (or not, as the case may be) among them, and the colonel then made his selection.

General Sir Walter Walker, one of the great stalwarts of the Gurkha Rifles for the past 50 years and who became their major general, as well as Commander-in-Chief of Allied Forces in Northern Europe, decided he was going to join; achieving it was another matter:

My headmaster at Blundells thought I was proper material for the army, although my mother wanted me to go to work for Imperial Tobacco where she had a pull. I went to Bristol and I saw the sort of job I'd have to do, looking at cigarettes coming out of machines, and decided to follow my grandfather and elder brother into the army. I passed into Sandhurst and aimed to go to India . . . the Gurkhas. I had a pull because my grandfather commanded 1/8th Gurkhas. My elder brother tried for the Gurkhas but was too tall. I played golf with an officer on leave from the Gurkhas, Francis Fisher. He watched me playing, he watched my table manners and what have you and obviously sent back a report saying 'fit for the 8th'. And then I stayed with the colonel of the regiment, and he wrote quite a long report on me and said it was nice to see that this young officer had clean fingernails. This was only the first part of the equation; you then had to pass muster in India before you could get into the Gurkhas. I'm not sure it was the best of systems because quite a few of my friends who rose to very high ranks in the army did not make it into the Gurkhas. They went into the Punjab regiments or Frontier Forces. Even so, the Gurkhas traditionally had an excellent officers' corps, and those I encountered when in due course I joined the 1/8th were extremely strict. For example, I eventually became adjutant to the commanding officer, General Bruce Scott (a colonel then), and he was a real disciplinarian. When we went around the lines, he would say: 'There is a cigarette stub there. Why is it there? Why has it not been cleared up before I came round?' He was as strict as that, and believed that such attention to detail would improve discipline and ultimately save lives. I am sure he was right. As far as his officers were concerned, he insisted that we knew not only the name of every soldier in the battalion but also his number. He would say: 'What's the name of that man over there?' If I didn't know, he would give me what I deserved – a rocket.

He was an absolute expert on frontier warfare and one learned much from men like that; stood me in good stead for later. Frontier warfare was, in a way, similar to fighting the Japs. If you made a mistake, you did not live to tell the tale. The tribesmen in the north-west were deadeye dicks with their rifles. If you withdrew from a hill in sloppy fashion, too slowly, you wouldn't get down under your own steam. I learned the techniques of the North-West Frontier when we went up to our perimeter camp and tried to ambush the tribesmen who were sniping at our camp at night. It was their favourite trick, picking us off one by one. In order to lay an ambush against tribesmen who can move as silently as butterflies, you had to be absolutely adept at leading your men and concealing them with the same stealth; the Gurkha is good at that, anyhow. You had to make certain that when the enemy entered the ambush, they were killed – otherwise *you* would be. And apart from the actuality of doing it, one read and read – reports of actions that had taken place earlier and the mistakes that had been made . . . and how it should have been done. Every week, our divisional commander held a study period for his brigade commanders and his commanding officers. It might be that you were studying ambushes, and you had to be ready. He would say, 'Walker, now what is the technique of laying an ambush?' and if you fluffed your lines you didn't last long.

Mistakes cost lives and so did lack of knowledge. It was

therefore important that one read up all aspects of these operations. What were the mistakes of the past? Why was it possible
when the enemy walked into an ambush, they were not all killed?
And one learned the techniques and developed them ... so that
you didn't fire until you had them all in the bag, or that you had
stops to get those who had not immediately entered the ambush
area and stops to get those who managed to retreat, so that they
were all killed. These techniques, learned with the Gurkhas on the
North-West Frontier, I carried forward against the Japanese in
Burma in the Second World War and against the Communists in
the Malayan Emergency ... and later as Commandant of the
Jungle Warfare School, which I raised in Malaya, and was able to
pass them on.

There were other aspects of life in the Gurkha regiments that were
drummed into Walter Walker at a very early stage, and the lessons are
still being learned by young officers in today's British army – that a
successful officer in command of Gurkhas had to earn the respect and
trust of his men. It was not something that could be ordered, forced or
bought. An officer who came into the regiments with any sign of
aloofness or offhandedness would find that the Gurkhas themselves
would not respond well. All officers, in fact, discovered that there was
always a period of time that had to elapse before they were accepted
by the Gurkhas: it could be two months, three months, sometimes six
months – but one morning the officer would awake and discover a new
level of reaction from his troops. He had finally been accepted. There
were a number of obvious actions that a young officer could take *en
route* to achieving this preferred status, not least consideration for the
Gurkha beliefs that all men are equal in their human form, although
that did not deter them from accepting authority and the orders of
senior ranks, which they followed with blind obedience.

The point was made crystal clear by another future stalwart,
Anthony Stean Harvey, who joined at the outset of the Second World
War when a fresh intake of officers was desperately needed:

I looked up books to try to get some idea of what the martial races
of India were; the only two I could find were the Sikhs who were
big six-foot [1.8-metre] boys with heavy turbans and very heavy

beards, and they frightened me to just look at. I couldn't see them taking orders from me at five feet six [1.6 metres]. The other martial race I read about were the Gurkhas, cheerful little fellows always laughing, about five feet [1.5 metres] with Boy Scout hats on . . . My first impression of them was how smart they were. My second was how enthusiastic they were, and my third was that I was going to have a marvellous life if I was able to stay with them, and that's what happened.

There were lessons for me, too. Certainly no British officers were accepted for a period of, say, six months, but if you were enthusiastic above all things and fairly straightforward . . . a very strict bond [developed] between Gurkhas, the Gurkha soldier and the British officer. Our part, which we gladly accept, is that we will do all in our power to look after the welfare and wellbeing of the Gurkha soldier. This means that his welfare must come before ours. It means on active service to make sure your troops are bedded and fed before you worry about your own. You have to lead, you have to show that anything you ask them to do you are prepared to do yourself. It means also in peacetime you help manage their affairs, particularly financial affairs. In return the Gurkha will give you unquestioning obedience, loyalty and, above everything else, friendship. But you have to demonstrate in the first place that you are prepared to play your part in it. Most British officers do. And provided there is total sincerity on both sides, it's a marvellous combination. You get obedience, loyalty, bravery, you get comradeship and you get an awful lot of fun. And I wouldn't change a day that I've gone through.

British officers had to learn the Gurkhali language. It was a first priority, and not just for the sake of being able to converse with their soldiers – many of whom at that time went through their entire military career without being able to speak any English – but, more important, give them orders in a language they understood. They had to show enthusiasm for doing so; the Gurkhas noticed those who were bored or lazy. Nor was this vital 'getting to know you' process a straightforward situation of understanding the Gurkha mentality, his thought processes and cultural influences. There were two distinct types of Gurkha whose character depended on the region from which they were recruited – either eastern or western Nepal. Regiments at that time generally recruited from one or the other, not both. The main difference between eastern and the western Gurkhas stems from their background, as Gordon Corrigan explained:

The westerner gets up in the morning, walks from his village, farms his strip of land and then walks back to his village when the task is completed, chatting on the way to anyone he might meet, so he is socially inclined. He lives in a community. The easterner lives on his own land so his next-door neighbour may be some distance away. The east was always far less developed. There are no roads, of course, and they are pretty remote. He is a bit more suspicious of strangers and in some ways more independently minded. He is also a much more sturdy character. From the point of view of the British officer, a westerner would come in whom I didn't know and his mental process would be: 'Ah . . . sahib is a senior man; good. He speaks the language well; good. He's all right.' The easterner's thought process would be the same except he will not commit himself to immediate acceptance: 'He may be all right . . . I don't know. I shall have to wait and see.' Thus, he reserves judgement until he has got to know you. The point being in both instances, however, that unless he made an effort to encourage the process, the British officer could well find himself frozen out, and he would doubtless receive a visit from one of the more senior Gurkhas who would tactfully point out the error of his ways.

It was not uncommon for young officers to come out to the regiments brimming with confidence and wanting to change the world. Most were decent chaps – the selection ritual didn't often throw up bad apples – but occasionally they went over the top. Long-standing Gurkha officers, though often still quite young, were not only father-figures to the ranks but were also masters of tact and guile who would put officers straight about life in general and offer some corrective advice about their faults. Occasionally, a 'few arrogant little sods' turned up, and they would be swiftly brought to heel in one way or another. If they were sensible, they would also learn to pick up tips from the experienced Gurkha NCOs and officers. Little intricacies of life that would not normally occur to them could be learned and save their skin. Example: picquets were inserted into the hillsides to give covering fire for the main body of men marching through a valley, and removing a picquet from its position needed to be performed with skill and care, with speed and with eyes searching the surrounds. Pathans would invariably be on hand to shoot or snatch any stragglers and attack the picquet on its way down. Normally, an officer would wait until his main company had cleared the area before moving out with the rear party. 'No, sahib,' the Gurkha officer would say, 'you go first. On the hillside the sahib has a tendency to look where you are going and it slows us all up and we will all get shot. You go on ahead and then we will not have to wait for you.' And so the officer would attempt to keep up with the main group, all crashing down the hillside, along goat passes nine inches (23 centimetres) wide with Pathans zapping away with their rifles above them.

Many young officers in India joined for that kind of action. They also had a good life during those halcyon between-the-wars days. Even the youngest and lowest had a coterie of servants and were assigned a Gurkha orderly who would attend to his every need, from having his tea and shaving-mug ready at daybreak to digging his foxhole in battle. The relationship between officer and orderly was usually close. The latter belonged to the former, and in a curious way vice versa. In sexually lean times, on the frontier and in faraway danger zones, this relationship occasionally formed a closer attachment for those officers who today would be termed gay. Homosexuality existed, as in every army, though appears not to have been widespread. One of the few former officers who have included the subject in their memoirs was John Morris, later to become controller of the BBC's Third Programme. He saw service with the Gurkhas in Palestine and France and later on the North-West Frontier. He chose 'a handsome teenaged boy . . . whose animal way of moving attracted me'. It was, however, another orderly, sensing his sexual leanings, who slipped into his bed one night after drink had been taken.

His own orderly actually saved his life. Morris was in command of a hundred men in a picquet that came under fire from a large force of Pathan tribesmen. Morris froze to the spot and would undoubtedly have suffered that well-known frontier mutilation, the fate worse than death, if his young orderly had not pulled him clear. As it was, 30 of the unit fell, many of them wounded and lying moaning on the ground. Morris pleaded with his commanding officer to be allowed to go back to the spot to rescue the wounded. His colonel refused, knowing full well that the Pathans would be lying in wait, just as they always did. The wounded were easy bait for a second ambush, and the colonel knew from experience that the shame of leaving wounded men to their mercies would merely be exacerbated by the further losses incurred in trying to rescue them.

One of the wounded men captured by the Pathans was set free soon afterwards and came running naked towards his comrades. His body had been horrifically mutilated in typical Pathan blood lust, his penis and testicles slashed to ribbons and his stomach slit open. This was not merely a demonstration of what the British soldier might expect if he fell into their hands. The night of the Pathan attack, as Morris lay anguishing over the day's events his orderly crept silently into his tent, stripped off his clothes, climbed into his bed and began massaging his body. Morris simply burst into tears. Hollywood made movies out of the sexual passions and infidelities of British officers in the Indian army, and it had to happen. They were often separated from their wives and families for months, sometimes years, and during the second half of the nineteenth century – during and after the great Indian Mutiny – it was considered unsafe for women to live there, especially if they were to be left alone for long periods at a time. Many officers had Gurkhali mistresses, the camp followers and widowed women who were allowed to live at the depot. But when India became safe again for English women, they, too, began to arrive in quite large numbers, from Calcutta and elsewhere, occasionally from England, some to be reunited with their husbands and others, the largest contingent, looking for eligible young officers to marry. They became known around the hill stations as the Fishing Fleet.

Regimental colonels generally did not care for these visits because they were a distraction to the men. Some regiments, such as the 5th Gurkha Rifles, even disapproved of marriage among its young officers – 'plenty of time for that sort of thing when you get back home to England' – and preferred to think that they would consider themselves married to the regiment.

And so we come to the Gurkhas themselves, and, without wishing to over-gild the lily, they were, and are, rather special, the word 'special' used time and time again during research interviews for these pages with the officers who came to their regiments to command. What they discovered was that the chaps were free volunteers, whereas in the Indian army – and the British army to some degree – they would confront many soldiers who had other reasons for being there, men who would arrive with their attention diverted by their assorted problems relating to their families, homes, debts, and their minds not always focused on the job at hand. That is not to say the Gurkhas were an easy bunch to deal with, and especially not the newcomers. These were wild boys, 16 or 17 years old, straight from the hills. They arrived from the back of beyond, most of them illiterate and some even unable to understand Gurkhali, having come from remote regions close to the Tibetan borders where they spoke a local dialect. They would for the most part be strong youths, weather-beaten, with long, shaggy hair matted and untamed. Some had illnesses that had not been discovered, and British officers had to learn to spot the sick boys who might have hookworm, tuberculosis – which was the scourge of the Nepalese hills – or chronic malaria, endemic in all Gurkha regiments. Those who did not appear to be filling out were weighed regularly, given extra milk and treated as well as the battalion medical orderlies could manage. Their feet had to be regularly inspected. Most of them had never worn boots, and within minutes of putting them on they were tripping up and falling over because they had lost their natural guiding instincts that thin hide sandals – or none at all – provided.

They laughed a lot, especially during their first days in the ranks when they should have been po-faced and silent; they had no comprehension of discipline or the need to stand completely still. Simple commands were met initially with bemused indifference. Nor could they be properly turned into the courageous fighters that they were soon to become by a swearing, swaggering English sergeant major typified in countless cartoons and movies. If they had been in the Foreign Legion, they would have been beaten senseless and left face down in the dust, bleeding in the heat of the sun until they understood that they had to jump to it.

Gurkha NCOs had their own methods and could certainly be stern when necessary. But generally the young Gurkhas were brought along in a manner that would never have been accepted in any other part of the British military. This has been no better described than in an

incident recalled by John Masters, who was interviewing one of the
new recruits during his early days in command of the training unit of
2/4th Gurkhas at Bakloh:

> The boy came into my office to give particulars of his home and
> family, and I was lighting a cigarette as he entered. Subadar Dallu
> standing behind him nearly exploded when the lad, too, pulled out
> a cigarette and asked me for a light and sat carelessly on the edge
> of my desk. I motioned the quivering subadar into silence and
> asked the recruit his name. He said, 'Punabahadur. What's yours?'
> The NCO had the delicate task of superimposing on his confident
> self-respect without injuring it or diminishing it, the discipline
> that turns a brave man in uniform into a soldier. I watched
> Havildar Sarbidan, only 34 but mannered like a grandfather, stand
> patient in front of his squad for weeks on end, slowly and tenderly
> bringing them to heel. Then, one day, he spoke to a recruit in the
> rear rank, the one who in the dim past had suggested that they
> would all like a rest in the shade. 'Well, Burkhabadur, *now* what
> would you do if you felt hot on parade?' Little Birkhe and the
> whole squad, appalled at the memory of their past misdeeds,
> stood blushingly silent and then began working out with the
> vicious all-out, all-together snap that later tore apart German
> panzers, Japanese guards and many evil theories.

The North-West Frontier and unruly provinces such as Waziristan were
fertile training grounds for the Gurkhas in the years running up to the
Second World War – there and at the other outposts where the battles
with tribes of various denominations kept the British and Indian armies
busy with intermittent bursts of uprising throughout the 1920s and
1930s. It was almost arrogant of the British to imagine that they would
be easily subdued; the Pathans and Wazirs had, after all, a rather longer
record of wars that they viewed as honourable and exciting, as
Alexander discovered to his heavy cost as he tried to force those passes
in 327 BC. In the towns and the cities, the troubles were largely
confined to civil unrest inspired by the Indian nationalists, continuing
their increasingly violent campaign to get the British out. Another level
of major engagements were the outbreaks of religious rivalry, which
were vicious and unpredictable. Just as the Gurkhas were never used in

Northern Ireland, they were kept away, as far as possible, from the internal strife and urban conflicts of India itself, remaining generally on the periphery to police the hills and the borders where tribesmen had no interest in who was running India. The Afghans, too, presented a fairly constant need for attention around the Khyber Pass and the border regions between the wars. Although the British signed a peace treaty in 1920 after the Second Afghan War, the next two decades set the future pattern of unmitigated turbulence in that country which the Viceroy of India feared would spread – and indeed was spreading – across the hills into what is now Pakistan. There remained the incessant barbarism in these skirmishes and battles on the frontier, and the torture and the blood lust were not necessarily confined to the Pathans or the Wazirs.

The Gurkhas were quite capable of similar tactics when their ire was aroused. One hot and busy day on the frontier in the summer of 1935, when temperatures were 50°C in the shade, A Company of 2/4th Gurkhas was clearing up after a skirmish with a heavyweight mob of tribesmen, having bayoneted several who were lying in the scrub, apparently dead. Two were not, and they reached for their guns and each shot a fine young Gurkha in the back.

The men of A Company were furious at this unsporting attack and weighed in with their kukris. Or at least Halvidar Balbir did, and when he had completed his mission he came running back down the hill, kukri dripping blood in his right hand and five heads of Pathans in his left. The eyes of Gurkhas mist over when they really get mad, into a lighter shade of pink. The halvidar had committed an illegal act, but there was on this occasion no stopping him or his men. The Pathans' headless corpses would be left as a note to their colleagues, but the truth was that they wouldn't give a damn. All was fair in war – except bombing the tribesmen from aeroplanes. They felt that really was against the rules, and the Pathans complained to the League of Nations. Meanwhile, they just went on with their sniping and attacks against the Gurkha patrols and camps, picking them off with their snipers or engaging lesser numbers than their own band in a fight. One more act of unspeakable cruelty would go in the log – as when a British officer ws badly wounded in a small battle on the hillside and repeated attempts by his platoon to reach him were driven back by the tribesmen. The next morning, the tribesmen had gone, but the officer was found, dead; his testicles had been chopped off and he had been flogged mercilessly, probably while still alive. Then his skin was pegged out on a rock. The anger surrounding such a discovery prompted a response in kind which, as far as the British army was concerned, was simply not done.

The discovery of the officer's body was used to inspire the platoon not to take any prisoners in the next battle with the Pathans, and if there were any, the jemadar said, he did not want to see them. Curiously, it was the jemadar himself who took a prisoner in a scrap a few days later: a wounded man left helpless with his leg shattered by a grenade. One shot would have sufficed, but the jemadar did the right thing and had the stretcher-bearers carry him into camp. His senior officer who had given the order for no prisoners went into a blind rage and ordered the wounded tribesmen to be pegged out on the ground, and every man who passed him was ordered to boot him in the balls. He died late in the afternoon, and his body was carried out and dumped in the place where they had found their own officer's mutilated body the previous day.

The taste of their 'own medicine' ploy did nothing to subdue the blood-letting of the tribesmen in the north. Any Sikhs or British captured were invariably beheaded and/or castrated, the latter operation often being done by the womenfolk. Their tortures became the stuff of pulp fiction, except that they were true, as all who served in these wild places and had seen the evidence in those years between the wars knew very well: death from a thousand cuts, salt in wounds, pegging open a prisoner's mouth and the women urinating on him until he drowned – they were but a few of the Pathans' list of things to do to the British and their lackeys, the Gurkhas.

Elsewhere, the Gurkhas were called on to assist when two massive earthquakes struck Nepal and north-west India around Quetta in 1934 and 1935 respectively. The 7th and 10th Gurkhas had a particular concern in the Nepalese quakes since they were centred on the eastern homelands of most of its recruits from the Rais and Limbus and rumbled all the way to Kathmandu, which was badly damaged. Many villages were simply swept away.

At Quetta, where the Gurkhas had large bases, the city collapsed in ruins and thousands were killed. The Gurkhas of 2/8th laboured long and hard in the rescue missions, one of their number, Rifleman Harkbir

117

Thapa, who had a particularly acute sense of hearing, saving the lives of many people trapped under the wreckage. Another, 2/8th hero Naik Nandlal Thapa, was awarded the Empire Gallantry Medal for repeatedly entering buildings that were in danger of collapse at any moment during the aftershocks, tearing at masonry with his bare hands and bringing survivors to safety. At the time the EGM was the highest award for gallantry when not under enemy fire, but when the George Cross was created in 1940 by George VI, Naik Nandlal's actions were still remembered, and he was awarded a GC in place of the EGM. He had by then retired and had returned to his home in Nepal, where he remained until his death in 1987 at the age of 84.

Towards the end of the decade, internal strife became endemic and frequent – Indians against Indians, Indians against the British, Muslims against Hindus. The uprisings were coming fast and furious, giving the clearest indication yet that the days of Empire and Imperial India were numbered. What would happen to the Gurkhas? A diversion delayed the inevitable. The Germans were at it again . . .

CHAPTER TEN

A Last Game of Bowls

Life for the Gurkha regiments in India had been, as one officer put it in a regimental history, as good as it gets. The 1930s had provided all that the Gurkhas and their officers could have wished for. The action that they and their British officers lusted for came in short bursts largely against the triblesmen on the North-West and North-East Frontiers, who became progressively less of a problem and casualties fewer than they had been for a number of years. Training in the battalions had been able to proceed at a more leisurely pace and, in consequence, with much greater emphasis on quality in both the command structure and efficiency and skill in the ranks. Commanders who had made their names in earlier campaigns advanced quickly to higher office, and a whole new echelon of military managers had taken over.

They, in turn, took control in an India where they could enjoy what, in the event, turned out to be the last gasp of traditional colonial lifestyle that went with the posting – the formal dress for dinner in the officers' mess replete with medals, the cocktail parties, the champagne cup and the brandies with their coffee under the cloudless, moonlit skies, surrounded by their orderlies and pleasant company. When they were not on their tours of duty on the frontier, there were the regimental balls accompanied by the regimental band, and nights of magic played out to the swing-era records of Duke Ellington, Benny Goodman and Artie Shaw. And there were the games, fishing, wild duck shoots, big game hunts, mountaineering expeditions to the Himalayas and, in some parts, polo, cricket and rugby.

For the Gurkhas themselves, the tail end of the 1930s had also been a time of variety with a taste of Western-style pleasures, such as they were in Imperial India, and sporting competitions and games in which they eagerly participated. Important religious festivals in the Nepalese calendar were fully observed, and sufficient numbers in the ranks, and an unending supply of willing recruits, provided a full complement in the battalions while at the same time allowing long leave to be taken in their homeland if they so wished.

The long trek to the hills for those who went back was still no quicker. There were no motorable roads linking Kathmandu to the Indian border. Those dignitaries who did possess a car, such as the British minister resident in the capital, had to have it literally carried aboard a wooden frame manhandled up hill and down dale by a team of 80 or so porters from Bhimphedi, where the road ran out, on the border to the Kathmandu valley. The journey usually took a week to ten days, depending on local hazards; only then could the car be put down on what passed as roads, and these were confined to the valley itself and around Kathmandu. Elsewhere, pneumatic tyres would have been ripped to shreds and no roads reached anywhere near the hills.

There had been a good deal of toing and froing across the border. As the end of the decade neared, the Brigade of Gurkhas had 20 battalions, well trained, well exercised and well rested, which was fortuitous given the news being picked up on the crackling radios in the depots. As the 4th Gurkhas at Loralai, in Baluchistan on the Afghan border, planned to begin their community week of summer celebrations in September 1939 – dog show, gymkhana, treasure hunt, ladies v. gents cricket match, picnics, dinner parties and finally a spiffing fancy-dress ball – Britain declared war on Germany. There were hasty consultations amid rumours of German bombers taking off in Siam that would fly directly across their path. Should the week be cancelled? The generals *in situ* at Quetta, 200 miles (321 kilometres) away, decided that the Gurkha riflemen could not shoot down the bombers even if they came their way and relented. And so, as John Masters put it, the 4th at Loralai was allowed to finish its game of bowls.

The Gurkhas were not to be hurried into battle. It was not that they weren't ready, very willing and unquestionably able. Neville Chamberlain's dithering War Cabinet in pre-Churchill London was slow to involve either the Indian army – which eventually provided two million personnel for the war effort – or the Gurkha battalions, in spite of an immediate offer of assistance from Nepal itself. In the month war was declared, the Nepalese Prime Minister, Judha Shamsher, offered to send eight battalions of his own Nepalese army to bolster the internal security of India if and when the British and Indian armies were required for the conflict with the Germans. It was not until after the evacuation of the remnants of the British Expeditionary Force from Dunkirk in May 1940 that the Indian army was finally mobilised and the British minister in Nepal was belatedly instructed to call on the Prime Minister and accept his offer of help. He also requested that the Indian army should be allowed a dramatic increase in its Gurkha recruitment to a total strength of 30 battalions.

It was only a beginning. Within months, the Brigade of Gurkhas was increased to 45 battalions, serviced by 10 training centres in India. As word spread among the Himalayan foothills, men who were on leave filtered back to their units, some only just having arrived home. They were to be joined by hundreds of others who began spontaneously to wander down from the hills, walking all the way to India, casually turning up at Gurkha depots and, in their usual polite and unassuming way, asking if they could volunteer. They were, wrote Major Duncan Forbes, 'like guests coming to a party'.

The response could not have been more encouraging for the British army if Winston Churchill himself had stood in Durbar Square with a loud-hailer and appealed for recruits. During the next four years 250,000 hill men came forward to serve the British in the Gurkha battalions of the Indian army on the front lines of Europe, North Africa, the Middle East, Persia, Iraq, Greece and Burma. And there was still the North-West Frontier, where the Pathans and the Wazirs, encouraged by the German onslaught, stepped up their own action with uncontrolled delight.

To embark on even a precis of the actions of the 45 battalions of the ten Gurkha regiments during the next five and a half years would require a volume of its own and still fail to do their story justice. We can only glance through some of the highlights, pick out some personal experiences and previously unpublished archives and record the heroics of the Brigade of Gurkhas and, in particular, the men whose bravery won them the Victoria Cross.

What became immediately clear was that the infrastructure to receive the additional manpower was sadly lacking, and it wasn't until

November 1940 that the first of the specially constituted training centres opened for business to prepare the raw recruits for the rigours of warfare, a process that would take a minimum of five months. Nor were existing personnel, whose recent experience had been on the North-West Frontier, sufficiently well versed in the mechanics of the modern army of Europe. Their weapons were often of First World War vintage, and they were very short on personnel who had experience of modern weaponry, mechanics or communications – in short something of a controlled panic was on. There would also be a grave shortage of officers, since the Gurkhas traditionally ran a tight ship, and teams of recruiters were alerted in the UK to find suitable men. Anthony Harvey was an insurance clerk when he enlisted in the British army as a private soldier in 1940, intent on gaining a commission which he succeeded in doing within the year. As a second lieutenant he volunteered for a new regiment just being formed, which the world would soon come to know as the Paras. Although he'd had his interview for the Parachute Regiment and had been accepted, his CO had been ordered to supply officers to the rapidly expanding Indian army; Harvey was one of the many seconded for the purpose:

I was going and that was that. There was no question of a debate about it, and 14 weeks later I arrived at the 5th Gurkha Rifles Regimental Centre at Dharamsala. There was a massive expansion on, and the few British officers that normally would have been in the Regimental Centre could not possibly have coped with the training or the administration . . . and therefore were glad to see anyone arrive. I was sent, along with all the other people on draft – several hundred of us – to an officers' training school at Bangalore, where we did a three-month language training course. The language they taught was Urdu, which was the *lingua franca* of the Indian army. When I joined my Gurkha settlement, I was called in by the CO and he said: 'I understand you have passed your Urdu examinations.'

'Yes,' I replied proudly.

And he said, 'Well, you can forget all that. We don't speak Urdu in the Gurkhas.' So from then on I had to study Gurkhali and very quickly, because by then I was a swinger – a junior company commander sent to command companies where the

122

commander had been killed or gone sick or on a staff course. I found myself constantly in detachments where there was nobody else who spoke English, and it was therefore a question of learning Gurkhali or not saying anything at all.

By the time Anthony Harvey was in operational mode, the Gurkhas were already at war on several fronts. Their very first encounter had something of the *déjà vu* about it. At the end of April 1941 they moved towards what was now called Iraq and had once been Mesopotamia, where their fathers and grandfathers had had such an eventful and costly engagement in the First World War. The government of Rashid Ali was supposedly pro-German and had Nazi advisers in numerous key positions. Under the command of the recently promoted Gurkhas' own 'Bill' Slim, the 10th Indian Division made short work of its invasion and soon surrounded Baghdad, took the surrender of the Iraqi government and installed a pro-British substitute. The operation was concluded without major bloodshed and secured for the Allies strategically important road, rail and air communications. From there, Slim moved to Persia, entering from the south with 1/2nd, 2/7th and 2/10th Gurkhas at the helm, while the Russians came in from the north. Resistance again collapsed, and the Middle East oil was under protective lock and key.

The good news was already being overshadowed by disaster in North Africa. The story began on 22 January when the ANZAC hat (they had no Union Jack) was hoisted up the flagpole at Tobruk, the vital North African port. General Archibald Wavell, commander of all British army forces in North Africa, successfully defended Egypt against an Italian invasion in 1940 and went on to boot them out of Libya, capturing 130,000 prisoners, 400 tanks and 1,290 guns. Around 500 Allied troops were killed and 1,300 wounded. It was a great triumph, although a temporary one. On 14 February the advance guard of General Rommel's Afrika Korps landed down the coast at Tripoli and within the month it was driving Wavell's army back towards Egypt. The British stood their ground at Tobruk, so as to deny this crucial port to German ships, and managed to hang on, in spite of a long siege, to take reinforcements by sea.

Among them were 2/7th Gurkhas, along with the 2/4th and 2/5th, who formed part of the Indian brigades. Later, as the Allies came under severe pressure, the 2/3rd and 2/8th were among the newest reinforcements rushed in. A strong countermove by the Allies forced the Germans on the defensive, pushing them back from the coast. As history now records, this most famous of the Second World War dramas was a long, drawn-out campaign lasting months, with no real movement of positions until Rommel launched his long-awaited second offensive on 22 May 1942. After a massive tank battle around Bir Hacheim, the Afrika Korps crashed the British lines and the Allies fell back for the defence of Tobruk against heavy German pounding. On 1 June 2/4th Gurkhas, then serving with the 10th Indian Infantry Brigade, was moved urgently to a position in that place called the Cauldron for what was their first major action.

They were equipped with two-pounder antitank guns which in the event proved woefully inadequate, their shells bouncing off the armour of the German tanks. The excitement of seeing action turned quickly into terrible frustration as the enemy advanced, unstoppable, and the battalion was overrun. A flavour of their desperate situation is captured in this extract from the regimental history:

> It was some time before we realised that no one who left our position ever did return. The outside world was dead and we were isolated. No reply came to our signals . . . we did not know that the brigade headquarters was no more, that the divisional headquarters had gone, that the Brigadier and CRA [Commander, Royal Artillery] who had lately left us were prisoners. As the sun went down we were lined up to be led off into captivity, the British separated from the Gurkhas, and the Gurkhas from the rest. The darkness descended upon us, in prelude and in presage of the months and years of tribulation to come.

A similar fate befell the 2/7th in the final battle for Tobruk. The Allies finally gave way on 21 June and for the time being surrendered the city, along with a huge amount of recently landed stores and equipment; 25,000 Allied troops went into prison camps. Among them were the entire 2/7th Gurkhas who had fought nonstop for two days until, isolated from the rest, their ammunition simply ran out. 'The men had been fairly bursting with confidence [and] their sense of superiority did not leave them until the end. After they had fought it out against overwhelming odds and lost, the stunned expression on their faces was a sight that few who saw it will forget.'

It was a sorry tale, too, for 2/3rd and 2/8th, who had an almighty dash to reinforce positions in the western desert as Rommel advanced from Tobruk along the coast towards Egypt, heading for Alexandria. The 2/3rd hit trouble almost as soon as they arrived, and their battalion 'box' formation was in part overrun and 200 men taken prisoner, although fortunately many of them managed to escape at Tobruk when the Germans were later pushed back. The 2/8th were in trouble on their first action, when a furious if confused battle against a powerful German-Italian onslaught threw them into disarray. There were many casualties and prisoners taken, although around 280 managed to escape and find their way to El Alamein, 100 miles (160 kilometres) away, where on 6 July General Claude Auchinleck's forces seized back the initiative for the Allies and threw everything they had at Rommel until his advance was halted and turned.

It was Auchinleck, incidentally, who later spoke in praise of the Gurkhas' steadfastness in what he admitted were 'high wastage roles' – i.e. a large number of men being killed, wounded or captured in double-quick time, because that was the style of the battle, pounding each other's position with artillery, and then moving in behind the tanks. North Africa was to be the scene of many Gurkha battles in the campaign that had progressively driven Rommel from one stronghold to another, to the point that by the spring of 1943 he was virtually surrounded in rugged, mountainous terrain in central Tunisia. The 7th Indian Infantry of the 4th Indian Division was to play a key role in the final act of the 8th Army's relentless pursuit of the Afrika Korps until its final submission in May 1943. The 4th Indian Division was commanded by an ex-Gurkha officer in the 1/2nd, General Francis Tuker, who used the three battalions of Gurkhas under his command to brilliant effect.

He used the 1/9th and the 1/2nd at the forefront of the push towards a crucial position. The overall objective was for the 4th Indian Division to take the Fatnassa heights in a silent night assault to enable the 8th Army to get behind Rommel's forces. Tuker's plan was for the 1/2nd and 1/9th Gurkhas to capture the summit of the heights. Once he had issued the orders for this objective, he wrote in his log with the genuine concern of an ex-Gurkha officer for his men: 'Perhaps I have asked too much of them and set them a task which is beyond human accomplishment.' It was certainly a daunting task, since the heights were alive with enemy nests as the Gurkhas set out on the six-mile (9.5-kilometre) march to their mission under the cover of darkness on the night of 5 April 1943.

They fanned out in companies, and although there were many heroes that night one man in particular made his own special contribution to the final result in the 8th Army's campaign against the Afrika Korps – one man who actually did influence the outcome: Subadar Lalbahadur Thapa of the 1/2nd Gurkha Rifles, and there is no better summary of his work that night than the citation that appeared in the *London Gazette* when he was awarded the Victoria Cross:

... during the attack on the Rass Ez-Zouai feature, Subadar Lalbahadur Thapa was second in command of D Company. The Commander of No 16 Platoon was detached with one Section to secure an isolated feature on the left of the Company's objective. Thapa took command of the remaining two Sections and led them forward to break through and secure the one and only passage by which the vital commanding feature could be seized to cover penetration of the Division into the hills. On the capture of these hills, the whole success of the Corps plan depended.

First contact with the enemy was made at the foot of a pathway winding up a narrow cleft. This steep cleft was thickly studded with a series of enemy posts, the inner of which contained an antitank gun and the remainder medium machine guns. After passing through the narrow cleft, one emerges into a small arena with very steep sides, some 200 feet [61 metres] in height, and in places sheer cliff. Into this arena and down its side numbers of automatic weapons were trained and mortarfire directed. The garrison of the outer posts were all killed by Subadar Lalbahadur Thapa and his men by kukri or bayonet in the first rush and the enemy then opened very heavy fire straight down the narrow enclosed pathway and steep arena sides. He led his men on and fought his way up the narrow gully straight through the enemy's fire, with little room to manoeuvre, in the face of intense machine-gun concentrations and the liberal use of grenades by the enemy.

The next machine-gun posts were dealt with, Subadar Lalbahadur Thapa personally killing two men with his kukri and two more with his revolver. This Gurkha officer continued to fight his way up the narrow bullet-swept approaches to the crest. He and two Riflemen managed to reach the crest, where Subadar Lalbahadur Thapa killed another two men with his kukri, the riflemen killed two more and the rest fled. Thapa then secured the whole feature and covered his Company's advance up the defile. This pathway was found to be the only practicable route up the precipitous ridge, and by securing it the Company was able to deploy and mop up all the enemy opposition on their objective. There is no doubt that the capture of this objective was entirely due to this act of unsurpassed bravery by the Subadar and his small party in forcing their way up the steep gully and up the cliffs of the arena under withering fire.

The task that once seemed to its commander beyond human accomplishment was complete. The 1/9th followed the 1/2nd in clearing the remaining obstacles, and before first light the 5th Brigade had pushed through. The 8th Army commanders were so unprepared for the move that they were unable to follow through quickly enough to secure the defeat of the Afrika Korps there and then. But it mattered not; the deed was done, and by the time of the surrender of the Axis forces in Tunisia in May, Rommel was already back in Germany.

As for Subadar Lalbahadur, his actions were clearly significant to the outcome and were recognised as such with some pomp and ceremony never previously afforded to a Gurkha soldier. In June 1943, with Tripoli safely back in Allied hands, King George VI arrived to make his presence felt among the troops. He drove through streets lined with men of the 4th Division and then presented medals to the recipients – including Lalbahadur. Later, he was brought to London, where his exploits had become well known. In a blatant PR exercise for the British army, he was put on show and handed around various military establishments and public events. At one, in the company of Field Marshal Lord Birdwood, he was brought before a large audience, drew his kukri and gave a demonstration of how he used it to kill the Germans during the exploits that won him the VC. As requested by the field marshal, the demonstration was accompanied by Lalbahadur's screams that clearly alarmed members of his audience.

Today, it would be seen as a somewhat demeaning display. At that particular time, it was not and Lalbahadur himself, unused to any form of Western ways, was very proud to have been fêted in the way he was; it was certainly something to tell the children and grandchildren. Born in western Nepal of the Magar tribe, he had served with 1/2nd Gurkhas since 1925 and had joined the war effort almost direct from an active tour on the North-West Frontier, where he was commissioned as a Gurkha officer in 1937. He remained with the battalion for the campaign in North Africa and for a short time in Italy. In 1944 he was appointed subadar major of the 5/2nd Gurkha Rifles in India. He retired in 1948 after his regiment moved to Malaya to become part of the British army. Other awards made to him included the Order of British India (First Class) and the Star of Nepal (Fourth Class). He was also granted the honorary rank of captain. Four of his sons, Tejbahadur, Nandabahadur, Ranbahadur and Pahalsing, all served in the regiment, the last becoming a Queen's Gurkha Officer. Captain Lalbahadur Thapa VC, OBI, died at Paklihawa, Nepal, on 20 October 1968, aged 62.

The serious losses suffered at every level of Gurkha regiments in the North African campaign was matched by simultaneous battles in the Far East after the Japanese entered the war in December 1941. The regions worst hit were those that had been seriously neglected by the London War Cabinet in terms of equipment, men and priority, and the crisis soon became all too evident. The Japanese, already on the march through China and South-East Asia, stormed on relentlessly, taking Hong Kong and British-held Malaya in the same month they bombed Pearl Harbor. By mid-February Penang had fallen, and the greatest disaster of all, Singapore, the great naval fortress and Britain's gateway to the entire region, surrendered. Among the 138,700 British troops killed, wounded or taken prisoner were the entire 2nd Battalions of both the 2nd and 9th Gurkha Regiments. Many of those captured were never seen again, having been forced to work on the railway of death, along with 45,000 other Allied prisoners, of whom almost 18,000 died.

Later in the month, there were further losses as the Japanese began their campaign to force the British out of Burma. Rangoon was abandoned in March ahead of the Japanese invasion force, which found the place a smoking ruin. The Allied forces, equivalent to two small infantry divisions, had to make one of the longest retreats in history to reach the solitary railway bridge across the Sittang river to get clear and back into India.

Five battalions of Gurkhas were among the British forces in retreat from Burma, and four of them were engaged in a fierce rearguard action as the column made its dramatic and costly escape to relative safety across the deep, fast-flowing river before the bridge was finally blown up to prevent the Japanese from pursuing them. Four of the Gurkha battalions, 1/7th, 3/7th, 1/3rd and 2/5th, were hit hard, losing 24 British officers, 34 Gurkha officers and more than two-thirds of other ranks, in excess of 2,000 men. Dozens of men were stranded on the east bank of the river after the bridge was blown. Most were believed captured or killed, although 40 men of the badly mutilated 2/5th Gurkhas straggled home weeks later, having moved north to look for places to cross. Although, as elsewhere, these casualties had to be set against the whole Allied totals, they were disastrous, and combined with the losses in North Africa put the whole Gurkha setup under severe pressure.

CHAPTER ELEVEN

Desperately Seeking Officers

The search for fresh officer material was well under way in Britain by late 1941 to replace the fast-dwindling Gurkha officer corps – an operation that ran alongside the signing of raw recruits into the ranks from Nepal. And before proceeding with this account of the Gurkhas' contribution to the Allied effort in the Second World War, it is worthwhile to divert our attention to a largely ignored group of young men who were taken, in some cases, virtually straight from school in the UK, shipped to India and put into rapid training programmes to take their places as officers in the Indian army and the Gurkha regiments as described by Anthony Harvey.

As with the majority of young men from Britain and its Allied nations who became instant warriors across the entire panoply of war, they had no previous military experience. Michael Marshall was another of those young men, still only 18 years old, and although his story is just one of many, it provides a poignant and at times moving insight into what represented a major departure from the norm for the recruitment of Gurkha officers. But as he himself admitted, the need dictated the method:

> When I was at school at Eastbourne College, who were evacuated to Radley, a brigadier of the Indian army came round in 1941 and spoke about the opportunities of joining the Indian army. And as the bursar of Radley was a retired Gurkha officer, prewar, I learned a lot about the Gurkhas from him. I also began learning basic Urdu from him, and when I left Radley in July 1942 I

131

immediately joined up. We, that is the group of people that I joined with, met at the Great Central Hotel, Marylebone, London, in July 1942. Every one, 250 of us from public schools, were made officer cadets, although for technical purposes we were attached to the Royal Scots regiment. Within three weeks we embarked for India on the troopship SS *Ruys*, which was a 29,000-ton Dutch cargo ship converted for trooping. The journey to India took eight weeks via Cape Town. We eventually arrived early in October at Bombay, went by train to Bangalore, where we started a course at the Officers' Training School which lasted six months. Towards the end of that course we were asked which regiments we would like to join, giving three preferences. Mine were the 4th and 5th Gurkhas and the 13th Frontier Force Rifles. I and two others were commissioned in the 5th Royal Gurkha Rifles. It was one of only two that served in virtually every frontier campaign, i.e. the North-West Frontier. I found out, previously knowing little about the regiment, that it was very highly thought of and was probably among the two best Gurkha regiments.

Marshall went up to the regimental centre at Abbottabad in the North-West Frontier Province. The regiment had been there since 1858 and for a newcomer it was an extremely impressive complex. The first question he was asked by his CO was whether he played rugby; his affirmative reply went down well. He joined the Abbottabad officers' club, playing squash and swimming, and had a 'very enjoyable time in an atmosphere which was strangely unwarlike'. There seemed to be no real pressure at Abbottabad at that stage, as if they were hardly aware that a world war was on. It was all still very Kiplingesque, although it soon began to change.

He began to learn Gurkhali and some of the finer points of working with the Gurkha soldiers. Gurkha officers and senior NCOs were impressive. They had been taken out of their battalions to train the troops, although new officers, especially non-regulars, were regarded as people who had to be suffered. There remained an overhang from the prewar process of selecting and training young officers. It was, he found, quite selective, and a number were transferred to other units or to staff jobs and didn't get sent to battalions. Quite a lot of this selection, Marshall believed, was in the hands of the Gurkha officers, who had a strong influence on the British officer permanent staff. This was particularly evident in an active service unit. Gurkha officers, some with up to 35 years' experience, were the backbone of the regiment.

Marshall received basic training in weaponry and in the general handling of men and tuition in the Gurkhali language. He had no inkling of what it was going to be like in the jungles or the mountainous regions where he would eventually see service. Nor was he told at that time that he was going to be posted to Burma when the Allies re-launched their offensive in May 1943 for what would become one of the longest campaigns of the war – so long that Field Marshal Sir William Slim's 14th became known as the Forgotten Army, fighting the Japanese in the jungles and paddy fields of Burma right until the last gasp of the war in 1945.

At the time of Marshall's arrival, the 5th Gurkhas were spread around the war theatres: the 1st Battalion was in the Middle East and eventually moved to Italy to be in place for the battle of Monte Cassino. The 2nd Battalion was in the retreat from Burma; the 3rd Battalion was still in India, as was the newly formed 4th, but both were destined for Burma as the fresh campaign got under way. He had been at Abbottabad for only three months when he was summoned to see his commanding officer. He was being posted to the 4th Battalion, which had just gone to the Arakan region on the west coast of Burma. Marshall and another young officer, Lieutenant George Malone, a southern Irishman, also had to take with them a reinforcement company of two Gurkha officers and 150 Gurkhas of other ranks.

Their journey by rail meandered across India, eventually arriving at Madras, where they embarked on a steamer to sail around the coast to Chittagong. There, they travelled on to Dohazari by train and from Dohazari marched for five days to Tumbru Ghat. From there they moved by river steamer to Bawli Bazer and then marched on a mule track over the Gopi Pass, on the Mayu Range.

At Gopi Bazar we got into sampans and were taken down to the Kalapanzin River to Taung Bazar, where the 4th Battalion was based. The entire journey from Abbottabad took 28 days. As we

133

arrived, standing on the bank of the Kalapanzin to meet us, was the CO, Colonel Norman MacDonald, the adjutant Captain J.C. Birch, and Subadar Major Mun Raj Gurung. Norman MacDonald had been commissioned in 1916 and had served in the Dardanelles. So had the subadar major. They were delighted to see the number of reinforcements we had brought with us because they had suffered some heavy casualties the previous week and casualties from illness were also building up. The monsoon had only recently finished, and this part of the Arakan was really a series of hillocks surrounded by water. The paddy fields then were about a foot [0.3 metre] deep in water and the four rifle companies of the battalion were spaced out on these hillocks of dry ground. All the rivers were still flooded, and one was permanently damp. Our position was about seven miles [eleven kilometres] from the supposed Japanese forward positions. Colonel Mac, as he was known by everybody, was a delightful man. He told me that he was posting me to B Company. Regretfully, the OC of B Company had been drowned four days earlier. He was a tea planter called Captain J.F. Turner and he'd been demonstrating to his men swimming the Kalapanzin River in full battle order. He was known to be a strong swimmer, and it was thought that somehow his legs had become entangled with weeds at the bottom of the river. There were no other British officers in B Company, and so I had to get on as best as I could.

In October I became a full lieutenant at the age of nineteen years four months. The battalion's task at this time was active patrolling. Each company took it in turn to send out either fighting patrols or standing patrols. These generally went out for three or four days at a time. As I was the only British officer in B Company, totally inexperienced, I soon learned what I ought to be doing. It was not easy. I had only a limited knowledge of Urdu and Gurkhali. On one patrol lasting four days I had with me ten men and Subadar Indrabir Thapa from B Company who was very experienced and always spoke to me in Gurkhali, and, if I didn't understand it, in Urdu. It was only when I got back to the battalion and heard him talking on the inter-company telephone system to the CO in perfectly good English that I realised that he had no intention of making my life easy, and he knew that the only way that I would properly speak Gurkhali was by speaking nothing else. I wasn't too pleased at the time, but I was very grateful afterwards.

Some of these patrols were fighting patrols, i.e. they went out with that intention. Others went out to previously determined positions in order to sit there and ascertain the movements of the Japanese so that a general picture could be built up for the brigadier. The 4th Battalion was in 114 Brigade of the 7th Indian Division and our brigadier was Michael Roberts, who was himself a 1st Gurkha. In October I'd gone out with a standing patrol. We were out at night going through paddy the whole way. At about two in the morning we were shot at by a Japanese patrol while crossing an open paddy field. Everybody got down into the water and stayed there for half an hour until they had gone. When we came out, we looked at ourselves and everyone was covered in leeches: most people probably had 40 to 50 leeches hanging from them. We spent a good half-hour removing them. So penetrative are some of these leeches that they can go through the laceholes in your boots, and you are quite unaware that they've in fact travelled up your legs until you feel them actually drawing blood. The most fearsome leeches which we came across were in the flooded chaungs and rivers where one often saw elephant leeches. These are some six to nine inches [fifteen to twenty-three centimetres] long and any cattle or buffaloes that you came across in the Araken were always hanging with leeches. The animals had no way of removing them. Our method of removing them was with a lighted cigarette.

In November the observation patrols finished and the battalion moved forwards. A number of actions took place on a company level immediately after Christmas, and in January 1943 the whole brigade, spread over a vast region, began the general advance through the foothills of the Arakan Yomas, with the intention of cutting Japanese supply lines to the south of the Mayu River and eventually to capture Buthidaung. During this period, Marshall was acting company commander of B Company and was eventually joined by a second lieutenant, Tom Briscoe. He had been at school at Christ's Hospital prior to his arrival, had been a captain at rugby and head boy. He and Marshall became immediate friends, only to be parted two months later when Briscoe was killed.

As we advanced through the foothills which were dense trees, not jungle, we had a series of brisk actions against the Japanese. One I well remember ended in a rather macabre way. It was an afternoon battle. D Company and my own B Company were involved. It was very close fighting and was the first time that I heard Gurkhas actually shouting 'Ayo Gurkhali', which is a very fearsome noise at close quarters and undoubtedly scared the Japanese. It was also the first time that I'd seen them using their kukris at close quarters. They use them very briskly and mostly went for the throat, often putting down their rifles and bayonets. The Japanese ran, but we suffered quite considerable casualties. They were not heavily dug in, and the Japanese never ran when they were heavily dug in. They used to see it out to the end. In this case they had only dug small foxholes which were in the form of trenches suitable for one man at a time. We killed probably 20 Japanese. And the next morning I was instructed to take two platoons back to this position to bury the dead. The macabre part of my story is that I instructed the jemadar to see that the bodies were buried, and I went off for some other purpose for half an hour or so. Rigor mortis had set in on the bodies left behind by the Japanese and would not easily go into the foxhole trenches dug by the Japs. When I came back, I found that instead of digging further graves, the Gurkhas were in the process of cutting up bodies and pushing them in. Of course, I had to stop this. It in no way concerned them, however, and they thought that I was being pernickety, I think.

Here, I can say one thing about the Gurkha, that he is in many ways the most delightful person. He has all the nicest character-istics of the British race, i.e. he likes playing games, he likes drinking, he likes women, he likes gambling. However, in my experience he has little feelings for the dead, either the enemy or his own comrades . . . no feeling of sadness and certainly none of remorse when they'd killed the Japanese. Hence the attitude they took when I told them to stop it and put their kukris away. At the time they were elated. And it's a very interesting fact that

Gurkhas when they are going into action at close quarters become bloodshot in their eyes and are a very fearsome adversary.

In another of these battles, on 4 February, a date that became engraved on Michael Marshall's memory, he was ordered to attack a Japanese position with C Company commanded by a close friend, Major Pat Beytagh. The two companies set off at 0630 in a typical early-morning mist that hung over the paddy fields in the Arakan like shrouds. They climbed up through the jungle to within 400 to 500 yards (365 to 457 metres) of what they thought was the Japanese position. Major Beytagh gave Marshall the order to attack with his company at about 0900 hours. The attack went in and brought a massive barrage of Japanese counterfire. Marshall's company used two-inch (five-centimetre) mortars and grenade dischargers. The Japanese did the same, but eventually the Gurkhas overran the position with a final charge and their battle cry. His company suffered one killed and thirteen wounded, one of whom was Lieutenant Marshall himself:

I was wounded in the back and arm by a Japanese grenade which fell behind me. We all carried morphine syringes in our kit. My orderly also had severe wounds in both legs by the same grenade but managed to extract the syringes. We were both injected. I think I was very lucky that I had in my haversack my binoculars, a compass and two grenades, which took most of the blast. I think without them I would have been killed. We were taken back to C Company. I wasn't aware really what was happening, but the Japanese position was being mopped up by my company. I can't remember how many Japanese bodies were found. I think it was three or four but the rest ran. I was then taken with the other wounded by stretcher-bearers back through the jungle to battalion headquarters.

From there on, the strangest events occurred. That very day the CO received a message from brigade headquarters that the whole brigade advance was to be halted and an immediate withdrawal ordered. So the whole of the action that had just taken place and all the previous month's work was to be aborted. The reason for this was that the Japs had during the night of the fourth assembled a task force of about 9,000 men to cut off the supply lines to the

7th Division. This Japanese force, complete with artillery and some light tanks, otherwise relying on the supplies that they planned to capture from the 7th Division, came through the mist in the paddy in the early hours of the morning. In the great fight put up by the 7th Indian Division, a series of brigade boxes were formed, heavily defended by artillery and tanks. The Japanese, expecting their usual victory, the capturing of supplies and the total retreat of all troops, were surprised to find that this time the boot was on the other foot. The admin. boxes were supplied by air in a system previously arranged by the 14th Army. The whole division stayed put, and the Japanese force in the end, without any captured food supplies or ammunition, was virtually destroyed.

For my part life did not become particularly pleasant. I was carried on a stretcher for the best part of two days to the admin. box, and when we arrived it was found that the field ambulance had been totally destroyed by the Japanese. All the wounded had been butchered on their stretchers. All the doctors and surgeons had been murdered save one, an Indian medical officer who'd been left for dead but in fact had feigned death and was able to tell the whole disgraceful story. Some of these wounded were those from my own battalion who'd been wounded in the various actions that had taken place in the days before.

I was in a temporary hospital with many other wounded, and I think it was after I'd been there for two or three days that I found I had got gangrene in my left arm. Many others wounded were also suffering from gangrene. And as there were no anaesthetics, limbs were being amputated without any anaesthetic, the only method being for two large British orderlies to knock the patient out with one punch to the jaw and after he'd been given a large tot of whisky. This occurred to my own superb orderly, who was wounded in both legs at the same time as I was. Both his legs had to be amputated and very regretfully he didn't survive.

There was only one surgeon at this stage who'd managed to hang on to his kit, and he was later awarded the DSO. He came to see me and told me that I would have to have my arm off. I think then one of the most fortunate things happened as far as I was concerned: one of my fellow officers, Captain Colin Mackenzie, came to see me and said that he'd got some of the latest sulphonanide tablets which no one else had, which he gave to me. They did the trick and I didn't have to go through what would have been I think an unpleasant experience.

On 17 February – and they had by this time built a landing strip in the middle of the box – I was fortunate enough to be evacuated by a light aircraft. It took the pilot and one other person. And I was flown out to Cox's Bazar. From there I was taken by ambulance to Chittagong and from Chittagong by sea to Calcutta, where I went into the main hospital for a week or so, and then by ambulance train to a major hospital at Dehra Dun for six weeks before taking sick leave in Kashmir.

After his recovery, Marshall went back to the regimental centre at Abbottabad and was immediately sent for jungle training near Dehra Dun – a prelude to what now lay in store. The 14th Army's new campaign in Burma was well under way. He returned to his battalion in September but a month later was back at Dehra Dun for a three-inch (7.6-centimetre) mortar course prior to his appointment as three-inch mortar officer. The reason for this activity became clear after Christmas; a major offensive was about to begin. The battalion joined its division at Manipur and was ordered to move down from Tamu to Kalewa through the Kabaw Valley, and then march on through the Gangaw Valley. The marching had to be carried out at night so that eventually they would arrive at the Irrawaddy, capture the town of Pakokku and cross the Irrawaddy for the continuation of the advance. They found Gangaw Valley to be one of the most unhealthy places in Burma, very dry, dusty and very hot. The march of around 400 miles (643 kilometres) took the whole of January. Pakokku was on the banks of the Irrawaddy virtually opposite Pagan, the site of a large number of ancient pagodas, one of the holiest places in Burma:

When we got to within four to five miles [six to eight kilometres] of Pakokku our four patrols found a heavily defended position at Kahnla. And here we had the biggest battle that the battalion had so far experienced. The Japs were well dug in, and the battle took all day. Eventually, we overran the position at about four o'clock in the afternoon, and many Japs had to be finished off in their foxholes as they refused to surrender. During the morning of the

139

battle, our new CO, Colonel John Turner, our previous CO having been promoted to brigadier in another division, was giving his orders when he was hit in the stomach by a sniper's bullet. I was three or four feet [0.9 or 1.2 metres] away from him at the time. Regretfully, he died that evening. He had come to us from the 7th Gurkhas and was well liked.

The battalion suffered considerable casualties during this action – 40 to 50 killed and wounded. The command of the battalion was taken over by Major Dereck Owen, who was also a regular and had joined the regiment in 1937. Shortly afterwards we crossed the Irrawaddy. The subterfuge masterminded by General Slim had succeeded as the main attack across the Irrawaddy was near Mandalay and the crossing of the 7th Division was relatively straightforward, although some units did suffer casualties. We landed at Nyaungu and the battalion position was close to Pagan. And I remember going and looking at the pagodas.

The new CO arrived. He also came from the 7th Gurkhas, Colonel Maconachie. We stayed at our position near Pagan . . . and this particular area of Burma was infested with snakes and there were a whole series of incidents, the worst being when the battalion's mess waiter, walking from the mess to the kitchen, trod on a puff adder, which is extremely venomous. The mess cook came out and chopped its head off immediately but the mess orderly died the following day. Quite close to this part of Burma, which is very dry, is an area well known for the numbers of king cobras, one of the very few snakes to attack on sight; the majority of snakes want to get out of your way as quickly as possible. It's only when you accidentally tread on them or surprise them that they go into the attack. One of the favourite pastimes of the Gurkha soldier when they find evidence of snake holes in the ground is to close up the holes, leaving one open. They push burning rags down one of the closed holes and wait for the snakes to come out of the remaining open hole. They then chase them with their kukris making much noise and thoroughly enjoy themselves in cutting them up.

In March I was appointed A Company commander with the rank of captain. From then began the general advance again. This time we were instructed to capture the oilfields starting at Pwinbyu and then going on to Yenanyaung, Maagwe and Minbu. In all these places we came across telltale signs of the 1942 retreat. Old burned-out British vehicles, burned-out light tanks, and of course the oil wells themselves which were demolished and set alight. The Japanese fought a tough rearguard action throughout, then occupying well-prepared positions. We were supported by the Carabineers' tanks. They were an excellent regiment and we had two squadrons fighting with us. But there was one rather poignant incident. I saw a young tank commander, and I saw his tank receive a direct hit to the right of my company position while we were advancing at Minbu. At the moment it was hit he was giving instructions standing up and was killed immediately. The whole tank burning in front of our eyes. Many years later when I was carrying out my professional work as a chartered surveyor, I was asked to advise a would-be purchaser of the structural condition of a Georgian house in Oxfordshire. While I was walking round the house I saw a photograph on the desk in the study of the then owner, a retired colonel, of a young officer in the Carabineers. I was having coffee with the lady of the household later in the morning and I asked her whether her husband had been in the Carabineers and she said, yes, he had. He had commanded it in the last war, in Europe. And then I said: 'Did you have a son in the Carabineers in Burma?' She said, yes, he was killed. It was the same person. I told her what I knew, and she said that she was extremely interested to hear but she felt it would be unwise if I said anything to her husband, who was then out of the house. She would tell him later, because he'd been so cut up at his son's death and he was now quite elderly. She thought it would be too much for him. I felt that was one of the most extraordinary coincidences of this life.

After we had done the mopping up in the oilfields, in May we were instructed to go down through Burma to the Pegu Yomas. On 28 May, still commanding A Company, I was appointed major two days after my twenty-first birthday. I can remember it distinctly because I thought at the time it would have been rather nice to have been a major at the age of twenty. In the Pegu Yomas the monsoon had begun in June and early July, and we had several actions. Although the Japs were retreating, they still fought like tigers. It was then, and for the first time, that the battalion started taking prisoners, mostly wounded Japs who had been left behind to rot. We came across some fearsome sights of Japanese soldiers suffering from massive gangrene, dysentery, beriberi *et al*. Very often their weapons had been taken from them or they'd been discarded, and one couldn't help feeling an element of pity despite all the things that they'd done.

In July Major Marshall was once again hospitalised. He had been suffering from the effects of amoebic dysentery for some considerable time but then went down with malaria. He was evacuated down to Rangoon, which had by then been captured, and was taken by hospital ship to Calcutta. During the voyage he developed hepatitis as well. So at that stage he was suffering from three different life-threatening diseases. Few of his colleagues escaped without some form of illness, and no wonder . . .

The Arakan was probably the worst for conditions. We were there immediately after the end of the monsoon. One was never dry, sleeping accommodation was made out of bamboo; they were called bashas and they generally leaked quite a bit. But the main factor was that going on patrols you were generally walking through paddy fields up to your knees in water for most of the time. Night-time was spent lying on only a groundsheet, and if it rained, which it often did, you were soaked to the skin. Most water had to be taken from chaungs; sometimes this was pure and other times it must have been infected because of the instance of dysentery. Many of my fellow officers had it so badly they never returned to the battalion. Also in Arakan, I would think that 50 per cent of the Gurkhas were affected by ringworm, and when we were in a rest position before Christmas 1944 the CO gave the order that no shirts would be worn in daytime, every man affected being painted with gentian violet, and a very strange sight the battalion looked at that stage.

From Calcutta General Hospital I was taken to the General Hospital at Secunderabad, and while I was in bed there we celebrated the end of the war. When I recovered I was granted convalescent leave because I'd also developed jaundice. I went to a convalescent home, one of the homes of Sir Victor Sassoon. It was a beautiful house, and I spent a pleasant time there. From there, in September 1945, I was allowed to rejoin my battalion. I made my usual trip to Calcutta, where I stayed at the Grand Hotel, which was the transit camp for officers. I then eventually was put on a flight to Bangkok, where I arrived about a fortnight after the battalion had arrived as the first troops to take over from the Japanese. The battalion was stationed at Bangkok University, and there was a general feeling of relief and jollity. I was informed I was to become camp commandant at 7th Divisional headquarters, which was in the centre of Bangkok, and six months later my old friend George Malone, who I arrived at the battalion with in 1943, turned up in my life again. He had progressed on the staff and was currently 14th Army camp commandant. He in fact was responsible for moving the 14th Army headquarters down through Burma until they arrived at Rangoon. He was going on leave and asked me to take over. The second coincidence – though only later evident (when *Bugles and a Tiger* was published) – was that when I arrived at Rangoon I found myself allotted a rather nice bungalow which was divided into two, and after I'd been there a little while the other portion was taken over by one Colonel John Masters. I got to know him quite well. He was extremely kind to me as a much younger man. He didn't stand on his rank or on his dignity, although he could have done having not only been a regular 4th Gurkha officer but having been an acting brigadier in the 2nd Chindits!

Marshall's time in Rangoon was brief and in April 1946 he went on leave to the UK, nearly four years after he'd left. In August he returned to India, and in October he went to the regimental centre at Abbottabad, where he remained until February 1947, when he demobbed, aged 22 years 10 months. He made an interesting final reflection on his time with the Gurkha battalions, short though it was:

British officers who served with Gurkha battalions as regulars before the war became rather unbalanced and starry-eyed about the virtues of Gurkhas. One got the impression that some thought the Gurkha could do no wrong. This of course isn't so. The Gurkha, I think I've indicated earlier, had many of the same vices and virtues of the British tommy, which is probably why they get on so well together, but, also, there was absolutely no doubting their courage . . .

CHAPTER TWELVE

VCs Galore!

After the 1942 retreat, the Allied forces back at their bases in India were rested after the shattering hike from Burma. The cost had been high – 13,463 casualties for the British and 4,597 for the Japanese. As Michael Marshall had witnessed, British forces had lost much of their weaponry and – short in the first place of decent equipment – now badly needed rearming. Many of the troops had no personal weapons and antitank guns were thin on the ground. It would be months before the commanders were ready to launch the new offensive described by Michael Marshall in the previous chapter, but by the end of 1942 a plan emerged to send columns into Burma to sabotage and generally harass the Japanese positions, cut their communications and supplies and perform hit-and-run attacks. It was the brainchild of Major General Orde Wingate, once described as the most eccentric general of the Second World War, although there were quite a few contenders for the title. He had the enthusiastic backing of Field Marshal Archibald Wavell, who was by then commander-in-chief of Allied forces in India prior to his appointment as Viceroy of India in 1943, when he brought Wingate in to command the 77th Brigade.

Deep penetration behind enemy lines wasn't a new idea. Several units had tried it. Some survived, including that formed by the ambitious, empire-building David Stirling. Having acquired 50 parachutes which fell off the back of a truck, Stirling used them as the basis for the formation of the Special Air Service, dreamed up a motto – Who Dares Wins – and made a name for himself racing ahead of the herd, miles inside enemy lines, raiding and pillaging, stealing and killing and causing general mayhem among the outposts of Rommel's Afrika Korps until his luck ran out. He was hauled off to Colditz, but the SAS went careering on without him.

Orde Wingate's scheme was more grandiose and controversial. He was a difficult, colourful and complex man. The son of a British officer, he was born in India and brought up in a family with strong Christian beliefs. He received a military education and was commissioned in 1923, later serving in India and then in the Sudan. He was transferred to Palestine in 1936 as an intelligence officer at a time when small bands of Arab rioters were regularly attacking both the British and the Jews. Wingate organised and trained special 'night squads', which successfully employed the tactics of surprise and mobility. His support for the Zionist cause was heavily frowned on, and in 1939 the British succumbed to Arab pressure: Wingate was transferred from the region that eventually became Israel and was barred from returning. His personal involvement with the Jews in Palestine was halted, but many of those he trained became heads of the Palmach, a unit of the Jewish underground army in Palestine. One of those who later became its deputy commander was Yitzak Rabin, eventually the nation's first Prime Minister to have been born in Israel and the first to be assassinated. Wingate returned briefly to Britain before being transferred to Ethiopia and was a major figure in liberating the country from the Italians. It was from this posting that he moved directly to India under Wavell. There, Orde Wingate developed his idea for a guerrilla force to attack the Japanese in Burma, using Gurkhas as the spearhead, and the London powerhouse needed little convincing. Churchill himself was very keen on swashbucklers. Wingate came up with the name Chindits for his force, which was a corruption of the Burmese word *chinthe* for 'winged stone lion', the guardians of Buddhist temples.

The original Chindit formation was officially known as the 77th Infantry Brigade, brought together for Wingate's first expedition. Under the title of Operation Longcloth, he assembled British commandos, 13th battalion King's Liverpool Regiment, 3/2nd Gurkha Rifles and 2nd battalion Burma Rifles, in all about 3,000 men, with hundreds of mules, oxen and elephants carrying their supplies. The Gurkha battalion was newly raised, which was exactly what Wingate wanted. He believed that fresh soldiers would be untainted by old ways and could be moulded by his training and theories of jungle warfare. The first thing he did was to split them up and mix and match the various battalions into sub-units. This, to the experienced British officer in the Gurkhas, was a travesty. Wingate ignored the protests, although it meant that the Gurkhas were serving under officers and inexperienced junior commanders who had no understanding of their ways or their language, and vice versa. The result was that many Gurkhas under his command ended up being used as just muleteers. He became one of the few people to actually criticise the performance of the Gurkhas, but regimental historians have not been backward in putting the blame on the man himself.

The first expedition had three objectives: to cut two main railway links from Mandalay and generally harass the enemy in the Shwebo area. The first objective lay 180 miles (290 kilometres) to the east. The Chindit columns were launched from Manipur in February 1943, and the main force reached the railway in two weeks without encountering any Japanese. They were to be resupplied at the target by the RAF. However, at the railway line two columns were ambushed and suffered heavy casualties. They managed to blow up the railway line in numerous places over a distance of 30 miles (48 kilometres), which would be heralded by war reporters as a brilliant achievement but, in truth, was overstated and the damage not sufficient to hamper the Japanese seriously. Nor did the media report the horrendous situation confronting the Chindit troops.

The Japanese were now alerted to the presence of a large British force, which they believed was a division of British commandos. They acted accordingly, piling troops into the area. The Chindits had managed to cross the Irrawaddy but then, under heavy fire, Wingate had to disperse his force, and so they were unable to be resupplied by the RAF, as arranged. The columns faced desperate weeks ahead: starving, lost in dense jungle, hundreds falling sick, wounded or killed under ambush; they were a sorry sight. Many suffered psychologically, and 12 young Gurkhas, very recent volunteers, had serious breakdowns to the point of having to be restrained, one howling like a dog and trying to eat his equipment. But the ordeal was not of their own making; some placed the blame on their commander. As Byron Farwell wrote: '. . . there was a psychopath directing these mad British expeditions behind enemy lines: Orde Wingate.'

A disorganised retreat became the only solution, and in that the Gurkhas were more fortunate than others, since many of them were under the command of an efficient ex-Sapper officer, Major 'Mad Mike' Calvert, later of the SAS. Even so, he finally had to split his force into groups of 40, with instructions to get back to India as best they could; 200 returned in comparatively decent order; 446 were lost, of whom only 150 were eventually accounted for. Overall, Wingate lost almost a third of his force. They had spent 12 weeks in the jungle and most had marched almost 1,000 miles (1,600 kilometres). Far from the picture drawn by newspaper reports at the time, the exercise was a dismal failure in almost every respect – other than the experimental value of testing British forces to the rigours of jungle warfare. It was also an appalling waste of lives for very little gain.

Even so, by the middle of the year the idea of the Chindits was revived, partly under pressure from the Americans. The Japanese were still showing no signs of wishing to progress further into the impenetrable Burmese landscape towards India, and the British were running only limited operations against them. But the Americans, under pressure in the Pacific, began agitating for a new theatre of operations to be opened up in the Far East. They wanted action from the British and from the substantial reservoir of Indian army manpower, which the ebullient US General Joe Stilwell claimed was being left idle, which was hardly true. At the summit conference in Quebec in August 1943, Churchill took along Orde Wingate, who revived his theories of long-range penetration. After some toing and froing between American generals, notably from Stilwell, who was to command US forces in the Chinese–Burmese theatre, Wingate was given the go-ahead by Allied commanders for a second expedition.

His vast new 'special force' would be formed for what was to become known as Operation Thursday, a complex and meandering proposal involving six brigades that were to be deployed by air into jungle locations. Its object, according to Wingate, was 'to insert a substantial force into the guts of the enemy' with the ability to penetrate deeply. Wingate would not survive to witness the outcome. He was killed in a plane crash on 24 March 1944. His body now lies in Arlington National Cemetery, Virginia. Brigadier Joe Lentaigne succeeded him, which was good news for the Gurkhas: he was formerly an officer with the 4th Gurkha Rifles. He now faced the daunting task of making the lumbering project work. Veterans from the original 77th Brigade were to be used, including survivors from the 3/2nd Gurkhas, along with the 3/6th, 3/4th and 4/10th. They were joined by battalions from more than a dozen British regiments. Each brigade had its own base close to an airstrip from which their columns would be sent to harass the Japanese. The Chindits put on a brave face and began what was to become an imprecise movement of men, machines and animals across the most challenging terrain under the worst weather on earth. Each column had its own objectives, although the initial fighting was in the hands of the 77th Brigade under the direction of recently promoted Brigadier Calvert, whose Chindit base at Henu soon attracted the attention of the Japanese and became the focal point of some harsh battles in which both sides took heavy casualties. The officer corps of the Gurkhas was, as usual, badly hit, leading as always from the front. The brigade had been in continuous action for almost two months and was expecting a respite when Joe Stilwell called for assistance, unable to manage with his Chinese-based force attempting a push towards the Japanese positions at Myitkyina. The 77th was ordered to proceed at once to capture the town of Mogaung, 165 miles (265 kilometres) away. The only way in was to walk, and it was the monsoon season. Calvert's brigade was already in dire trouble. Casualties had been high, sickness was rife from malaria and dysentery and the troops were already exhausted. But what Stilwell wanted, Stilwell got, and the column set off on what was to be another harrowing march through dense jungle in torrential rain.

They arrived at their map reference on 8 June and battle commenced. The Japanese were well dug in, and the scrap went on for 16 long days until finally the Japanese pulled back, which was fortunate for Calvert. His force of 2,000 'effectives' was down to 806 men, and falling. Although it was a triumph for all concerned, the 3/6th Gurkhas came out of it with praise and high honours – including two Victoria Cross awards. The first went posthumously to Captain Michael Allmand, who had been charged with leading his company into attacking a key bridge that the Japanese held with a stout defence.

The Gurkhas lost 30 men in the fight for control of the bridge, which they eventually won. Captain Allmand had stepped forward when GHQ India called for officer volunteers for the second Chindit expedition. Educated at Ampleforth, he was two months short of his twenty-first birthday. Over the period of the battle, Allmand took part in a number of actions in spite of his poor physical condition and limping badly from trench foot, which had affected many of the troops. He was killed in the final battle for the bridge, as his citation explained:

> Lieutenant (acting Captain) Michael Allmand was commanding the leading platoon of a company of the 6th Gurkha Rifles . . . and was ordered to attack the Pin Ilmi Road Bridge. The enemy had already succeeded in holding up our advance at this point for 24 hours. The approach to the bridge was very narrow as the road was banked up and the low-lying land on either side was swampy and densely covered in jungle. The Japanese, who were dug in along the banks of the road and in the jungle with machine guns and small arms, were putting up the most desperate resistance. As the platoon came within 20 yards [18 metres] of the bridge, the enemy opened heavy and accurate fire, inflicting severe casualties and forcing the men to seek cover. Captain Allmand, however, with the utmost gallantry charged on by himself, hurling grenades into the enemy gun positions and killing three Japanese with his kukri. Inspired by the splendid example of their platoon commander, the surviving men followed him and captured their objective. Two days later Captain Allmand, owing to casualties among the officers, took over command of the company and, dashing 30 yards [27 metres] ahead of it through long grass and marshy ground, swept by machine-gun fire, personally killed a number of enemy machine gunners and successfully led his men on to the ridge of high ground that they had been ordered to seize. Once again on 23 June in the final attack on the railway bridge at Mogaung, Captain Allmand, although suffering from trench foot, which made it difficult for him to walk, moved forward alone through deep mud and shell-holes and charged a Japanese machine-gun nest single-handed but he was mortally wounded and died shortly afterwards. The superb gallantry, outstanding leadership and protracted heroism of this very brave officer were a wonderful example to the whole battalion and in the highest traditions of his regiment.

Nor was that day of 23 June 1944 yet complete in its acts of acclaimed heroism. Rifleman Tulbahadur Pun had just turned 21. After completing his recruit training in the regimental centre, he joined the 3rd Battalion for the Chindit expedition. On the same day Captain Allmand was killed and in the same action against the railway bridge, Tulbahadur Pun earned the battalion's second Victoria Cross, as his citation described:

> Immediately the attack developed the enemy opened concentrated and sustained cross-fire at close range from a position known as the Red House and from a strong bunker position 200 yards [183 metres] to the left of it. So intense was this cross-fire that both the leading platoons of B Company, one of which was Rifleman Tulbahadur Pun's, were pinned to the ground and the whole of his section was wiped out with the exception of himself, the section commander and one other man. The section commander immediately led the remaining two men in a charge on the Red House but was at once badly wounded. Rifleman Tulbahadur Pun and his remaining companion continued the charge but the latter, too, was immediately badly wounded. Rifleman Tulbahadur Pun then seized the Bren gun and, firing from the hip as he went, continued the charge on this heavily bunkered position alone, in the face of the most shattering concentration of automatic fire, directed straight at him. With the dawn coming up behind him, he presented a perfect target to the Japanese. He had to move for 30 yards [27 metres] over open ground, ankle deep in mud, through shell-holes and over fallen trees. Despite these overwhelming odds, he reached the Red House and closed with the Japanese occupants. He killed three and put five more to flight and captured two light machine guns and much ammunition. He then gave accurate supporting fire from the bunker to the remainder of his platoon which enabled them to reach their objective. His outstanding courage and superb gallantry in the face of odds which meant almost certain death were inspiring to all ranks and were beyond praise.

Rifleman Tulbahadur Pun received his Victoria Cross from the Viceroy, Field Marshal Lord Wavell, at a special parade held in Delhi on 3 March 1945. He later joined the 2nd Battalion, 6th Gurkha Rifles, after partition and saw service in Malaya and Hong Kong. He rose to be regimental sergeant major of his battalion before retiring to his village on a pension with the honorary rank of lieutenant (QGO) on 14 May 1959, later visiting the UK for the reunions of holders of the Victoria and George Crosses.

The Chindits remained in operation throughout 1944, softening up the Japanese in parallel to the new offensive of the 14th Army under the command of Field Marshal Slim. The return to Burma by the Allied forces was the start of a long, brutal, bitter campaign that lasted a full two years, still being fought well after the war in Europe ended with Germany's surrender on 8 May 1945, and thus the 14th became 'the Forgotten Army'. The move across the Burma landscape was a strategic masterpiece, but there was no easy solution to the outcome, as the Japanese themselves found, day after day after day. They had been timid about advancing towards the Indian border, but now the 14th was coming after them. And this time the Allies were stronger and better prepared.

As Walter Walker, then a lieutenant colonel commanding the 4/8th Gurkhas, explained:

> We were fighting a first-class enemy in the Japanese, who were far better fighters than the Germans. They were first-class jungle fighters and that is why we were driven out of Burma in the first place. We had to learn the technique – their technique – and we had to stand and fight. And when we did, they resorted to other methods – they tied TNT to their stomachs and threw themselves in front of tanks to blow them up just as their kamikaze pilots flew suicide missions – and people tend to forget, if they ever knew, that there was no fighter like a Jap fighter. They were also incredibly cruel and ruthless. I've seen my Gurkha soldiers' bodies after they've done bayonet practice on them – my soldiers who had been taken prisoner and then tortured like this. It was not a pretty sight.

The Gurkhas, as we have seen, were not averse themselves to a bit of blood-letting, but their defence is that body mutilation only ever came after an enemy soldier was killed in battle and was never done to prisoners. Once in the Burma campaign, one battalion commander offered a reward for each Japanese head brought in. One havildar came back one day with six ears and laid them on the ground; he said the heads had been too heavy to carry. Walter Walker experienced the situation where a Gurkha patrol brought back to camp the head of a Japanese officer, killed that day in a skirmish; he apparently had 'a wispy beard and drooping moustache'. The head was nailed to a tree, and new Gurkha soldiers who had never seen a Japanese soldier dead or alive crowded round to view it. After two days, when it began to stink, Lieutenant Colonel Walker ordered it to be removed and buried.

The regimental history of the 1/10th also records an instance that reflects the general unwillingness of Gurkhas to take prisoners, which was a particular aspect of the modus operandi that was similar to the French Foreign Legion's, who themselves never took prisoners unless it was absolutely necessary. They tended to be an incumbrance on long marches, miles from anywhere; nor for that matter did the Japanese unless it suited them. A platoon from the 1/10th under Jemadar Lalbahadur Limbu went out to deal with a group of 80 Japanese with wounded soldiers who were resting in the jungle a couple of miles away. The Gurkhas ambushed them using two sections, one forward and one behind, and attacked using bayonets and kukris. The Japanese fled and ran straight into the second section. At least 40 were killed and Lieutenant Colonel D.D.M. McCready, commenting on this action, noted: 'There was a great blooding of kukris in this small action and, significantly enough, in spite of the number of Japanese wounded, no wounded were brought back.' Jemadar Limbu was awarded an immediate Military Cross. Encouragement for the 'kill' came from the top, and Walter Walker had his own method of instilling into his men the necessity of disposing of as many Japanese as possible:

When I took command of the 4/8th it did not take me long to realise they were war-weary and at a very low ebb. Their CO and adjutant had been killed, and frankly they were not up to the standard I was used to . . . and although they were weary I worked them very hard. They were not mutinous and realised I was trying to train them like racehorses . . . to try to ensure that when they went into battle they were not killed. I published one golden rule in orders every night and it stuck in the minds of the men. I would say to them: 'What is the golden rule today?' The phrases I used were designed to try to instil in my men a fighting spirit; that they must kill every single Jap that they encountered. And that there is no question of retreating in the face of the enemy; that I would accept nothing but victory, and if they obeyed these golden rules then they would live. If they didn't and became lax when they were out of sight of their commanders, then they might not live to see another day. And that is what I did. Not only did I publish the golden rule of the day in orders . . . it was plastered over the camps that we occupied, until every man knew it was a code of conduct.

Medals in the Burma campaign came thick and fast, and it is worth noting that during the whole of the Second World War, of the 100 Victoria Crosses awarded, 31 went to men fighting in Burma, and, of those, 9 were won by men of the Gurkha regiments. The citations for all of them, as already demonstrated, tell stories of individual bravery of the highest order, and while it is not possible to give details of all (see Appendix III), I have selected three more for the record, taken not from the senior levels but ordinary Gurkha soldiers from the ranks whose deeds were simply remarkable.

Rifleman Ganju Lama was 17 when he was enlisted into the 7th Gurkhas in 1942. He was unusual in that he was not an ethnic Gurkha, nor was he a Nepalese subject, but as things were then, the recruiters were prepared to accept any volunteers who closely resembled Gurkhas. After training, he was sent to the 1/7th Gurkha Rifles, then ensconced at Imphal, scene of one of the biggest 14th Army battles. Within weeks of his arrival, Ganju had been awarded the Military Medal for his part in an attack on a Japanese patrol, killing several of them. The following month, in June 1944 and then 19, Ganju's unit was part of the 48th Indian Infantry Brigade, 17th Indian Division, along with the 2/5th Gurkhas in a major engagement of the enemy, which was supported by tanks on both sides. Ganju himself saved what looked to be a tricky situation and in doing so became known as the man who single-handedly took on three tanks firing at point-blank range – and won, as his citation explains:

On the morning of the 12 June, 1944, the enemy put down an intense artillery barrage lasting an hour on our positions north of

154

the village of Ningthoukhong. This heavy artillery fire knocked out several bunkers and caused heavy casualties, and was immediately followed by a very strong enemy attack supported by five medium tanks. After fierce hand-to-hand fighting, the perimeter was driven in one place and enemy infantry, supported by three medium tanks, broke through, pinning our troops to the ground with intense fire. B Company, 7th Gurkha Rifles, was ordered to counterattack and restore the situation. Shortly after passing the starting line it came under heavy enemy machine-gun and tank machine-gun fire at point-blank range which covered all lines of approach. Rifleman Ganju Lama, the No. 1 of the P.I.A.T. gun, on his own initiative, with great coolness and complete disregard for his own safety, crawled forward and engaged the tanks single-handed. In spite of a broken left wrist and two other wounds, one in his right hand and one in his leg, caused by withering cross-fire concentrated upon him, Rifleman Ganju Lama succeeded in bringing his gun into action within 30 yards [27 metres] of the enemy tanks and knocked out first one and then another, the third tank being destroyed by an antitank gun. In spite of his serious wounds, he then moved forward and engaged with grenades the tank crews who now attempted to escape. Not until he had killed or wounded them all, thus enabling his company to push forward, did he allow himself to be taken back to the Regimental Aid Post to have his wounds dressed . . . It was solely due to his prompt action and brave conduct that a most critical situation was averted, all positions regained and very heavy casualties inflicted on the enemy.

Ganju Lama was rescued by his own unit and was taken to hospital. He was eventually traced through the chain of evacuation, told he had been awarded the Victoria Cross, and was presented with the medal by Lord Wavell, in the presence of Admiral Lord Louis Mountbatten, Field Marshal Slim and members of his own family. After Indian independence in 1947 Ganju joined a Gurkha regiment that remained within the Indian army and in 1965 was appointed ADC to the President of India.

Bhanbhagta Gurung, one of many of that name that the 2nd Gurkha Rifles enlisted was, it will be recalled, on hand to meet Major Gordon

Corrigan and his band of travellers – the author included – at the Gurkha Welfare Centre at Gorkha in October 1998 when he was 79 years old. He was born in the Phalpu in the district of Gorkha and joined the 3rd Battalion, 2nd King Edward VII's Own Gurkha Rifles, at the age of 18. He was among the first Chindit expedition and spent much of the next two years with the 3/2nd Gurkhas, part of the 25th Indian Division, in action down the Arakan coast in a number of assault landings. In February 1945 the battalion landed at Ruywa and after heavy fighting came upon a brigade of the 82nd West African Division attempting to evacuate its casualties but held up by the Japanese at a feature known as Snowdon. On the night of 4 March, B Company of the 3/2nd Gurkhas was ordered to capture the ground dominated by the enemy. One of Bhanbhagta's fellow riflemen was killed in an attempt to rush one of their positions single-handed. The whole section was pinned down by a tree sniper who was inflicting casualties by the minute.

Bhanbhagta, being unable to fire from the lying position, stood up, fully exposed to the heavy fire, and calmly killed the enemy sniper with his rifle, thus saving his section from suffering further casualties. The section advanced again, but when within 20 yards [18 metres] of the objective it was attacked by very heavy fire. Bhanbhagta, without waiting for any orders, dashed forward alone and attacked the first enemy foxhole. Throwing two grenades, he killed the two occupants and rushed on to the next, killing the Japanese in it with his bayonet. Two further enemy foxholes were still firing on the section, and again he ran forward alone and cleared these with bayonet and grenade. During his single-handed attacks on these four enemy foxholes he faced continuous machine-gun fire from an enemy bunker. He went forward alone for the fifth time, leaped on to the roof of the bunker and flung two No. 77 smoke bombs into the bunker slit. Two Japanese rushed out of the bunker coughing. Bhanbhagta killed them both with his kukri. A remaining Japanese inside the bunker was still firing a light machine gun and holding up the advance of No. 4 Platoon. This time Bhanbhagta crawled inside the bunker, killed the Japanese gunner, and captured the light machine gun. Bhanbhagta ordered the nearest Bren gunner and two riflemen to take up positions in the captured bunker, and, as the Japanese attempted to counterattack, the small party under his command ripped into the advancing enemy troops, inflicting heavy casualties.

His regiment gained the battle honour 'Tamandu' and some months later Rifleman Bhanbhagta was decorated with the Victoria Cross at Buckingham Palace by King George VI. After the war his company commander tried to persuade him to continue serving, but he chose to return to his village where he had a frail widowed mother and a young wife and children. He left his battalion in January 1946, with the honorary rank of havildar. His three sons followed in his footsteps to serve in the 2nd Battalion of his regiment. He was honoured by his own country in 1945, when he was awarded the Star of Nepal, Third Class. His company commander, later colonel, D.F. Neill, described him as 'a smiling, hard-swearing, gallant and indomitable peasant soldier, who, in a battalion of very brave men, was one of the bravest'. When we met him in 1998, it was apparent from all around him that those thoughts had not diminished.

Another hero of the same tribal name, the diminutive Rifleman Lachhiman Gurung, became one of the most famous of all the Gurkha VCs when, years later, he was photographed on the steps of 10 Downing Street with the then Prime Minister John Major, after an appeal fund was started for Gurkha pensioners including Lachhiman and Bhanbhagta by a group of supporters led by the *Sunday Express* and its then editor, Brian Hitchen, a long-time Gurkha fan. Lachhiman's story is one of the most astonishing of all when, alone in his trench, blinded in one eye and with one hand blown off by a grenade, he continued to hold off a Japanese onslaught.

Lachhiman, a tiny, slender man, was recruited into the 8th Gurkha Rifles in 1941, although he was past the normal age, thought to be around 24 years old, and was under the minimum height, standing just four feet eleven inches (1.49 metres). In peacetime he would never have been accepted as a volunteer; in fact he had tried before but had been rejected. He passed his recruit training and was posted to the 4/8th Gurkha Rifles in Burma and came to the war in the final crucial stages when bitter battles were still being fought in spite of the surrender of the Germans. The 4/8th was part of the 89th Indian Infantry Brigade in the 7th Indian Division, advancing south along the Irrawaddy against the retreating Japanese forces.

Three days after his arrival in the battle zone, Lachhiman was to take part in some very rapid action when B and C Companies were ordered to hold an important position on the west side of the river near the village of Taungdaw, which was vital to the Japanese withdrawal. The Japanese fought with what was described as 'fanatical fury' to break through, with wave after wave of suicide attacks. The key position was held by No. 9 Platoon of C Company almost 100 yards (91 metres) ahead of the remainder of the company. The citation for his VC takes up the story:

On the night of 12/13 May, 1945, Rifleman Lachhiman Gurung was manning the most forward post of his platoon. At 0120 hours at least 200 enemy assaulted his company position. The brunt of the attack was borne by Rifleman Lachhiman Gurung's section and by his own post in particular. This post dominated a jungle path leading up into his platoon locality. Before assaulting, the enemy hurled innumerable grenades at the position from close range. One grenade fell on the lip of Rifleman Lachhiman Gurung's trench. He at once grasped it and hurled it back at the enemy. Almost immediately another grenade fell directly inside the trench. Again this rifleman snatched it up and threw it back. A third grenade then fell just in front of the trench. He attempted to throw it back but it exploded in his hand, blowing off his fingers, shattering his right arm and severely wounding him in the face, body and right leg. His two comrades were also badly wounded and lay helpless in the bottom of the trench. The enemy, screaming and shouting, now formed up shoulder to shoulder and attempted to rush the position by sheer weight of numbers.

Lachhiman Gurung, regardless of his wounds, fired and loaded his rifle with his left hand, maintaining a continuous and steady rate of fire. Wave after wave of fanatical attacks were thrown in by the enemy and all were repulsed with heavy casualties. For four hours after being severely wounded Lachhiman remained alone at his post, waiting with perfect calm for each attack, which he met with fire at point-blank range from his rifle, determined not to give one inch of ground. Of the 87 enemy dead counted in the immediate vicinity of the company locality, 31 lay in front of this rifleman's section, the key to the whole position. Had the enemy succeeded in overrunning and occupying [his] trench, the whole of the reverse slope position

158

would have been completely dominated and turned. This rifle-man, by his magnificent example, so inspired his comrades to resist the enemy to the last, that, although surrounded and cut off for three days and two nights, they held and smashed every attack. His outstanding gallantry and extreme devotion to duty, in the face of almost overwhelming odds, were the main factors in the defeat of the enemy.

Lachhiman was evacuated to hospital, but he lost his right hand and the use of his right eye. On 19 December 1945 he was decorated with the Victoria Cross by the Viceroy of India, Field Marshal Lord Wavell, at the Red Fort in Delhi. His proud father, then aged about 74 and very frail, was carried for 11 days from his village in Nepal to be present at the Red Fort to see him decorated. Lachhiman continued to serve with the 9th Gurkha Rifles who remained in India after independence in 1947. He was promoted to havildar but retired on completion of his service, returning to his village in Nepal. One of his sons subsequently became an officer in the 8th Gurkha Rifles.

Before leaving this summary of events in the Second World War, mention must also be made of the Gurkhas' involvement in the Italian campaign in which two further VCs were won during costly battles at Monte Cassino which were being fought in parallel action to the activity in Burma, bringing the Gurkhas' total of VCs won during the conflict to 11. The Gurkhas paid dearly, as indeed did all the Allied forces involved in this long and bitter struggle against crack German troops in this final phase of enemy resistance in Italy.

Amid the mayhem of death and destruction there were moments of black humour, as Anthony Harvey recalled as he made his way to the Italian front line direct from the regimental training centre with a reinforcement draft for the 1/5th to replace heavy casualties in a battle called Mozzogrogna. He was immediately put in a rifle company as a learner and went on patrols locating German positions. His first taste of real action was during the last battle of Monte Cassino. At the time Harvey was in the reinforcement company, well back from the battle lines, while young officers like himself took it in turns to get their 'battle inoculation'. Harvey was still in the reinforcement camp, acting as assistant adjutant, when he heard that a third assault on Monte Cassino was coming up. He recalled:

The first two attacks at Cassino had been disastrous, and the New Zealanders and the Americans and the 4th Indian Division had lost really horrendous casualties. This was the last one and was the one that was preceded by the bombing of the monastery which made it successful. I had asked to be sent forward to the battalion but no one would give me permission, and so I just left one day and hitchhiked back to the battalion. They weren't expecting me. The CO was dug into the side of a road almost into a hedgerow. And I crawled up and reported to him and his first words were: 'Where the hell have you come from?'

I said: 'Well, I've just reported up from the reinforcement camp.'

He replied: 'Well, you'd better get into that village. The company commander's just been shot in the arse.'

I said: 'How do I get there?'

He just looked me in the eye and said: 'Crawl, you bloody fool. How else do you think you're going to get there?' I started to crawl towards the village only to be joined by a Goanese mess waiter who was going to crawl all the way forward to this battle area which was being shelled – with a plate of sandwiches for the company commander. Extraordinary! Anyway, we crawled on through and we passed some dead bodies. I recognised one Gurkha officer who was particularly good. He'd been shot through the throat. I took over from the company commander who was on a stretcher ready to be evacuated. They had done the bulk of the work, but we were overlooked by a thing called the Platform, and the Germans were dug in and we couldn't move without them firing on us. We had been supported throughout the campaign to date by the Canadian tank brigade. Somewhere down in the water meadows I saw one tank struggling to get up to our village. I got in touch with a Canadian sergeant in charge, and I asked him if he could come up and crunch through the rubble which had once been the village of Sant Angelo . . .

And so it went on. One battle scenario replaced another in rapid succession and one of them was the setting for the first of the Gurkha VCs in the Italian campaign: Rifleman Sherbahadur Thapa, of the Chettri tribe, one of the tribes enlisted by the 9th Gurkhas. He was posted to the 1/9th Gurkhas in Italy with a reinforcement draft in September 1944. He came to the war as the Germans were defending a position stretching from east to west in northern Italy, known as the Gothic Line. His battalion was involved in heavy fighting near the town of San Marino. On 17 September 1944 the 1/9th was ordered to seize three commanding positions, the last of which was not captured until the early hours of 19 September, by which time the forward positions of the battalion had run out of ammunition:

Sherbahadur Thapa was a number-one Bren gunner in a rifle company which just before dawn came under heavy enemy fire. He and his section commander charged an enemy post, killing the machine gunner and putting the rest of the post to flight. Almost immediately another party of Germans attacked the two men, and the section commander was badly wounded by a grenade, but without hesitation this rifleman, in spite of intense fire, rushed at the attackers and, reaching the crest of the ridge, brought his Bren gun into action against the main body of the enemy who were counterattacking our troops. Disregarding suggestions that he should withdraw to the cover of a slit trench, he lay in the open under a hail of bullets, firing his Bren gun from his exposed position on the crest of the hill because he knew they would not have been visible from the slit trench. By the accuracy of his fire . . . this isolated Gurkha Bren gunner silenced several enemy machine guns and checked a number of Germans who were trying to infiltrate on to the ridge. At the end of two hours both forward companies [of the 1/9th] had exhausted their ammunition and, as they were by then practically surrounded, they were ordered to withdraw. Rifleman Sherbahadur Thapa covered their withdrawal as they crossed the open ground to positions in the rear and himself remained alone at his post until his ammunition ran out. He then dashed forward under small arms and mortarfire and rescued two wounded men who were lying between him and the advancing Germans. While returning the second time he paid the price of his heroism and fell riddled by machine-gun bullets fired at point-blank range. The great bravery of this Gurkha soldier was instrumental in saving the lives of many of his companions, and his outstanding devotion to duty contributed largely to the severe reverse which the enemy eventually suffered when our troops counterattacked. His name will live in the history of his regiment as a very gallant soldier.

In March 1945 at a ceremony held outside the Red Fort in Delhi, Field Marshal Lord Wavell presented her son's Victoria Cross to Sherbahadur's mother, who had travelled from Nepal especially for the occasion.

The 4th Division had been in a rest situation and returned to battle early in November. Anthony Harvey was a 'swinger' company commander – one sent in to replace an injured or dead company commander – having taken over A Company of the 1/5th Gurkha Rifles, which was sent out on to Monte San Bartolo, the objective of a future attack, to scout the steep approaches. It was known that the position was occupied by German troops who had the approaches covered by machine-gun posts. The platoon had moved up the spine of this particular feature. It wasn't terribly high, said Harvey, but high enough compared with the roads underneath. The leading scout, whose name was Thaman Gurung, was working his way to the summit when he came upon Germans in a slit trench preparing to open fire on the main section. Thaman Gurung, who had just turned 20, charged with his kukri, but he didn't have to use it: the Germans were so surprised they surrendered and were sent down the hill to the rear section of the platoon. Their capture alerted the Germans on the other side of the crest, and as Thaman crept back towards them he saw they were preparing to open fire. Within a very short time mortarfire of some intensity came down on the Gurkha positions. In full view of the enemy troops, he dashed across the bullet-swept crest firing his Tommy gun into German positions until his ammunition ran out. Then he threw his two grenades, darted back to the leading section, collected more grenades and hurled them at the Germans, thus creating a diversion for his section to withdraw. His citation completed the story:

Meanwhile the leading section which had remained to assist the withdrawal of the remainder of the platoon was still close to the summit. Rifleman Thaman Gurung, shouting to the section to withdraw, seized a Bren gun and a number of magazines. He then, yet again, ran to the top of the hill and, although he knew well that his action meant almost certain death, stood up on the bullet-swept summit in full view of the enemy and opened fire . . . It was not until he had emptied two complete magazines and the remaining section was well on its way to safety that Rifleman Gurung was killed . . . His superb gallantry and sacrifice of his life [allowed] his platoon to withdraw from an extremely difficult position without many more casualties, bringing valuable information that resulted in the whole Monte San Bartolo feature being captured three days later.

Anthony Harvey, being there, has, like the rest of the platoon, particular cause to be thankful for the actions of Thaman: 'There is no doubt that he saved our lives, and long after the action a court of inquiry was set up and all the witnesses were sworn and made to tell what they knew about it, as a result of which an application for the award of the VC was made and was granted. It was thoroughly deserved.'

And so one more story of courage was prepared for the regimental histories that today stand as a lasting contribution to the Brigade of Gurkhas' contribution to the Allied cause in the Second World War. Apart from the many British officers killed, 250,000 soldiers from the Nepalese hills had served the British Crown at its hour of need in 42 Gurkha infantry battalions. Of these, 7,544 were killed, 1,441 posted as missing, presumed dead, 23,655 wounded (although the last figure was thought in reality to be considerably higher) and 2,734 received bravery awards.

PART THREE

Never Say Die

The unravelling of the vast force of Nepali hill men who had fought so loyally for the Allies and who, by and large, wanted to remain in their employ was probably a greater headache to those charged with demobilisation of the troops than most other elements of the British and Indian armies. The Indian army started out as a force of 200,000, but during the six years of war utilised the services of almost two million; 250,000 of them were Gurkhas, recruited into various elements of the Allied forces, paramilitary roles, police and civilian tasks. From the moment the war ended, the build-up began to what would become the most emotional and difficult period in Gurkha history, played out against the explosion of anti-Imperialist, pro-nationalist and bloody religious struggles across the Indian subcontinent and South-East Asia.

CHAPTER THIRTEEN

Partition – In Every Sense

The days of Empire and the British Raj were numbered, and the Labour government of Clement Attlee, after much dithering and changes of mind, finally set about dismantling British rule of the nations and their lands collected like trophies since the beginning of the seventeenth century. Ahead lay years of shocking civil unrest, murder, mayhem and jungle warfare across the whole of what was once called the East Indies, which the Allies had just saved from Japanese occupation and whose war dead lay scattered across this unforgiving terrain in their tens of thousands. The Gurkhas would find themselves in the unhappy position of becoming piggy in the middle of both the uprisings and the politics.

The first of a series of setbacks came after the celebration of the homecomings. The Gurkha soldiers were confronted with the harsh reality of postwar life – that almost 60 per cent of those still serving would have to return to their homes. Twenty battalions were to be axed immediately. To this was added the disappointment of men released from prison camps only to discover that the remaining battalions were at full strength and the many older Gurkha officers would find difficulty in re-establishing themselves at their wartime level. The homeward path to the Himalayan foothills became well trodden by disheartened men, many disabled by their wounds, sick from the diseases picked up during the war and in the prison camps, and many of them without any form of pension because they had not served long enough to qualify (these received only their back pay and a demobilisation package). It was all very hurried and unsatisfactory, left too often in the hands of insensitive Indian civil servants. There were the medals – literally thousands of them. Chandra Bahadur Gurung, former lecturer at Tribhuvan University, Nepal, recalled in his 1998 book *British Medals and Gurkhas*:

> At the end of World War II when as a child, I returned with my parents to Nepal from Abbottabad where my father had served . . . It was so common in my village for children to play with British medals they were known as *khopi*, a child's plaything. Medals were seen everywhere, in hundreds and thousands. They seemed to have little value but as time passed, medals became scarce . . . they were lost, stolen or smuggled away from their original owners as were other trophies of war and valuables some households possessed such as Japanese Samurai swords... [consequently] in Nepalese villages nowadays, it is very hard to find war medals.

There was, however, still gainful employment for many – a fact ensured by the chaotic state of postwar cities across South-East Asia and the demands of boisterous nationalist politicians calling for 'Asia for Asians . . . self-government *now*!' The luckiest of the Gurkha battalions was the 2/5th, which was given an immediate prestige posting to Tokyo to become part of the Commonwealth Occupation Force for which no expense was spared. New uniforms, new transport and new weapons were ordered to put on a good show for the Japanese. Elsewhere civil unrest and a general lapse in the control of law and order meant the dispatch of Gurkhas to many parts of the Far East and beyond.

Lord Louis Mountbatten, departing his job as Supreme Commander of South-East Asia, signalled their continued presence when he said prophetically, 'I am afraid you are in for a sticky time, old chap', as he waved goodbye to one of the administrators left to sort out the mess. He departed to the sound of a cliché, the rumblings of discontent in India, Malaya, Indonesia, Burma, Borneo, Korea, Vietnam . . . all of which would ensure that there would be an abundance of work for idle hands as the Communists, inspired by the march of Mao Tse-tung across China, rose up to kick out the Imperialist forces. Within months of the end of the war, the slaughter began, and over the coming decade all of those countries were engaged in new battles, this time confronting a largely Communist-inspired struggle against Imperialist rule.

The British, above all, were slow to appreciate that the Communist leaders it had armed in Malaya against the Japanese, and indeed had fêted and honoured as war heroes and allies, were now ready to fire on British troops and murder the colonialist settlers with the guns kindly provided by the Allies. Muddled policy and tardy reaction merely exacerbated the problems. The most volatile of all the nations, the jewel in the crown of the British Empire, was being torn apart by nationalist ardour and religious fervour which combined to ensure the bloodiest of all situations. If that wasn't sufficient, hordes of Pathans were moving out of the North-West Frontier – ever brisk to snatch the moment of opportunity – eastwards in raiding parties on Kashmir, not so troublesome now as in the past, but more interested in loading their camels with booty and returning quickly from whence they came. All in all, big trouble was brewing.

Mountbatten was soon on his way back to become the last Viceroy of India, the man chosen to discover a solution to Indian woes and implant it in the nation within a given period of time in the summer of 1947. The deal was partition: the creation of the independent nations of India and Pakistan and in consequence the end of the British army in India and the division of the Gurkha regiments. Before that happened, the Gurkhas were again in the forefront as India engaged in its own full-blown and appalling religious warfare between Hindu and Muslim with barbarous side action from the Sikhs.

John Thornton was two weeks short of his nineteenth birthday when he was commissioned into the 3rd Queen Alexandra's Own Gurkha Rifles and reported to their regimental centre at Dehra Dun in September 1946. For the first five weeks, his job was to see that no soldier going on discharge was billed for shortages of kit and to ensure that they all had a double issue of clothing to take back to Nepal. The commandant had decreed that the veterans of Africa, Italy and Burma would not go short. Later, he was posted to the 2nd Battalion stationed at Wah, a small town 50 miles (80 kilometres) west of Rawalpindi. A cement works stood next door. Everyone and everything was permanently covered in a film of fine white dust. Rumour and counter-rumour was rife of countless conflicting stories of ethnic violence. The lid, said Thornton, was about to come off – and it did, on the night of

7 March 1947, when 293 people were slaughtered in the Punjab and troops were sent to Amritsar.

Across India, the powder-keg situation threatened to blow anywhere, at any time, and the Gurkhas were running into trouble at almost every step of the way. They were in the thick of it when independence and partition were announced on 15 August, giving cause for the massive movement of refugees from the atrocities being committed on both sides of the new national boundaries in what would today be described as ethnic cleansing. In four months to December 1947, the official figures said that 8.5 million people, almost equally divided between Hindu and Muslim, left their homes and trekked across the newly defined border between India and Pakistan 'in the largest migration in history'. Millions of souls never made it, slaughtered in the cruellest of civil strife ever witnessed. John Thornton recalls the work of just one of the Gurkha battalions involved:

Our main task was to patrol the countryside around Saghoda, a large city 200 miles [321 kilometres] south of Rawalpindi. We were to stop attacks on villages and to bring back running refugees to a control RV [rendezvous]. We were issued with six-wheel Dodge trucks that were superb cross-country vehicles. A pall of black smoke on the horizon meant another village was burning. Sometimes we got there on time, mostly not. If we didn't, then every man, woman and child was dead, the men mostly on the village perimeter where they had died fighting. The women, with their children, had preferred to commit suicide by jumping into the village well. Sometimes there would be so many bodies in the well that it overflowed. On the few occasions we arrived on time, we had absolutely no hesitation in shooting every attacker.

To this day, the smell of burned hair still brings back vivid memories of the slaughter. As we became more experienced, we would smuggle a couple of sections into a threatened village. Any attack was met with maximum force. This had a considerable deterrent effect and attacks on villages lessened, although the main reason for this was that either we had evacuated all Hindus and Sikhs or the villages had already been attacked and destroyed. When we had gathered the refugees together, our next task was to escort them to India. Saghoda was too far away to take the overland route, so the 150,000 refugees were to await evacuation by air. As it took some time to gather the necessary aircraft, we were tasked to escort foot convoys to the Indian border. We left a small rear party in Saghoda and moved about 150 miles (241 kilometres) east, where other refugees were concentrated.

These foot convoys were horrific. Each consisted of some 100,000 men, women and children. Each one stretched for about 20 miles (32 kilometres) and moved like a caterpillar: by the time the head of the convoy stopped, the rear had only just started to move. It was always on the move. We had some 80 men to protect a column, and it was continually attacked. Groups armed with axes and guns would wait for a gap in our defences before rushing into the convoy. Everyone would be slaughtered and their belongings looted. The young girls, particularly aged between 12 and 15, were abducted. Lucky ones were forcibly converted to Islam and taken as slaves. The unlucky ones were raped and then horrifically murdered: impaled on bamboo stakes or tied to charpoys and sawn in half while still alive.

It was no wonder we showed no mercy. We soon realised that wearing Gurkha hats gave the murderers our positions, so we changed to steel helmets. Next time the gangs attacked, they shouted out: 'Don't fire! We are your brothers – we are all of Islam.' We realised that the previous convoys had been escorted by Muslim troops wearing tin hats and many had obviously colluded with thugs. We went along with them and encouraged them to move towards us. When they were close enough, we shot them. Attacks eased off after that. Our convoy crossed into India six days later. We handed the survivors over – about half the number we had set out with – and were told that it had been a successful convoy! We moved into India and picked up a mass of Muslim refugees headed west to Pakistan. The same happened in reverse: we shot down Hindus and Sikhs to protect Muslims.

We returned to Saghoda and helped in the airlift. Dakotas had arrived from all corners of the world. They were stripped of seats and each one carried about 80 refugees squatting on the floor. While we had been away, two Gurkha civilians appeared at our rear party, a grandfather and his grandson, aged 12. The old man had worked at the remount depot after service in the Great War. The whole family, except these two, had been slaughtered. I was determined to get them on the airlift but met with strong resistance from those coordinating the passenger lists. The organisers were Hindu civil servants, who were obviously taking bribes to fix the list. I was getting nowhere, so I took drastic action. I arrested the chief civil servant and took him back to our camp in Saghoda city. I told his number one that if the two Gurkhas were not on a plane within 24 hours, I would arrest him also, and then would release him and his chief in the middle of the Muslim city. Grandfather and grandson were on the next plane out. We had a whip-round for them and handed over about 300 rupees. I never heard of them again, but could only assume that they made it back to Nepal and their distant relatives. With the airlift finished, we moved back to Rawalpindi and comparative calm. Life became normal and social life was resumed.

For weeks the rumours circulated around the jungle telegraph of the British military as to the future of the Gurkhas: the prophets of doom said they were all washed up and would be disbanded; others said quite the opposite; that Britain needed the Gurkhas now more than ever before. The issue was raised in the British Parliament, where Attlee assured repeated questioners that Britain still intended to maintain Gurkha troops; the numbers were at that time not known. Eventually, it became clear that all existing Gurkha regiments would continue in business, but only four would remain under the banner of the British army: the 2nd, 6th, 7th and 10th. They would leave India in January 1948 for a new base outside the country, in Malaya, and would never return. The remaining six, the 1st, 3rd, 4th, 5th, 8th and 9th, were to stay in India and become part of the Indian army (see Appendix II). All British officers of those regiments would transfer to the other British regiments, not necessarily Gurkha units, their places to be taken by Indian army officers. There would, henceforth, be no British officers serving in any unit of the Indian army.

The decision was final; no debate, no consultation at officer level and no appeal. It was heartbreaking news and caused great anguish among British officers and Gurkhas alike. It would not be an exaggeration to say that tears welled up in the eyes of some long-serving British officers faced with the prospect of being parted from their beloved battalions. As one colonel wrote: 'It is not our regiment going to India that hurt; it was our separation from it.' Anthony Harvey recalled the moment of the decision in his own regiment, the 5th Royal Gurkha Rifles:

> The British officers were all absolutely convinced that we would be chosen for HMG. We were the only *Royal* Gurkha Rifles, we'd won four VCs in the Second World War and we were a racing certainty to be one of those chosen – or so we thought. I've always suspected – and I'm sure I'm right – that Pandit Nehru thought the same and that he wanted the 5th, and since he was Prime Minister of India he got them, and suddenly I discovered that the regiment I'd gone to war with and grown to love very much was not going to HMG. We had a long meeting of British officers, finishing at four in the morning. We decided that we would advise all Gurkhas, including Gurkha officers, to stay where they were and not to opt as individuals for HMG but to keep the battalion together. All that they would lose was their British officers.

The reaction in Britain that the 'Royal' regiment was being given away was none the less one of shock; there were cries of 'disgraceful!'

As for the Gurkha ranks, it was a confusing and bewildering time, not least because their officers were unable for many weeks to produce conditions of service that would apply on the changeover. Finally, a letter was sent to officers in Gurkha regiments under the signature of the Adjutant General of the Indian Army which carried this following last paragraph: 'Every single soldier is being given the choice of whether he wishes to remain under the War Office, under the new Government of India, or neither, so there is no question of forcing them to serve under one or the other. Whatever they do, will be of their own free will.' This edict was the result of a tripartite agreement between Britain, India and Nepal in which the terms and conditions of the Gurkhas' future employment by either country was to be set in stone and could not be deviated from (which in itself proved to be a millstone in later years).

There were very mixed feelings among the Gurkhas themselves. If bets had been taken, people would have lost their money if they'd put it on a veritable dash to retain their 132-year-old association with Britain, as many were predicting. In the event, the desire to remain soldiers of the British army was considerably overestimated, partly because of the manner in which it was being presented and partly because many did not want to leave the regimental centres of India.

Feelings were running high. The 1/2nd Gurkha Rifles, for example, had to be 'persuaded' to remain under the British flag. General Sir Francis Tuker, himself an old 2nd Gurkha, personally addressed the battalion and told the men that if they remained in India they would have to hand back the regimental truncheon given to the battalion by Queen Victoria in place of a third colour. It would have to be returned to her grandson, King George VI. Tuker talked them out of staying in India, although it was touch and go. In the 2/7th, only 53 men in the entire battalion elected to stay in British service. In another battalion, only one man stepped forward, but quickly stepped back again when he saw he was a man alone. British officers observing this mass exodus from their ranks viewed it as a depressing betrayal that so many of their men should opt to serve under Indian army officers, viewed with disdain by many, rather than remain with them. Some cried openly. The much-vaunted bond between the British officers and the Gurkhas born of years of mutual respect and loyalty seemed at this moment of crisis to count for nothing. Yet much of the situation was discovered later to be sheer misunderstanding and confusion – and that the Gurkhas themselves thought the officers were deserting *them*. As Major L.E. Pottinger, who transferred to the 6th from the 9th, later wrote:

> ... their British officers were walking out and leaving them during conditions of near chaos ... they could not believe that the all-powerful British Raj, which had only recently beaten the Germans and the Japanese, could be so base as to abandon them. When they realised what was happening, they were resentful, and who could blame them?

Even General Tuker admitted that 'we mishandled the whole business', and untypical animosity emerged as the deadline for the changeover approached. John Cross, then a young officer, recalled the scene at Rangoon at the beginning of January 1948 – the date of the final handing over of regimental colours – when Burma, too, had gained her independence and those Gurkhas who were going to the Indian army prepared to leave:

> So anaesthetised by the subcontinent crumbling, we had given too little thought to what we would find in our battalions. We had seen Gurkhas, strong in patience and fortitude, discipline, loyalty, trust and respect, showing the brighter side of their characters. Now we were in for a nasty shock, as we experienced the darker aspects of their make-up. In retrospect, my initial views on Gurkhas had undoubtedly been over-rosy and, not before time, these were now rectified. My basic approach to them never changed and my fundamental faith in them never faltered . . . [but] the men who opted to serve in India sailed on SS *Ethiopia* and were in ugly mood. They carried Indian Congress banners and spat in the colonel's face when he went to see them off. They shouted pro-Indian and anti-British slogans and taunted those left behind. I recalled the colonel's words of wisdom: a good Gurkha cannot be bettered but there is none worse than a bad one. This was the first time I had come across Nepalese nastiness and it saddened me . . . Only years later did I fully understand my feelings: the living legend that is the military mark of the Gurkhas' greatness is, to an extent, the reflection of the high calibre of British officers who have served selflessly with them for many years . . . and [they] feel lapses from a normally high standard in a very personal way.

There were no actual mutinies but many occasions for overt challenge to authority and discipline in the coming months, and other more serious incidents. One evening at the new base in Malaya, a hand grenade primed and with the pin out was rolled across the floor of the Gurkha officers' club, although fortunately it failed to explode. A spot check of men's kits revealed other unauthorised grenades and ammunition.

Further discord was promoted by outside influences. Letters and pamphlets purporting to be from the Communist Party of India and the

Nepal Congress Party – pressing for reforms in its own government – regularly appeared containing poisonous, vulgar and threatening words for the attention of the Gurkha officers.

The appearance of such literature scared many, especially those who had witnessed similar reprisals in India, and certainly caused anguish within the ranks for some time. It was simply too much to expect that the pressure for change across the whole of the Indian subcontinent and the Far East should not in some way affect Nepal and, indeed, while the British were clearing out of India, the preparations for a revolution there were already being planned. Fears were widespread of violence of the kind that had engulfed India, but in 1951 the Nepalese government was overthrown and control wrested from the Rana family, whose hereditary Prime Ministers had ruled with an iron hand over a one-party system for 104 years. The King of Nepal was restored to the throne and became the country's ruler.

The Gurkhas who opted to stay in India went on to establish themselves as a permanent and vital part of the nation's armed forces. India continued to recruit in large numbers, far more than the British, to the point where in 1997 it had a complement of around 120,000 men. There were seven Gurkha regiments, each with five battalions and four training centres located in various parts of India. Each training centre has one battalion strength of Gurkha soldiers. This provided a total of around 40,000 men in the Indian Gurkha Brigades and training centres, and a similar number were serving in other Indian army units, such as the Assam Rifles and the Jammu and Kashmir battalions. The remainder serve in numerous other police and paramilitary forces of the Indian government. Almost sixty per cent are recruited from Nepal, the rest coming from Gurkha families who settled in the subcontinent. Since partition, Gurkha battalions have been involved in military operations as part of the Indian army against Pakistan in 1947, 1965 and 1971 and China in 1962. They are more or less permanently available for operations against the Tamils in Sri Lanka, notably in the 1987 uprising, although their deployment, as is the case with the British regiments, is governed by the 1947 tripartite agreement.

In the remainder of these chapters, therefore, the Indian army Gurkhas play no further part in the proceedings since our focus is on the British elements. We pick up the narrative as the new era dawned for the officers and men of the remaining Gurkha regiments for whom the opportunity to demonstrate how much they were needed by the British army was already staring them in the face. What became known as the Malayan Emergency, a Communist-led revolution against Imperialist rule, had been simmering since the end of the war and came to the boil on 16 June 1948 when Chinese Communists murdered three British rubber planters. The perpetrators of the crimes were Britain's former allies, one known as the Malayan People's Anti-Japanese Army. Now it was called the Malaya Races Liberation Army but still run by its Communist Chinese leader, Ching Peng MBE, who apart from getting a medal from King George VI had also marched in the 1946 London Victory Parade. He declared war on the British following the formation of the Federation of Malay States in February 1948 under a British High Commissioner. Ching had behind him a well-disciplined organisation and an army of 5,000 men run on formal military lines. The British government ordered an immediate state of emergency, declared the day after the murders. The 'Emergency', as it was known – never referred to as a 'war' – was going to be over by Christmas but lasted almost 11 years against an enemy known as Communists terrorists – CTs for short – who were the forerunners of a long line of such warriors who gave Western governments a real run for their money through the 1950s and 1960s.

The CTs were well versed in jungle warfare, and in Malaya the jungle was nicknamed by British troops as the green hell. The Malayan peninsula, stretching 400 miles (643 kilometres) between Thailand and Singapore, had a hot and wet climate, with four-fifths of the land area covered in dense tropical rainforest. This harboured all nasties imaginable, including leeches, ticks, scorpions, snakes and very large caterpillars, which all, combined with the sheer effort involved in hacking away at creepers and vines and wading waist-deep in mosquito-blown swamplands, created a task and a half for any army.

The rush into action was on even before the Gurkha regiments had settled in their new bases in Malaya and Hong Kong. Even so, they went straight to it, as Anthony Harvey, who was by then with the 2/6th which he later commanded, explained:

I was there in '48 when the CTs walked into a planter's office, tied him in his chair and blew his head off. They were Chinese

Communists, nothing else, and they were against Imperialism. They were the same people who were holed up in the jungle during the war when we dropped in British officers and a lot of supplies, including arms and ammunition. These Chinese sallied out and blew up Japanese convoys and attacked their camps. Now they planned to do the same to the British – they deemed it right in '48 to throw us out and take over as a Communist state. Because they had killed unarmed men and attacked the planters' wives and children, the Gurkhas had nothing but contempt for them. And although they surrendered to us and we took them in, probably the Gurkhas would not have been averse to a spot of harsh treatment. They were, however, skilful guerrillas, very clever indeed, and very brave up to the point of death.

In short order, the Gurkhas were massed in Malaya, six battalions, and some of them were still in poor shape. It was, after all, only six months since the great shake-up, and battalion commanders had had no time to train up new recruits or assess their new officers. Few remained who were trained for the rigours of jungle warfare, learned during the latter days of the war. Walter Walker, soon to command the 17th Gurkha Division, was instructed to write a pamphlet on the techniques of tracking and ambush which became the basis for the Jungle Warfare School, hurriedly set up in Malaya as the Emergency began to spread. In the meantime the Gurkhas faced long and monotonous patrols which were largely a game of hide-and-seek; the CTs were hiding and the British were seeking. The CTs emerged every now and again, carried out acts of savagery and simply vanished again. Occasionally there were skirmishes and shoot-outs but no successful conclusion was in sight.

By March 1950 the CTs had taken a hefty toll – 863 civilians, 323 police officers and 154 soldiers had been killed. The terrorists had also suffered, largely at the hands of the Gurkhas, and their casualty figures were 1,138 killed, 645 captured and 359 surrendered.

Coincidentally, in Hong Kong at that time was a British staff officer well known to Gurkhas who had served in Burma at the time of the Chindit operations – 'Mad Mike' Calvert who had finished off the war as commander of an SAS brigade in north-west Europe. In May 1950 General Sir John Harding, Commander-in-Chief of Far East Land

Forces, sought out Calvert and asked him to make a detailed study of the problems facing troops in Malaya and to report back as soon as possible. Calvert took off for the jungle, made a 1,500-mile (2,413-kilometre) tour, unescorted and along routes infested with terrorists. He visited villages, spoke to their head people and then prepared a long summary of his findings and these became the basis of the Briggs Plan.

General Sir Harold Briggs was director of operations. His plan was a two-phase operation: first, to close down 410 Malayan villages, most of them shanties inhabited by Chinese, and move the inhabitants to fortified regions thus out of contact with the terrorists, and, second, to embark on an ambitious plan to interrupt and eventually deny food supplies to the guerrillas in their jungle hideouts. The Gurkhas would have a major role in both, first in the undertaking of harassment patrols in the jungle and second by linking up with a newly created SAS-style force, to be led by Mike Calvert. In both aspects, there was a secondary role of making contact with the indigenous people of the jungle regions and winning their trust.

The long-range Gurkha patrols began almost instantly and were intended to put them into the jungle for much longer periods than the seven days which was considered the maximum time for infantry to be out in those conditions, and even that was a struggle. To deny the guerrillas food meant being around the places they were most likely to obtain it from. Anthony Harvey remembers: 'They could live on a handful of rice a week and could certainly do things that we British could never have done. Then, I began with a six-week patrol which was very exceptional, and we could only do it because we were supplied by airdrops. The Gurkhas were carrying 80 pounds (36 kilogrammes) apiece and the officers 50 pounds (22 kilogrammes) and for a little short-arse like me that is really hard work in those conditions. If we had not been air-supplied we could not have done it.'

While the Gurkhas set to work on the intensive jungle patrols as well as internal security operations as directed by London and the British High Commissioner in Kuala Lumpur, Mike Calvert set about raising his troops by posting an invitation for applications for special duties in a special force for the Malayan Emergency. Many who came aboard were former wartime operatives in the now disbanded squadrons of the SAS, among them one of Calvert's best officers, Major

John Woodhouse, later to command 22 Special Air Service Regiment, and a collaborator with Walter Walker in the solutions to the wider terrorist threat as it spread into Borneo. For the time being, however, the Gurkhas and the newly formed unit under Calvert, to be called Malayan Scouts (SAS), were working closely together, and by mid-1952 the general military operations were beginning to make some headway into tracking and arresting the elusive CTs.

By then, General Gerald Templer had taken over as High-Commissioner following the assassination of the previous incumbent and, though he was a tough operator, he introduced a policy known as 'hearts and minds'. It was Templer's view that pouring troops into the jungle was not the solution; the answer lay in winning the hearts and minds of the Malayan people with kindness, gifts and, where necessary, some unofficial corruption. However, the sheer hard graft of tracking and searching for the terrorists still had to be completed. One of the first of these politico-military operations was entitled Operation Hive, involving two SAS squadrons, a company of the 1st Fijian Infantry Regiment and the 2/7th Gurkha Rifles centred on the region of Seremban. The 2/7th's history records what happened and the extent of the action:

> Op. Hive was designed to saturate a selected area with troops so that the terrorists' mode of life would be completely disrupted. A concentrated programme of police checks on roads and the new villages was planned in detail with the aim of driving the bandits back to the jungle food dumps, where they would be forced to eat valuable reserves. Then, the military units would move to specific areas, where it was hoped by intensive ambushes and patrols to force out the terrorists once more into the open or into the many stop [ambush] positions established on likely tracks in the jungle. A lot of men were required to close the chinks in the jungle, many more than were available... searching for about 100 bandits hiding in an area exceeding 600 square miles [1,554 square kilometres].

In the event, only 16 terrorists were killed during Operation Hive, and some Gurkha officers believed that not all of them were attributable to Hive. In other words, it was a vast and frustrating undertaking for a small result. Templer himself visited the control centre and was

Then as now, decades apart but the aim is the same – the hopefuls line up to join the British army during the hill selection programme. The picture below was taken by the then officer commanding the Gurkha Training Wing, Major Gordon Corrigan in 1997. (*Gordon Corrigan*)

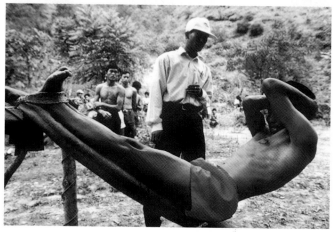

The hill selection of new recruits is a dramatic process. Watched by anxious relatives, the hill boys who want to join the British army are given a number, weighed, examined, tested, and then put through gruelling physical trials. In 1998, there were jobs for only one in every 300 applicants. (*Gordon Corrigan*)

An oasis of calm, part of the recruitment and training centre of the Brigade of Gurkhas at Pokhara, in the shadow of the Annapurna range, Nepal. (*John Parker*)

In training, a batch of new recruits gather for their first training session… and, in the end, are turned out in precision fashion. (*Soldier*)

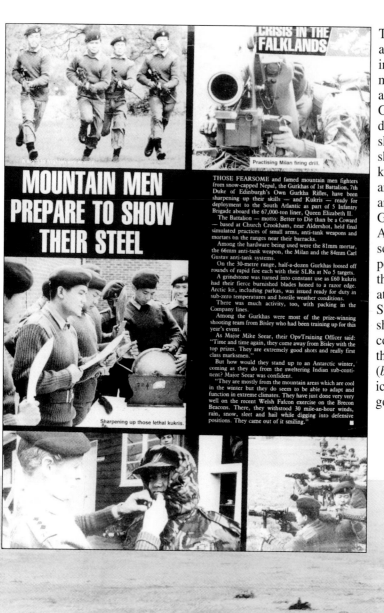

The Falklands – and pre-publicity in *Soldier* magazine (*left*) about the Gurkhas' decapitational skills and sharpening their kukri blades went around the world and put the fear of God into Argentine soldiers, to the point that the very thought of their attack on Port Stanley helped shorten the conflict. Yet even the Gurkhas (*below*) found the icy terrain tough going.

Jubilant men of the 1st Bn, 7th Duke of Edinburgh's Own Gurkha Rifles capture an Argentine anti-aircraft gun. (*Soldier*)

The homecoming – the Gurkhas' home-town of Fleet turns out to give them a rousing reception on their return from the Falklands.

Service in Nepal: Brigadier David Morgan, charged with closing the Brigade of Gurkhas base at Dharan, directed his men in relief and rescue work after a severe earthquake struck the country in 1989, for which he was presented with the Wilkinson Sword of peace.

The contraction and amalgamation of Gurkha regiments began in the late 1960s. Here, in 1994, the Duke of Edinburgh oversees the disbandment of his 'own' regiment, the 7th Gurkha Rifles, originally formed in 1902.

The 6th Queen Elizabeth's Own Gurkha Rifles, originally formed in 1817, was another of the casualties of 1990s cutbacks. It was also disbanded as a regiment in 1994 and reduced in manpower to become the 1st Bn Royal Gurkha Rifles. The renowned Gurkha Band, however, survived. (*Soldier*)

Smiling faces, but in the middle of controversy over pensions and redundancy. Rifleman Bhanbhagta Gurung, who won a VC for his bravery in Italy in 1944, with Lt Lalbahadur Gurung (no relation, other than tribal name), one of the many Gurkhas made redundant after 26 years' service, photographed by the author at Gorkha, Nepal. (*John Parker*)

First into Kosovo after the NATO bombardment, soldiers of the 1st Royal Gurkha Rifles guard the route north along the Kacanik Pass towards Pristina. (*Crown Copyright*)

impressed. He said tersely, 'Stick to it', which was taken as praise, inasmuch as he was under pressure to halt the operation and return the Gurkha battalion to its normal duties. Lessons were learned and new plans formulated. Some of the most successful operations in the Malayan campaign, however, came in joint air and ground assaults – the Gurkhas on the floor of the jungle attacking bandits and the SAS jumping into the trees from Dakotas. From these, the Gurkhas and the SAS formed a relationship that would last well into the 1960s and beyond as new challenges appeared on the horizon for both.

The Gurkhas remained the key operatives in the Malayan campaign as far as firepower was concerned and, in spite of the years of frustration chasing an unseen enemy and an exceedingly high manhour/kill ratio, the military units involved were competitive throughout in their 'body-count'...someone, somewhere was keeping a tally, and the 1/10th Gurkhas went home the winners, having notched up 300 'kills'.

CHAPTER FOURTEEN

SAS and Claret

In the years since Partition and almost continuous patrolling in the jungles of Malaya, the Gurkha regiments settled to a pattern that in many ways reverted to its past, in its customs, in the selection of officers and now, with the opening up of Nepal in the 1950s, the Ministry of Defence approved the building of two recruitment centres at Pakhlihawa in the west and Dharan in the east. No expense was spared and both were to be magnificent oases of British military life in the midst of the spectacular landscape that surrounded them, with barracks, training grounds, excellent sports facilities, their own communications and transport and, at Dharan, a first-class hospital fully staffed by British medical teams and made available for community use. Recruitment was resumed at the centres with the annual expeditions into the surrounding hill country by the galla wallahs, met as always by thousands of willing and eager young men. This was good news for the British, whose forces had been – and continued to be – heavily deployed in trouble spots around the world, ranging through Korea, Egypt, Aden, the Persian Gulf, Cyprus, Kenya and a large contingent in Germany to meet the possible threat of a Soviet invasion across the Rhine.

It meant that the Gurkhas became a predominant force in the policing and quelling of the Communists' terrorist activities in their old stamping grounds of the Malay peninsula, Brunei and, in the 1960s, Borneo. National service was producing a regular flow of British troops assigned to general army regiments, and for the first time the Gurkha battalions themselves began recruiting from the pool of officer material that the system was turning out. Some, like Sir John Nott, Defence Secretary of the Thatcher government at the time of the Falklands crisis, remained only for the duration and then went off into politics. For others, it became a career move – as with Tom Blackford, who was later to become commandant of the 7th Gurkhas, which he joined as a junior officer from Sandhurst. His story – similar to many who came in at that time – is in many ways a curious echo to the past when, it will be recalled from earlier testimony, including that of Walter Walker in the 1930s, potential officers had to pass through an intense vetting procedure to secure a place. It also highlights another fact, mentioned in the acknowledgements, that many young British officers seeking to join the Gurkhas in the 1950s were motivated to do so after reading the account of John Masters in his book, *Bugles and a Tiger*, first published in 1956. Masters' early days in the regiment ran parallel to the experiences of others 30 years later, as Tom Blackford well remembers:

I was called up for national service in 1956 and reported to the Royal Signals at Catterick . . . all I knew was that I wanted to go into the army but had no idea which bit. My father had been a Sapper during the war and that was pretty much my connection with the military. I applied for a commission, passed selection, reached Sandhurst in September of 1956. The course in those days was two years. At some stage we were asked to make a choice of regiment which we would most like to join. I was a bit naive and so I asked a chum of mine what he was going into. He said with some pride: 'I'm joining the Gurkhas.'

At that point I'd never even heard of the Gurkhas and told him as much. He went into his room and came back with a book and, thrusting it at me, said, 'Read that!' It was John Masters' *Bugles and a Tiger*, and I went away and read it. It fired me up, and I knew then that it was exactly what I wanted. The idea of serving in the Far East was very appealing. I went to see the Gurkha rep at Sandhurst and he said: 'Join the queue. There are about 26 ahead of you and only 3 places.'

I shall never forget the day of my interview. We were taken to the staff college at Camberley and in a big anteroom there were chairs in each corner and in them sat Field Marshal Viscount Bill

184

Slim, Field Marshal Sir John Harding, Field Marshal Sir Gerald Templer and General Totty Anderson, who was originally 6th Gurkha: it was a pretty daunting experience, a very junior officer totally unprepared for this grilling. We were shunted around and for whatever reason I shall never know I got one place in the 7th Gurkhas, my friend got another place with the 6th Gurkhas and a third chum of ours whom I had got to know very well went into the 10th Gurkhas. At the end of Sandhurst, in August 1958, I did two courses, and in January 1959 I sailed from Southampton and a month later arrived in Hong Kong to join the 2/7 Gurkhas who were just in the process of moving down from Malaya to an island just off Singapore. That was my arrival in the regiment and spent two fantastic years to start with but, like so many things, the course that you did in those days did not actually train you or prepare you to command soldiers, and especially not Gurkha soldiers. It was all slightly lofty, and I came down to earth with a bump. I was made a company officer, but I couldn't speak the language and I really didn't know whether it was breakfast or teatime.

Like many before him, Tom Blackford was soon to discover the peculiarities of working with Gurkha soldiers, and it was impressed on him that the only route to becoming a successful officer in the Gurkha battalions was the experience of doing it. He, too, discovered, as John Masters had vividly described, that the way to get on good terms with his men and overcome the language barrier was to demonstrate a willingness to understand them and their methodology. In his case, the necessity came rather more quickly than he had anticipated when his company commander went away to staff college.

It was only a short time after my arrival and I was summoned before the CO and told, to my great surprise, that I was taking over the company. That panicked me not a little because I still couldn't speak the language and, quite frankly, there were times when I simply did not know what the hell was going on. Fortunately, it isn't a difficult language to learn, and one could master the essentials fairly quickly. The difference with the Brigade of Gurkhas in this selection process of officers was not simply one of ability. The Gurkhas, the soldiers themselves, look to their officers for total commitment to themselves. While not wishing to belittle service in other British regiments, the relationship between the British officer and the Gurkha soldier is very different – almost what I would call a family kinship. It is not father and son, but as if they were all relations in some peculiar way. It is a very intangible thing and you cannot quite put a finger on it. A British officer never quite knows at what point – or why – he will have been accepted by the Gurkha soldier. One day, and for no apparent reason, something you might be saying to them would be treated with a reaction you had never experienced before; they might be laughing their socks off, for example. Suddenly, it dawned on you: you're in. They are a family and they live and operate as such, and the British officer is drawn into it over a period of time, perhaps six months. This family analogy is quite often displayed in the arrival of sons of former officers and men.

The pattern is repeated to a lesser degree among British officers. My own son followed me in and is still serving, instructing at Sandhurst, although in his case it was a logical step because he had, through me, been following the Gurkhas around since birth. There were, of course, some British officers who never quite jumped that divide, largely through the constraints of their own personalities. They were in the main probably those who did not stay very long anyway and were intent on career moves that would take them in another direction. It was a question of attitude and, whereas even the most junior British officer was technically senior to the most senior Gurkha officer, i.e. the Gurkha major, it was a very, very foolish young officer who tried to lord it over a senior experienced Gurkha officer. Those officers who did come on too strongly were rather quickly persuaded otherwise.

My one regret, I suppose, was that I joined the regiment at a time when we had just finished operations in the Malayan Emergency and one didn't have the sort of thrill – like many of my predecessors who had joined just before me – of arriving from England, being kitted out and sent down into the jungle for six weeks or more in antiterrorist operations. It is a wonderful way to learn about Gurkhas as soldiers and start picking up the language.

However, on my first tour – and in those days a tour lasted two and a half to three years' duty – I became intelligence officer as well and at the end of it took an enforced six-month leave.

In fact, I was away for more than a year at the time because I did two courses and got married. I rejoined the regiment in Hong Kong in the tail end of 1962, the year when the Borneo Confrontation began, and we interspersed our period of duty with operational tours in Borneo. This meant we could get back to some honest-to-God soldiering.

Indeed it did. The Confrontation, as this new outbreak of jungle warfare was euphemistically called by both sides, had its beginnings in 1961 when Communist activists inspired a local uprising in Brunei which spread into other British-dependent territories on the island of Borneo. Military analysts were predicting a Communist domino effect throughout South-East Asia; in this instance, however, it was the acquisitive eyes of Indonesian President Sukarno that lay at the heart of the trouble. Britain was responsible for the defence of the Sultanate of Brunei and the colonies of North Borneo (later Sabah) and Sarawak. Those states, it was hoped, would join the Federation of Malaya to form a powerful and stable alliance. The 'Mad Dr' Sukarno was doing his damnedest to prevent it.

The three British protectorates shared borders with Kalimantan, the Indonesian region of Borneo which accounted for three-quarters of its land-surface. Sukarno was intent on taking control of the remainder, to add 7,500,000 inhabitants to the 100 million he already ruled. His further ambition, inspired apparently by the Japanese in the Second World War, was to take over the whole of the Malayan states and with it the plum target of Singapore. In 1961 he was poised to continue his expansion, and the British government approved a hurried, if limited, military response and sent in an initial force drawn from the Gurkhas, the Royal Marine Commandos and the Queen's Own Highlanders.

Before long, there would be 28,000 men deployed, topped up with Australians, New Zealanders and what proved to be a very active contingent of the Special Forces. The latter consisted of 22 SAS – one of whose squadrons was commanded by Major Peter de la Billiere (later British commander in the Gulf War) – and pretty well all of the Special Boat Service, whose numbers included a young officer named

Paddy Ashdown. The Special Forces were rolled in at the instigation of Walter Walker, who apart from being Major General, Brigade of Gurkhas, was appointed director of military operations in Borneo, he being the foremost military expert on jungle warfare in the British army. Media reports wrote of him as an 'enigmatic' and 'eccentric' figure which he largely put down to sources at the Ministry of Defence whose noses he had put out of joint on occasions and had made no secret of his indifference to some of their edicts; to use his own language, he was under sufferance from fart-arses who, in due course, took their revenge by delaying his knighthood for several years.

The British public, in the grip of the Swinging Sixties, showed little interest in a military action that wasn't even to be called a war. Walter Walker was the principal architect of a most successful campaign, with very low casualty figures, innovative in its use of Special Forces in conjunction with the Gurkhas and which set the pattern for the future yet, in the event, trundled quietly into history. One of the reasons was the severe restriction placed on Walker's troops by Westminster after Sukarno had agreed to abide by a United Nations resolution on the island. All the while, he was building up his own troops, and using the Communist guerrillas as a blind, to make incursions across the border.

Walter Walker, therefore, was governed by strict terms of engagements, specific and limiting, which were drawn up to comply with UN requirements and avoid engaging British forces in a long and costly jungle war in a terrain that was naturally hostile and, in parts, still uncharted. Later, as the British force faced increasingly bold attacks, counterstrikes and cross-border actions were sanctioned. The overall penetration depth allowed was just 5,000 yards (4,572 metres), although this could be increased to 20,000 yards (18,288 metres) for specific operations authorised by Walker himself: 'It was a ridiculous situation when you think about it – how can you expect a patrol hacking its way through dense jungle to actually measure 5,000 yards [4,572 metres]? They might go 7,000 or 9,000 yards [6,400 or 8,229 metres] . . . or even more.'

They were known as the Claret Operations, colloquially called 'the golden rules', which was another echo from Walker's past, when he used to teach his Gurkhas one such rule a day. No cross-border operations could be for the purpose of retribution, and the MoD was insistent that absolutely no member of the British forces should be taken prisoner and absolutely no British casualties, dead or alive, should be left behind in case they might be photographed and produced as evidence to the world of British attacks. Initially, only the Gurkhas and the SAS were to be used in cross-border offensives. The Gurkhas especially had had the Walker principles of ambush and jungle warfare drummed into them – more golden rules: instant recognition of human tracks, urine, crushed grass, footprints, broken twigs and so on. When they made camp, no rifleman was allowed to eat, smoke or unscrew his water bottle without his platoon commander's permission. At night, sentries prodded any man who snored, and whenever the company was on the move a recce section led the way, their packs carried from behind.

The Claret Operations had to be logged and remained classified for many years, until they were finally released into the public domain in the 1990s. Because they were kept secret for so long and no one could discuss them, the Confrontation did not rate among the more celebrated victories of the British armed forces, even though it was just that. And they were carried out in one of the worst regions on earth for conventionally trained troops – the island where in 1995 a team of British soldiers on a training expedition, equipped with all modern aids, became hopelessly lost.

The Gurkhas, spearheading Walter Walker's force, fought in wild, dense, watery and mountainous terrain, far more hostile than Malaya and worse than the French and the Americans faced in Vietnam. Walter Walker's other key element was to use the SAS at the forefront of intelligence-gathering over what was effectively an 800-mile (1,287-kilometre) front. He would then combine their operations with those of the Gurkhas, with whom they had successfully worked the same strategy in Malaya. Indeed, John Woodhouse, second in command of the SAS and now the CO of 22 SAS, was just as keen as Walker was for them to work with the Gurkhas again, although conditions did not allow a replication of earlier activity, as Walter Walker explained:

> The SAS had their own technique when they dropped into trees during the Malayan Emergency and I thought they would be able to do the same in Borneo, but I was soon straightened out by John Woodhouse. He was a very shrewd man and saw immediately that I had this enormous frontier to cover and that the Indonesians

could penetrate it wherever they wanted. It was he who advised me to use his SAS in an eyes-and-ears role, but with a sting. He developed four main fighting patrols, which consisted of a commander, an expert in explosives, an expert in communications (and working the special set they had) and a medical orderly. They went deep across the border, gave villagers food and medical supplies and got information in return. They had an excellent communications system – far better than ours – through which they could get right back to John Woodhouse and pass the information; he in turn passed it to me. Years later, I met my opponent on the Indonesian side. The first thing he asked: 'What sort of radio did you have that enabled you to tell exactly where my troops were and when they were going to cross the frontier?' I was able to tell him the truth: that the SAS won the hearts and minds of tribespeople by arranging to protect their villages, and the villagers did some spotting for us. Their communications gear enabled the information to be forwarded on instantly. The first principle of jungle warfare, in those conditions, was to win the hearts and minds of the people, not destroy their villages or use scorched earth policies as the Americans did in Vietnam.

The arguments about such matters could go on ad infinitum. At the end of the day it was the battalion commanders who had to do the mopping up. In 1963, as the Borneo Confrontation swung into feverish activity, the Gurkha units were confronted by frequent bursts of sporadic and sustained action.

Captain Len Holmes was a sergeant with the Special Boat Service at the time and, after several operations, returned to Sematan on the west coast which had been the scene of earlier skirmishes. What originally had been a small camp for 42 Commando had mushroomed into a large defensive compound manned by a company from the 2/7th Gurkhas, and it was from there that the SBS once again began inserting teams into observation posts near the border where they could report any incursions. The Gurkhas intrigued all British forces who came into contact with them, Len recalled. Apart from their own reconnaissance duties, the SBS was used to resupply the long-range Gurkha patrols with ammunition and food. The two groups had much in common in their operational tactics, one obvious exception being that the Gurkhas were never particularly keen on waterborne operations. Although on the face of it the sideline task of resupplying the Gurkha patrols provided them with the security of being based within the safety of a Gurkha compound, it turned out to be one of the most hazardous they'd faced, and not always from the enemy, as Len Holmes explained:

The Gurkhas, few of whom spoke English, insisted that we identify ourselves by giving a special bird call. I can assure you it is extremely difficult to whistle anything when you're standing alone in the pitch dark trying to locate a bunch of trigger-happy Gurkhas. Life in the Gurkha compound was far from happy. Although they themselves are delightful, childlike warriors, living among them produced many problems, minor ones but still disconcerting. Our food was produced separately as theirs is too highly spiced for our consumption and we had a navy cook using two primus stoves producing meals from food bought locally. Washing had to be done at different times as our nudity offended their modesty. Most of us were only getting a few hours' sleep each night and were only in the camp for a rest one day in four, yet we still had to man the compound defences at stand-to each night and morning. The British officer in charge of the Gurkhas was also senior to our officer and clearly did not believe that the Special Boat Service were as special as his Gurkhas. That, coupled with his overbearing attitude, produced a rebellious response from our chaps. It is fair to say that only a great deal of common sense on the part of our team and a visit from our brigade major, who managed to curb some of the Gurkha officers' inflexibility, prevented a most unpleasant incident.

In all other respects the Gurkhas and the SBS shared a common philosophy. Their raids were by stealth, to the last moment, then all hell would break loose. Not long afterwards, a Special Forces recce team directed the Gurkhas towards an Indonesian army camp by a riverside. When the Gurkhas arrived, they discovered they were vastly outnumbered. They watched and waited until daybreak, when the Indonesians had a breakfast of spit-roasted pig. The patrol edged close and prepared to launch the attack:

A 3.5-inch (8.9-centimetre) rocket flared across the river and exploded among the breakfast party. Their hut disintegrated in a ball of flame, the men hurled in all directions. As the two assault platoons moved in ... they were confronted by a number of totally naked, panic-stricken enemy rushing from it. These were quickly dealt with and, covered by fierce fire from the support group, we assaulted the base. Resistance had ceased, but a number of dead lay scattered about the camp and blood was everywhere.

These outbreaks of violence, often on the run, were sufficient, once again, to produce numerous examples of Gurkha heroics – and one outstanding example was recognised by the award of the Gurkhas' final Victoria Cross. Lance Corporal Rambahadur Limbu, then 26, came from the village of Chyangthapu in Yangrop Thum, eastern Nepal. He joined the 2/10th in 1957 as it neared the end of a ten-year stint of antiterrorist operations in the Malaya Emergency and later moved on to Borneo. In November 1965 the 2/10th was ordered to dominate a position 5,000 yards (4,572 metres) inside the border between Malaysia and Indonesia, in the Bau District of Sarawak. Lance Corporal Rambahadur Limbu's company confronted a strong enemy force located in the border area entrenched in platoon strength on top of a sheer-sided hill. He could see the nearest trench and in it a sentry manning a machine gun. He inched himself forwards until, still ten yards (nine metres) from his enemy, he was seen and the sentry opened fire, wounding a man to his right. Rushing forwards, he reached the enemy trench in seconds and killed the sentry. Under heavy enemy fire, he gathered his own group together and proceeded to attack. Two of his men fell seriously wounded. Knowing that their only hope of survival was immediate evacuation from their exposed position so close to the enemy, the lance corporal made three attempts to rescue his comrades, crawling forwards in full view of at least two enemy machine-gun posts. For three full minutes he continued to move forwards but, when almost able to touch the nearest casualty, he was driven back. After a pause he hurled himself on the ground beside one of the wounded and, calling for support from two light machine guns that had now come up to his right, he picked up the man and carried him to safety. Without hesitation, he immediately ran back to the top of the hill, again moved out into the open between intense bursts of automatic fire, which could be seen striking the ground all round him, until he eventually reached the second wounded man. Picking him up and unable now to seek cover, he carried him back as fast as he could through the hail of enemy bullets. It had taken 20 minutes to complete this action. For all but a few seconds he had been moving alone in full view of the enemy and under the continuous aimed fire of their automatic weapons. Finally rejoining his section, he was able to recover the light machine gun abandoned by the wounded and with it won his revenge, initially giving support during the later stages of the assault and finally killing four more enemy as they attempted to escape across the border. The hour-long battle fought at point-blank range with the utmost ferocity by both sides was finally won. At least twenty-four enemy were killed at a cost to the attacking force of three killed and two wounded.

Lance Corporal Rambahadur Limbu was presented with his Victoria Cross by the Queen at an investiture at Buckingham Palace in 1966. He was accompanied only by his young son Bhakta, five years old, as his wife had died in the British Military Hospital in Singapore earlier that year. Rambahadur Limbu became a QGO and, in the rank of captain, was appointed to be one of Her Majesty's Queen's Gurkha Orderly Officers (QGOO) in 1983. On completion of his duty, he was made an MVO and retired in 1985 with the honorary rank of captain (GCO).

In a way, the citation to the Gurkhas' last VC was itself a tribute to the overall administration of the Indonesian Confrontation by Walter Walker and his successor, General George Lee. In the entire campaign, lasting almost four years, 2,000 Indonesians troops and guerrillas were killed in action. British losses were spectacularly light: 19 killed and 44 wounded, while the Gurkha battalions suffered 40 dead and 83 wounded. Defence Minister Denis Healey went on record to describe it as one of the most efficient uses of military force he had ever seen and averted 'a tragedy that could have befallen the whole corner of a continent if we had not been able to hold the situation and bring it to a successful termination'.

And so the Confrontation ran to a satisfactory conclusion as far as the British were concerned and was more or less over when acting Captain David Morgan returned to his unit, the 1/7th Gurkha Rifles, after spending a year in New Guinea on an exchange with an Australian officer, seconded to a native regiment who spoke pidgin English. He came back in time to clear up one further outstanding matter, concerning one of the terrorist leaders named Sumbi, still free and number one on the British 'most wanted list'.

Captain Morgan had, before he left for New Guinea, been involved in the formation of the first Gurkha parachute company since the war. He got the job of organising a P company by virtue of the fact that he had taken a parachute course while at Sandhurst, before joining the Gurkhas in 1960 having undergone the 'trial by field marshal' ordeal as described by Tom Blackford. When he returned to his battalion after the jaunt to New Guinea it was still on operations in Borneo, and he was running resupply patrols to forward companies before being seconded back to the parachute company. The unit hadn't exactly set the world alight and was being totally revamped.

The SAS offered to lend a hand with training, and they eventually formed a company for long-range penetration and patrol work, with men from both the 7th and 10th Gurkhas which were run on the same lines as the SAS, with a tracker, an explosives expert, a communications man and a medical orderly. The Gurkhas were also being tested on various manoeuvres, such as putting small groups of them out on their own with a corporal or a sergeant for up to six weeks at a time. When the Confrontation was formally ended, one of the four-man Parachute Company patrols was out forward, scouting around, when through an excellent piece of observation one of its members found coffee beans on the floor of the jungle.

They stopped and, using the point where the coffee beans were found as the central point, scouted around in a circle and found tracks, which they estimated were two days old, of several men. So they followed up. David Morgan explained:

> It turned out to be Sumbi, a Communist guerrilla and jungle warfare expert (trained in his youth by the British). What transpired was a remarkable story. The best men from two companies began tracking Sumbi and his group, who were getting slower and slower while the Gurkhas were getting faster and faster. The trail was heading north between our forward company position and straight for the area 'controlled' by yours

truly. Our first attempt at stopping Sumbi was a really gallant failure. The ambush was beautifully positioned by the commandant and the recce platoon commander, Lieutenant, now Captain, (QGO) Kulbahadur Mall, on the ridge line which our prey was using. Unfortunately for us, Sumbi, with what can only be described as divine foresight, camped about 1,310 feet (400 metres) short of the position. That night he decided that he had gone far enough in a crocodile formation, and the following morning he split his party in two.

The further Sumbi went north, the more he came into support company's area and the more our base at Long Semado became the centre of attraction. At one time I had 14 platoons under command and on another had no less than 84 sorties on the all-weather strip in a day. We were very busy. Any prisoners caught were sent to Long Semado for interrogation. Quite early on in the operations we caught two Indonesian section commanders who knew where their great leader might be heading. An official interrogator at Long Semado failed to break their story of innocence. That is until Major Moore arrived on a fishing trip.

'Why,' he said with a slight grin, 'don't you shoot them?'

I said: 'You can't bloody well shoot them.'

'No, no,' said Moore. 'We'll just pretend we're shooting them . . .' And that's what we did.

The Indonesians were held separately close to an 82-foot (25-metre) home-made range which we had built overlooking a river. We marched a mock firing squad out to the range, within earshot of the bunkers where they were held. The firing party commander roared, 'Right turn, quick march', and our little charade party marched smartly down to the range. Each Indonesian would then have heard, 'Halt, right turn, aim', and 'fire'. On the last a volley of shots rang out. Another pause, and then the *coup de grâce* – a single shot, followed by words of command which brought the squad up the hill and past each 'cell' before dismissing. The effect was shattering.

Each thought the other had been shot for withholding information and started talking. They basically told us what Sumbi was up to and where he was. The report went straight back to London. They were most keen on rounding up this particular party. They were apparently aiming for Brunei, where they intended to lie low for a while before starting another uprising.

One glorious morning we heard that Sumbi had been caught. He arrived at Long Semado for a few days' sojourn, during which time he was to be questioned by the entire interrogation team: four army sergeants and a naval lieutenant. After our previous efforts it was surprising to see how gentle they were with Sumbi. He was permanently handcuffed but his questioning seemed to be standard – no rough stuff, no tortures. There was a time limit to be met. We had about five days to break Sumbi and get his story. After that he had to be handed over to the Malays. The team went at him doggedly on a shift basis, day and night. On the evening of the fourth day I returned to the mess for a beer and found the whole interrogation team sitting despondently in silence. They had failed; Sumbi was talking, all right. He was cocky and arrogant but all that was offered was known to be lies. 'You should get him drunk,' I said laughingly. 'In vino veritas or whatever.' The naval lieutenant slipped off the table with a start . . .

Lieutenant (QGO) Kharkabahadur Rai, our antitank platoon commander, was in camp. He was cunning, quick and a Malay-speaker, but above all he was quite capable of looking after himself in a drinking match. We called him in. He would go to Sumbi's bunker, chat to him, talk about his family and so on and then casually ask him if he would like a quiet tot of rum. We left the actual detailed planning of the conversation to Kharkabahadur and sent him off. It worked. It wasn't long before Kharkabahadur arrived back in the mess with an empty army mug; a bottle of rum had been demolished. The team vanished out of the mess and set about their business with added zest. I suppose it was about four a.m. when I was woken by the team leader. Sumbi had broken down, had told everything and the naval lieutenant was to fly out as soon as possible with the 'Sumbi saga' in his hand. I was to retain a copy in case his helicopter failed to make it.

We agreed on a codeword which he would send to me telling me that he was safe, and once I got this I was to burn the duplicate. Later I got the codeword and destroyed the precious envelope without reading what it contained! The one thing that remains in my mind of those few days was the contrast in Sumbi's behaviour. When he arrived he was proud, upright and defiant. When we walked him to the helicopter he was fatter and possibly fitter, but a thoroughly defeated figure. His head was bowed and shoulders slumped as if to say, So what, I did my best. Alan Jenkins, who led the hunt for Sumbi, got an MC for that which, as far as I know, was the first time an MC was awarded without a bullet being fired.

CHAPTER FIFTEEN

Court-Martial the General!

Walter Walker was in trouble with the Ministry of Defence even before he left Indonesia for a post with NATO. The trouble, unsurprisingly, was simply that he had chosen once again to speak his mind on an issue about which he had very strong views: the Gurkhas. Even before the Indonesian Confrontation was at an end, it was learned that there was a proposal afoot to cut the Gurkha numbers in the British army by more than a third over the next four years. The battalions – having made substantial contributions to bringing the Communist threat to British interests in South-East Asia to a satisfactory conclusion – were now to be kicked in the teeth by the British government and its Ministry of Defence. They had, in effect, worked themselves out of a job. It was also not untypical of British civil service planning that having, not long before, completed the building of two superb Gurkha recruitment centres in Nepal, the MoD was now proposing to cut the numbers likely to pass through them and thus put at least one of them well on the way to being redundant. Quite dramatically, as Chandra Bahadur Gurung wrote, the Gurkhas were introduced to a new English word that they had previously not encountered and had difficulty in understanding: *redundancy*.

In 1966 there were eight Gurkha battalions remaining, along with logistics battalions, such as Gurkha Engineers, Signals and the Transport Regiment – in all, totalling around 16,000 men. The new Labour government inherited plans for the Gurkha cuts from its predecessors and became even more ambitious in their intentions to reduce Britain's military commitment across the globe, as well as pulling the rug from under remaining bits of the British Empire. The MoD (or the War Office, as it was until recently called) made the recommendations as to where the axe would fall. The Gurkhas, whose position had suddenly become tenuous due to the success of their most recent campaigns in Malaya, Brunei and Borneo, were to suffer heavily. Walter Walker blew his top. It wasn't as if the Gurkhas had actually finished their job against Indonesia yet . . .

> I first heard about it in the middle of a campaign – let me remind you, in the middle of a campaign. I naturally resisted, particularly when I found out that the King of Nepal himself, with whom we had a treaty, had not been consulted. And that was going on behind his back. So I fought hard against it, and for fighting hard I was hauled over the coals to such an extent that I was withdrawn in the middle of an important operation and flown home to be threatened with a court martial! It wasn't until I retired and I was at a dinner party when the former Secretary of State for the Army came across and said, 'I've never been able to apologise to you for what the Chief of General Staff threatened to do to you, without any reference to me as Minister for the Army. We would never have allowed you to be court-martialled. Please accept my apologies.'

General Walker was spitting with rage when the numbers were finally revealed: the Gurkhas were to be cut by more than a third over a four-year period to 1970 – all by redundancy and natural wastage. The figure was dramatic in that the battalions had already been hacked since their transfer from the Indian army to the British army in 1948 – when there were 36,000 men. By 1966 just over 16,000 remained, and they were to be cut again, the majority by compulsory premature release on terms that were not especially generous. From the Nepali point of view it was in every respect a catastrophic decision – as General Walker well knew from the regular treks he made into the hillsides, visiting his former soldiers who had returned to their villages, many living on a small pension, and some receiving no pension at all. The incoming foreign currency was also essential to the Nepali economy. This, said Walker, was a slap in the face to a tiny nation who had stood by Britain in her darkest hours.

The Gurkhas themselves were downhearted for many months, with rumours circulating in the villages that the British would not be recruiting any more of their young men; it was not true, but clearly the annual intake would be cut by about half. The fact that this proposal became known while the Indonesian Confrontation was still on infuriated Walter Walker, and for a while it did seem that he would be court-martialled for his outspoken response. It never came to that, but the people back in London who had threatened it and were prevented from proceeding did get their revenge. He learned of it by accident one day during a visit to Borneo by Lord Louis Mountbatten.

As Mountbatten came down the steps of his plane, he shook hands with Walter Walker and said: 'I'm sorry about your K [meaning knighthood].' From Walker's response, Mountbatten gathered that he knew absolutely nothing about the row and said within the hearing of the rest of the line of military VIPs waiting to greet him: 'You were put in for a K and it was turned down by the Chief of General Staff because of your resistance to the proposed cuts of the Brigade of Gurkhas. We then put you in for a CMG and that was turned down, and you are now going to get a DSO.'

Walker replied: 'But a DSO? I have two already.'

He got it anyway, and the citation for the gallantry medal was worded so that it appeared that he was constantly under enemy fire while flying continually over the jungle close to the Indonesian border. To rub salt into the wound – not that Walker claimed to have been wounded by the pettiness of his superiors – General George Lee, who succeeded him as director of operations in Borneo, was awarded a knighthood. Walker was not, at least not until much later.

But, as Walter Walker himself insisted, his 'K' – as Mountbatten put it – was irrelevant, as was the ridiculous threat to haul him before a court martial. The fact was, the protestations of himself and others over cuts in the Gurkha regiments were totally ignored, and the enforced redundancies went ahead much to the chagrin of long-serving officers, not to mention the Gurkhas themselves.

In England, Gurkha supporters rallied and pointed out the great strain that might well be placed on the already overloaded public service in Nepal. Many suggested, and were able to produce figures to prove, that the Indian nation was doing far more than Britain in providing for the wellbeing of its retired Nepali soldiers. The Gurkha

Welfare Appeal was launched in Britain and raised £1.5 million, a substantial sum in comparable values to today, and it led to the formation in 1969 of the Gurkha Welfare Trust for the specific purpose of providing relief for poverty-stricken Gurkhas and their dependants (see Appendix I). Today the Trust, now headed by Prince Charles, has a wider brief to provide financial, medical and community aid to alleviate hardship among Gurkhas and their families.

Many, of course, did not require assistance, nor do they now. They are quite comfortable in their retirement, although it has to be said that they are in the minority and generally the better off are those who managed to clamber out of the ranks to be commissioned as Queen's Gurkha Officers, some lately going to Sandhurst. Overlooked so far in these pages is the fact that the Gurkhas have another life beyond the British and Indian armies – that of their families and village communities in the regions of their birth where even today rigid lifestyles and customs are maintained, although it will become apparent that those who chose the military career discovered that it dominated their lives, from entry to retirement, and only those fortunate enough to reach officer level can really enjoy any true family relationships. Many former Gurkhas and a number of men currently serving in the Brigade of Gurkhas were consulted by the author for their recollections. They were all very happy to talk; few had complaints and out of the many who provided me with their own personal insights, for which several in-depth interviews were taken, the broader picture – in the man's own words – emerges and demonstrates the way in which an ill-educated hill boy can become a fairly well-to-do retired Gurkha officer. Major Dal Bahadur Gurung, one of the thousands of that name who have served the British Crown in the Gurkha regiments, spent his entire service in the 6th Gurkha Rifles.

In retirement, he is running a trekking and expedition company from Kathmandu along with other ex-Gurkhas and remains an agile man, deaf now through years of being in the midst of artillery fire, but still very capable of running up the side of a mountain. His early career is anchored back in the days of Walter Walker's jungle excursion units but, as will be seen in what he calls 'a three-hour tour of my life', there were other times about which he was far more proud. The remainder of this chapter is devoted to his story.

Dal's whole family, ancestors of both his mother and father, were linked to the British army, and the connections could be traced back to beyond the middle of the nineteenth century. Both of his great-great-grandfathers joined the Gurkhas of the East India Company; his great-grandfather was born in India and he, too, joined the British army. He visited Nepal when he was on leave and decided to bring his family back to Nepal when he retired from military service and settled near Pokhara. It was tradition then for retiring soldiers to keep their uniform, and Dal's great-grandfather wore his often, and always when he went to collect his pension. At that time there were only two places where ex-Gurkha soldiers could collect their pension. One was in northern India and the other was at the British Embassy in Kathmandu:

It used to take my great-grandfather seven or eight days to walk there from his home, and he always put on his uniform and medals to go there. One time when he arrived to collect his money, he was confronted by a member of the ruling family of Nepal, the Ranas, who enquired of him: 'What uniform is that you are wearing? Where did you get it?'

My great-grandfather replied: 'Well, sir, this uniform was not given to me by your government. It was provided by the British government for service in their army in India.'

'Then,' said the Rana, 'you had better go back there.' He was very angry at my great-grandfather's impudence and had him exiled back to India immediately, taking the whole family with him. They trekked for days back to the border and into Indian territory, and there they settled. My grandfather was born in India and joined the British army, and my father followed him. Unfortunately, my father expired at the beginning of the Second World War. My grandfather brought us all back to Nepal, to the hills above Pokhara, when I was about six years old. He taught me to read and write, and I went to school for only five years, to class seven.

My mother was 31 years old and my eldest brother was 16. So my grandfather looked after us from then on. When I was seven years old, my brother enlisted in the Gurkhas in 1942, and my second eldest brother enlisted a year later, leaving myself, my sister and younger brother at home. When my brothers came home in their uniforms, it was a true family occasion. Everyone was very proud, and my grandfather said I should enlist as soon as I could. The next year, when I was only 15, the recruiting officers came as usual looking for young men to join up. I was one of the boys selected, but my mother said: 'No, you are too young.' Next year, when I was 16, the recruiting officers came back again and I ran away with them.

The officers briefed me before I went to see the selection people and I was to tell them, when they asked how old I was, that I was 18. At that time the British recruiting depot was across the border into India and we had to walk for five or six days to reach it. There, after a couple of days of medical tests, I was recruited into the British army and was then transported by train to a depot near Calcutta which took three days. So in October 1952, at the age of 16, I was a Gurkha of the British army. We spent three days in Calcutta and then we were taken aboard a very large ship and sailed for five days to the training base in Malaya. I had 12 months' training before I went to my regiment in November 1953, the 6th Gurkha Rifles.

Quite soon afterwards, I had two new experiences: the jungle and a ride in a helicopter, which was quite exciting for a young man who was only just past his seventeenth birthday. They had new Wessex helicopters which took us deep into the Malayan jungle, where we set up camp and began our exercises and patrols. After only three days, we were on one of our patrols when one of the soldiers, an experienced man, discovered tracks. He called me over. As I was a new soldier, he wanted to show me what to look out for; we had to be very watchful and move around silently, like stalking tigers. I began to move back to my position when he signalled me to be quiet. Then he raised his sub-machine and fired and shouted to me to do the same. I could not see anyone, but I fired anyhow. Then, my friend moved cautiously forward into the undergrowth and there were two bodies of enemy soldiers lying there. He had killed them both, and I had not seen either of them. They would undoubtedly have killed us, given the chance. That was a good lesson for me. That operation lasted for 31 days. We normally carried enough rations for five days, fairly meagre food carefully measured each day. After that, fresh supplies came by way of an airdrop from a Dakota.

We would have to radio our position, chop away the under-growth and create a drop-zone. We had put in a request for fresh meat; for one thing there are certain aspects of the Gurkha soldiers' religion that affect what they eat (no beef) and how it is slaughtered. So they dropped us live chicken in the basket. Well, most of the time they became entangled in the trees. Sometimes, the baskets broke open and the chickens would come fluttering down, squawking, and we were all running around trying to catch them. Other times, the baskets were just hanging there, high in the branches, and the birds were going cock-a-doodle-do and we had to climb up and get them down. One of the baskets was hanging from a very tall tree, high in the ceiling of the jungle. We tried to chop it down, but we could not, and one of our men had to get up and release the chickens. It was not funny at the time!

We carried out patrols in the jungle many times, and during my second year there the Communists had stepped up their ambush tactics. The whole company went into the jungle in search of them, and after two days my company commander decided to split us into three platoons each with around 25 to 30 men, each going off in a different direction. The problem was, of course, that we had only one radio and so rendezvous points were earmarked from map references, which was pretty difficult in the jungle, I can tell you. If we did not show up, they would then come looking for us. What we did not know was that the Communists were between us, and we walked straight into the middle of an ambush. One of the men spotted tracks. My platoon commander sent scouts to crawl forwards. The jungle was so dense that you could not see many feet ahead. The scout reported back that the enemy were close by; we had already dropped to the ground, lying face down and silent. My platoon commander gave the signal for us to prepare to open fire, and we did, giving them everything we had got. Our firepower must have been bigger than theirs because they ran. We escaped without casualties and completed the operation, and returned to camp.

We never knew how long we would remain; time and time again we went off on our patrols responding to intelligence regarding the movement of the Communists. This remained the case until my first leave since joining the army, which was in 1955.

Dal's group was the first to be flown out; normally they went by sea. They were all weighed and given instructions on embarkation of the aircraft. They flew from Singapore to Calcutta, with stops for refuelling, and then a three-day rail journey brought them to the Nepalese border. At that time, Hindus living in Nepal had to undergo a period of purification, which lasted for five days, before they re-entered the country and travelled on towards their village. Under normal circumstances the journey would now be on foot, but while he had been away a light aircraft flight had been introduced from Kathmandu to Pokhara, where his grandfather and mother were waiting to greet him for the first time in three years.

My mother had written to me to tell me that when I came home on my first leave, I would have to get married. I was only 19 years old and I protested. My grandfather explained that if I did not marry, the girls for a young man of my age would be spoken for, and I would end up having no family. I could not, of course, disagree or argue. They had selected my bride, and I did not even see her before we were married. She was only 15 years old, and because there was no school in her village she had never received any formal education. We were married soon after I returned home and then, as the six-month leave neared its close, we were parted as I once more had to begin my trek across the country, back to Calcutta to rejoin my regiment in Malaya. Before I left, my wife informed me she was expecting our first child – which was something all newly married Gurkha soldiers aimed to achieve before they returned, and then they would try again next leave, too.

The situation there was much the same. We were still patrolling the jungle and still hunting the Communists. For me, it lasted another two years until 1957, diving in and out of the jungle on long patrols. The jungle apart, Malaya was a beautiful country, some breathtaking scenery, and the Malays were very nice people; I thoroughly enjoyed it. Then we went to Hong Kong, which was another new experience, and there I remained, largely on training exercises, until 1959 when it was time for another long leave – six months back in Nepal to see my wife and family.

In July 1960, on his return from leave, Dal discovered he had been selected to go to England with a training squad. He was already a corporal and section commander, and coming to England was a 'glorious experience'. He joined the demonstration company and took part in numerous military tattoos and demonstrations, at Warminster, Bath, Winchester and Edinburgh, a tour that lasted almost nine months. The Gurkhas, he said, always put on a good show. He was in the meantime promoted to sergeant and in the second year became a platoon commander and rejoined his unit in Brunei during the Confrontation.

We soon found ourselves in action, with various skirmishes and firefights. On one occasion when we were on our patrol, we received word over the radio that our base company was under attack, surrounded by 80 enemy soldiers. We hurried back to launch a counterattack and the Indonesians ran as we moved in firing from the hip. Two of my soldiers were killed. They had to be pursued and the whole company moved off back to the same area again. We stopped at the border. One platoon stayed there; the other moved across to recce the enemy positions. The operations lasted about two days. The jungle was exceedingly thick and impossible to penetrate in places, let alone see very far ahead. You never knew when you might be walking into an ambush. We came upon the Indonesian camp, but it was across a river and surrounded by dense jungle. It was impossible to put it under observation. We circled it best we could but could not get close enough. The company commander decided that once again we should set up an ambush. My platoon was sent off to put itself in position. It was very difficult to establish a place and all that the ambush entails – settling your firepower into a killing zone and giving them covering fire. Anyway, we found our spot where we could expect the Indonesians to proceed and settled in. We were there for two days in total silence. On the morning of the second day, they arrived . . . ten enemy soldiers. We killed eight of them.

We returned to our base camp and then took a brief respite, a visit to the cinema in a small town nearby. There was a new English film showing – *Bridge over the River Kwai* – and a group of us went to see it. It was very interesting. Several of our men had relatives involved in that, but they weren't mentioned. While I was there, there was some shouting: 'Number 12 platoon . . . you must come out.' They wanted us back immediately. I arrived back at camp around three o'clock in the afternoon. There were two helicopters fired up and waiting to go. My platoon was going back into action. We were all prepared, as a matter of course, for immediate action, and the helicopters took us to a place about 35 minutes' flying time away. We were dropped back on the border with Indonesia to begin immediate patrols. There were reports of heavy Indonesian troop movements, and we were out in the jungle night and day.

On the nineteenth day we were preparing to pull out, and we invited some local villagers to come to our camp that afternoon for a meal to clear up what food we had left because we were leaving the next morning. At around six in the evening I felt it best that the villagers should return home, and we ourselves began preparing our evening meal. Suddenly, a barrage of mortar-fire opened up around us. The Indonesians had surrounded our camp. We all dived for cover and fired back, although there was little chance of hitting them. They were firing from a good distance, well covered, but as a precaution we had encircled our camp with mines and trip alarms and they could not get close. We exchanged fire for about 15 minutes when their firing stopped and we stood by for the whole night expecting them to launch fresh attacks. We were on our own. Our radio was out and we could not get support. We just had to stay put. It was pitch black; you cannot see anything, and cannot go forward or back. The following morning, at daylight, we recced best we could and found no sign of the Indonesians. We hung around for a little longer and decided to chance it and make our way back to company headquarters, which we managed with some speed; we could not allow ourselves to be trapped, with no food and running short on ammunition.

In September 1964 we were pulled out and returned to Hong Kong – and then five months later we were sent back again, to exactly the same place we had exited from on the border. My old platoon commander had become company commander and I had replaced him. We had three platoons in the company. I was told to take my platoon to the other side of the border. It was again a very difficult location, in the middle of dense undergrowth. Personally, I am against following tracks. I prefer to go by bearings where possible. If you follow tracks, you can be walking into an ambush; it was a favourite trick of the Indonesians – and ourselves for that matter. We set off at 8 a.m. and by 3 p.m. were close to the site but couldn't see a thing; if we could not see it, how could we attack? Now, the same must apply to their side. This was quite a large camp, and regular supplies and airdrops were virtually impossible in this place.

There was a very big river close by and we decided that their supply route must be the river, so rather than proceed further into the jungle and very likely walk straight into trouble I decided that the best solution was to set up an ambush at the river. We returned to our base camp and I briefed my company commander on the situation. He wasn't very happy, but in the end, he said: 'OK, OK, sergeant, we'll do it your way.' That night after supper I gathered the men together. There were 24 of us in my platoon, and I selected 14 to come with me to the riverside to provide the firepower for the ambush. The rest would cover our backs. Then along came my company commander and said: 'Right, sergeant, I will go with the spring group.' In other words, he wanted to lead the ambush at the head of the firepower. He had not been at the briefing, but none the less he took command of the attack. In due course the Indonesian supply boat came in and their soldiers emerged from the jungle to unload. Nobody opened fire. The problem was that I had told my gunners at the briefing that I would open first. My company commander called me forward: 'Why did no one fire?'

And my gunners said: 'Why didn't you open?'

I had to explain to the commander that I had said I would open. Fortunately, within a very short while another boat appeared, a much better prize. It was a larger boat which carried ten Indonesian soldiers along with their supplies. They had to get out and push it to the side of the river, about 65 feet [20 metres] away. I waited until they were alongside, and then the other came out to meet it. Then I opened fire, which was the signal to the rest of my men. We killed them all. When it was over, I blew my whistle and ordered them to stop firing and we moved forwards. We scouted around and then moved out, heading back to our base camp, and the sector brigadier came over and asked me how many Indonesians my platoon had killed. I told him 18 in all, during the present tour, and he said, 'Well done', then got into his helicopter and flew away.

We had spent six months in the jungle before we were pulled out and returned to Hong Kong. I was due to go on my fourth leave, but by then India and Pakistan were at war and we were unable to take the normal route from Hong Kong direct to Calcutta and so had to fly to Singapore and then sail on to India. It took me a month to get there. When I arrived at the transit camp, I received a message that I was to go the following morning to see one of the officers there. I had no idea why and was wondering all night what it was about. When I went to the office the next morning, I was presented with the news that I had been awarded an MiD (Mention in Dispatches). My section commander and company commander were both awarded MCs for the Brunei campaign. So that was my souvenir from Brunei and something for me to show when I finally arrived home on leave a week or so later. I was very proud.

After my leave, I returned to my regiment in Hong Kong and went immediately on a platoon commander course to Malaya, returned to base on completion and the following year I was promoted to lieutenant (QGO) and appointed platoon commander. We remained in Hong Kong until 1971, when the regiment returned to Brunei, now peaceful, and I became a captain at that point, but what is called a QGOO [Queen's Gurkha Orderly Officer], which meant I was to go immediately to the UK for duty at Buckingham Palace. I stayed in England until 1973, and it was a marvellous experience for me. I was so delighted at being close to the royal family and to the Queen. The QGOO is a special appointment for regular duties at the palace, such as when there is an investiture you stand in the investiture room on either side of the Queen. Of course, many Gurkha officers have performed this duty. But I can hardly describe the feelings of pride when you receive that news and it is explained what you will be doing. So close to the Queen . . . it was fantastic.

The only problem was that you had to stand to attention, not move a muscle for two or three hours. For this duty I was awarded the MVO [Member of the Royal Victorian Order], which was presented to me by the Queen herself on the second floor of Buckingham Palace. She was lovely; so warm and charming. It was the highlight of my life in the British army.

Back in Hong Kong I became a company commander and in 1978 promoted to Gurkha major. There were further tours to the UK and then Belize, and I also became captain of the Bisley shooting team which was quite a responsibility, quite a big job! The reputation of the regiment depended on it. I returned to Hong Kong as one of the senior Gurkha officers of the regiment and remained there until 1982 when I retired after 30 years' service.

Dal then went on private assignment to the Sultan of Brunei. This is what is in effect the Sultan's private army. There were no formalities between the government of Nepal or the UK, and the arrangement was quite separate from the British government's own military commitment to Brunei. Many Gurkhas (and British ex-SAS) have served in Brunei under private arrangements – and still do. Dal was appointed a full major by the Brunei government, first as company commander and then as battalion commander, with special duties at the Sultan's palace, and he remained in the Sultan's service for a further ten years, until 1992 when he returned finally to Nepal.

My wife had been with me for much of the time since I became an officer. She had lived with me in Hong Kong and again in Brunei. My eldest son was born in 1956, which you will calculate was the result of my first leave home after joining the British army, when I got married. I asked him many times what he planned to do and did not encourage him to join the army. But he did so, and joined his grandfather's old regiment, the 1/2nd Gurkha Rifles, and as I speak has the rank of captain and is back in Nepal teaching British officers Gurkhali, now with the 1st battalion, Royal Gurkha Rifles. My second son was partly educated in England, where he did his A-levels, and then he went to university in America, where he now lives. My elder daughter married a British soldier and is living in England, and my second daughter, who loved Hong Kong, is now working there and plans to marry shortly.

Dal's story is one that reflects the success that could be achieved by those who become Gurkha officers. For the riflemen themselves, it is a far less glamorous life and certainly a less comfortable retirement, returning as they are bound to do to Nepal for a fresh start in life. For the majority, it was a journey back to the land when still comparatively young. For Major Dal, years in the service of the British army and to the Sultan of Brunei had left him with the air of a British military man, and as we shook hands and parted following our conversation in October 1998 he ushered me towards his Land Rover with the words, 'My driver will take you to your hotel'.

CHAPTER SIXTEEN

From Hong Kong to the Falklands

Tom Blackford was linked to Hong Kong throughout a career with the Gurkhas spanning almost 30 years, apart from the early 1970s, when he took a staff tour in the UK and later in Germany before taking command of the 7th Gurkhas in May 1979. But there is a sting in the tail of his account of his last years with the battalion – an outcome that robbed him of involvement in what was undoubtedly the battalion's finest hour in modern times. In 1974 the British colony became the only permanent base in the Far East for all Gurkha battalions following the closure of its bases in Malaysia, while at Brunei a defence agreement with the Sultan after the end of the Confrontation provided for a Gurkha battalion to be maintained there until 2003, when the agreement was renewed.

Throughout the 1970s, Gurkha battalions saw rotational service in Hong Kong, where they faced the increasingly difficult problem of illegal immigrants crossing over from China. From a trickle in the early part of the decade, the flow became a torrent, threatening to deluge the already overcrowded colony, and by the late 1970s the British army had deployed five battalions along the border. Tom Blackford's battalion was almost continuously engaged on rounding up illegal immigrants while based in Hong Kong during that period:

We did nothing else. It was simply a case of deploying your troops to cover as much ground as possible, with particular attention to all known crossing points. We posted a standard brick of four men – a commander, two catchers and a radio

213

operator – and once those guys were on the ground there wasn't much to do except sit and wait. It was all very predictable. You knew that before very long the immigrants would arrive and the brick would arrest them or call for backup if there were large numbers. On one occasion one of my companies, B Company, caught 1,800 illegal immigrants on the border road over a period of 36 hours. They never stopped coming: nonstop. We then handed them over to the police, who took them down to a compound and later put them all in buses and drove them back to the border. Many of them would just wait a few days and try again. The soldiers actually got very adept at recognising them. 'Caught you last week,' they would say. And the immigrant would smile, hoping to be let in but, of course, there could be no favours.

It was pretty soul-destroying work and often quite sad. Depending on where we were deployed at the time, you would catch an enormous number of people, and literally hundreds of them were truly pathetic cases. We, the Gurkhas, could not judge them. We were simply the instrument of arrest, and in a two-year period the battalion caught 27,500 illegal immigrants. They always reckoned that the attrition rate was about one to three or one to four, which gives you a fair idea of the ones that got through. [The figure peaked in 1979 when 90,000 flooded across the border.] We had a system that every morning we would fly around the area of operations and pick up any illegals who were out in the open, particularly in the marshy areas between China and Hong Kong which were difficult for them to cross.

They had no idea of the tidal flow and they would get stuck. You could hear them yelling and crying out in the dark. The following morning you would as often as not be picking up bodies. It was very distressing for all concerned, and not least for our troops, who were assigned not only the role of border guards and arresting officers but also corpse collectors. Apart from the many dead people we found, there were others who became violent and attacked the soldiers who were trying to help them, but the Governor at the time was pragmatic about it and said that if we were attacked then we should return the compliment. I think, however, the battalion as a whole prided itself on its restraint in

214

these situations. Everyone realised that these were desperate people who had got so close to succeeding that the disappointment of being arrested or the trauma of getting stuck in the mud and marshland became too much to bear. I think only twice did we fire in anger, using live rounds fired over the heads of a mob; no one was ever shot during our time managing this unhappy business. The job had to be done, and we were there and did it.

Meanwhile, the 10th Gurkhas faced a similarly difficult time stepping into a passive role during the 1974–5 troubles in Cyprus. The Greek National Guard led a coup d'état to depose President Makarios who, threatened with assassination, fled the island. Eight days later, Turkish troops invaded the north coast, landing at Kyrenia and enforcing a partition of the island, causing many thousands of refugees to move into Greek-held territory. The Gurkhas, along with other elements of the British army, had the unenviable task of virtually placing themselves between the two warring factions – as they had done in India – and protecting British personnel and installations, such as their Eastern Sovereign Base area, and assisting refugees, regardless of their nationality. They received particular praise for defusing what threatened to be a nasty incident when 2,000 refugees began to march towards Turkish positions following the capture of a Greek shepherd. Major M.G. Allen led a platoon of his C Company, supported by armoured squadrons from B Squadron, into the Turkish line of fire and stayed there until the potential for a dangerous flare-up had passed.

Back with the 7th in Hong Kong, Tom Blackford ended his tour of command in October 1981 with the rank of lieutenant colonel and moved over to take charge of officer recruitment before his direct connection with the Gurkhas ended in the mid-1980s when he was offered a post at Sandhurst, subsequently as deputy college commander. He handed command of the battalion to David Morgan and that, said Tom, proved to be the second biggest disappointment of his life (the first being that he arrived too late for the Malaya Emergency), for he would miss active involvement in the Falklands conflict.

For David Morgan it was the challenge of his life, coming hard on the heels of his appointment to commandant. Since Borneo, he had held a number of posts, including that of training officer at the turn of the 1970s, when there were amalgamations of battalions following the cuts to the overall Gurkha strength in the British army. Later, he became brigade major of the 48th brigade, which was known as the GSO2 Gurkha Field Force, and at the time was also heavily involved in anti-illegal immigration operations in Hong Kong. He had three years in that role and 'my feet didn't touch the ground . . . very hard work, up all hours, long days, no weekends. There was, as everyone now knows, an incessant flow of illegal immigrants arriving in Hong Kong at that time. The Gurkhas were the front line against that invasion, and we had some quite delicate humanitarian issues as well as the normal military-cum-policing roles to contend with. They gave me an MBE at the end of that, which I felt I thoroughly deserved.'

It was a very successful period for the Gurkhas in Hong Kong. They won a good deal of respect from all concerned, but by no stretch of the imagination could it be said that the battalion – or David Morgan himself, for that matter – was prepared for what was to happen in the coming months. The battalion had moved to the UK for a two-year tour in May 1981, housed at the former wartime barracks at Church Crookham, which became the permanent base for a Gurkha battalion in the UK in 1971 after the pull-out from Malaysia. Everything had gone smoothly and the 7th had won Bisley, which was just about its most demanding task. Command changed hands from Tom Blackford to David Morgan in October, and the battalion settled down to working with the newly formed 5th Airborne Brigade at nearby Aldershot, consisting of the 2nd Battalion of the Parachute Regiment and the 7th Gurkhas. Later the 3rd Battalion of the Parachute Regiment, housed at Tidworth, went to Aldershot to complete the brigade before training got under way in the early spring of 1982.

It was planned as a rapid reaction force that could respond to any call, although at the time the most likely places seemed to be some small dependency, perhaps in Africa. But then there came the rumblings of trouble far away in the South Atlantic and a group of Argentinian scrap dealers took possession of South Georgia. A full-scale Argentinian invasion of the Falkland Islands followed, and Prime Minister Margaret Thatcher ordered her military chiefs to send a Task Force to get them back at once. When it became clear that the 1/7th, as part of the British 'ready to do anything at any time brigade', could be part of a force to retake the islands, A Company was in Cyprus while B Company was in Belize. A Company was recovered swiftly, but it took much longer to replace B Company and get it back under command.

Lengthy discussions followed as to the logistics of the deployment to the Falklands, but before they could even begin to come to fruition the 5th Airborne Brigade, which had worked so hard together and was beginning to function well as a formation, was split asunder. The 3rd Battalion and then the 2nd Battalion of the Parachute Regiment were taken away to bolster 3 Marine Commando Brigade, which by now was preparing to sail to the Falklands. There was a suspicion among the officers and men of the 7th Gurkhas that they would be left behind in the UK. David Morgan recalls:

The original 5th brigade should have gone together. The reason the 7th Gurkhas did not go at the outset was that the Foreign Office were farting about with trying to get written permission from Nepal to send the Gurkhas to war on Britain's behalf. The Foreign Office have always done this, right from the First World War. Whenever any trouble arose, they wrote to the King of Nepal. I would think they were getting rather fed up with repeating what the then king said at the beginning of the Second World War, something like: 'Of course you may have our men. What are friends for? If you win we will win with you, if you lose we will die with you.' However, thanks to the sterling efforts of our Defence Attaché in Kathmandu [Keith Robinson, himself a former Gurkha] and many others in more influential positions in the Ministry of Defence, orders were received to move to Wales and exercise for a short period of time with two new battalions to the brigade, the 2nd Battalion of the Scots Guards and the 1st Battalion of the Welsh Guards. I have a lot of time for the Guards but the whole ethos of them and us, as it were, was so totally different as to be almost incompatible. We were doing section attacks with live ammunition and we were having to teach the Guardsmen how to fire machine guns. In hindsight I felt we should have been pushed to the forefront immediately as the key attacking force.

This view seems to have been shared by Margaret Thatcher who, when told that the MoD was sending a Gurkha battalion, replied: 'Only one battalion?' Meanwhile, during their wait for embarkation orders, the media was invited *en masse* to Aldershot to report on the Gurkhas' preparations for war. This single event was to have what David Morgan described as an astounding effect on the outcome of the conflict – one that had much to do with the final surrender of the Argentine forces at Port Stanley. Photographs of the Gurkhas sharpening their kukris and action shots of them charging across a field were published around the world:

> That publicity was to expand far beyond our belief and expectation. We eventually found evidence in Goose Green of young Argentinian conscripts reading their equivalent of *Soldier* magazine in which were huge headlines about the terrible Gurkhas who get high on drugs, eat babies and kill prisoners. It was extraordinary and hardly a confidence-builder for those young troops waiting with bated breath for the arrival of this murderous band of cutthroats in British army uniforms. It also became an integral part of the surrender, and there is no doubt that our reputation would, in the event, save many hundreds of lives, not least among the civilians and their families.

The 7th returned to Church Crookham to receive new equipment, including radios that no one, except Signals Officer Kit Spencer, had seen before, and more machine guns. David Morgan asked for and received two GPMGs (general-purpose machine guns) per section, and tactics involving this increase in normal firepower were practised. In addition, eight .5 Browning medium machine guns were issued to the motor transport platoon, which would be underemployed since there were few roads in the Falklands and no shipboard room to take vehicles in any event. These heavy, powerful weapons would be useful if there was to be any fighting at distance or in supporting assaults when no other firepower was available. The weight of the guns and ammunition would be a problem. The new MILAN antitank missile system was also introduced, which increased the firepower of the battalion.

Eventually, the day dawned when the battalion was ordered to board the *QE2*, piped on board by the Pipe Major and cheered by the Guards who had already embarked while the Gurkhas themselves stared in amazement at the size of the enormous ship. They lined the decks as the ship left the dockside at Southampton to much patriotic music and flag-waving. No one there knew that the ship's engines needed urgent repair and that once the liner had sailed past the Isle of Wight she would have to stop for several hours while the necessary maintenance was effected.

On board, there was an air of anticipation, and for most of the young soldiers it was to be their first engagement in a real combat situation. They began a daily programme of training that lasted from dawn until nightfall, involving fitness, minor tactics, weapon-handling, even TEWLs (a new form of training exercise designed to tax officers' command, control and communication skills, TEWLs standing for Tactical Exercise Without Land).

Work-outs were interspersed with some light-hearted breaks. The Gurkhas, not being used to life at sea, were receiving instruction on their respective boat stations in the case of emergency; they were doing it blindfold and became tangled up with a cocktail party organised on the same evening by the Scots Guards. The most memorable event of the trip south, however, was the battalion's eightieth birthday party when every member of the 7th Gurkhas, including recently attached personnel, joined in an evening of singing and dancing that, according to David Morgan, 'seemed to weld them into a team that was without doubt the toughest, most professional, happiest and most dangerous fighting unit in the world. It was a mood that would stay with the battalion throughout the campaign and beyond.'

They came down to earth on arrival at the Falklands, where they were immediately confronted by the survivors of the missile-hit HMS *Sheffield* being transshipped on to the *QE2*, which was to be used as a hospital ship. The battalion with most of its gear crowded on to the North Sea ferry, the *Norland*, which had just delivered the men of 2 Para to East Falkland, all the way from Great Britain, and was now to take the battalion to the same drop-off point. Before long, the small ferry, with some 650 bemused Nepali soldiers on board, was steaming out of the natural harbour heading for San Carlos Bay – and straight into the fury of a South Atlantic gale, building to Force Ten. The ferry was tossed around like a toy, with green water crashing over the bridge 74 feet (22.5 metres) above sea-level, and most of the Gurkhas were severely seasick. It was a ghastly voyage, and David Morgan's greatest fear was that if a missile of the Exocet variety hit the ferry, the loss of life would have been horrendous:

> There was one published description of the sight of the men landing at San Carlos which said, 'The Gurkhas came ashore like heat-seeking ferrets'. The truth was that the speed with which the men disembarked had much more to do with getting away from the dreaded sea and on to an environment that they understood. They had been at sea for 21 days, and they were elated that active operations now beckoned – on land! D Company, under the tough, experienced Major Mike Kefford, was to reinforce the southern perimeter of the bridgehead, together with a section of mortars, while the remainder of the battalion was to fly south to relieve the victorious members of 2 Para in Goose Green. Unfortunately, the whole air move had to be carried out by the sole surviving Chinook helicopter and, although very strict instructions were given to the pilots, companies ended up in the wrong places. It was not until well after dark that all companies reported that they were in their correct positions.

Goose Green itself was a shambles. There were 500 disgruntled Argentinian prisoners locked up in sheep-shearing sheds who were very frightened that their new guards were Gurkhas, having read the magazine that featured an article headlined 'Los Barbaros Gurkhos' which described in sordid detail how Gurkhas took no prisoners. These dispirited men were flown out to San Carlos and the 'barbarous Gurkhas' could then get on with the job at hand.

The victorious men of 2 Para were exhausted after an epic battle and many of its soldiers suffered from trench foot, a condition common during the First World War although rarely seen in modern times. The Paras were to move forwards, leaving the Gurkhas to clear up the combat battlefield, construct new defensive positions and dominate the whole of the southern half of East Falkland by using a series of short, sharp, heliborne patrols. A patrol from the Recce Platoon ran into an Argentinian group armed with antiaircraft missiles. The Gurkhas forced them to surrender by simply drawing a single kukri and brandishing it aggressively. Later that kukri was to be auctioned to raise money for charity and fetched £300!

D Company was ordered to move to Goose Green to boost defences, joining the remainder of the battalion. They were supposed to be flown up by helicopter, but after a long delay David Morgan could wait no longer and told them to march to their new position, in spite of being weighed down by ammunition and equipment. The journey took 36 hours. Most infantryman in the South Atlantic carried a heavy burden but none quite so heavy as the Gurkhas, who were armed to the teeth with a far higher ratio of automatic weapons, including ammunition for the mortars and medium machine guns. It was estimated that some men were carrying in excess of 140 pounds (63 kilogrammes), which in most cases was considerably more than their own body weight.

The relative calm of Goose Green ended when the brigade commander decided that he would send a Gurkha company forwards to act as a brigade patrol sub-unit to find out what the enemy defences around Stanley were like. D Company, having had a short rest after their march from San Carlos, was chosen for the task and set off with elements of 2 Para on the evening of 7 June on the only means available, the elderly Falkland Islands steamer MV *Monsunen*. The ship moved agonisingly slowly along the coast in darkness to avoid being seen by enemy planes, and some 150 men, without life jackets or life rafts, were eventually delivered by a Royal Navy crew. That done, the move up to the assembly area for attacks on Tumbledown and Mount William got under way, and during the final preparations for the attack the battalion was under sporadic but heavy artillery fire. Battalion headquarters was sprayed harmlessly with shrapnel, but on 11 June four members of B Company, including Second in Command Captain (QGO) Dalbahadur Sunwar, were wounded and were evacuated. It was during this particular incident that RMO Captain Martin Entwistle earned a Mention in Dispatches for assisting the wounded under fire. OC A Company, Major David Willis, had his trench and most of his gear destroyed by a direct hit while he was away on a recce. Meanwhile, the Argentinians had chosen to defend Tumbledown and Mount William with a marine battalion.

David Morgan and the CO of the Scots Guards agreed a plan: the Guardsmen would attack Tumbledown and the Gurkhas would take Mount William, placing the battalion in an ideal position to move down on to the capital, Port Stanley, if resistance continued. First, a minefield along the Gurkhas' intended approach had to be cleared, for which Sergeant Wrega won the Military Medal for his bravery in undertaking this hazardous task.

The plan went awry when the Guards' attack fell behind schedule, which meant that the move of the Gurkhas from the forming-up point was also delayed. It was daylight by the time the battalion had reached the position from which D Company was to carry forward the attack, and in spite of ferocious fire put down by Royal Artillery and Royal Navy guns, the single-file line of Gurkhas moving across the start line was spotted by the enemy, who opened up with heavy mortarfire that began to cause casualties. A further eight men were hit, two being seriously wounded. Typical of the reaction was that of Captain (QGO) Bhuwansing Limbu (son of legendary Gurkha Major Bagbir Limbu), who was D Company's second in command. Under heavy enemy fire, he turned to his company commander, Mike Kefford, and said in impeccable and accented English, 'Jolly exciting this, isn't it, sahib?'

A further delay was caused by some well-aimed shots from a hidden sniper, and David Morgan went forward to see what was causing the hold-up only to come under fire himself, one round missing his head by inches, while another hit D Company's Captain Keith Swinton, who was standing behind him, in the chest. Swinton was convinced he was done for with a bleeding hole through his body in the midst of essential organs, but when he got to the medical treatment centre he was put to the back of the queue. The round had passed within an inch of his heart and missed all his other vital internal mechanisms, and he was back at work within a remarkably short space of time.

The Argentinians decided that they had endured enough: streams of their soldiers were seen heading towards the Scots Guards to give themselves up, or even back to Port Stanley. David Morgan was told by Brigadier Sandy Wilson that the way was open for the Gurkhas to march on Port Stanley.

> . . .we were right on the doorstep of Port Stanley at the key moment and were the only uncommitted battalion, ready to move on the town. Having completed our own objective, which was to take Mount William, I reported to Sandy Wilson that William was now secure and he said: 'OK . . . the town is yours.' In other words, the Gurkhas were to move on Port Stanley, where 7,000 Argentinians, heavily armed, were waiting. We were already

moving when the next message came over the radio ordering me to halt our advance. We were not to go into Stanley. The Argentinians had surrendered.

It was the most disappointing event that could have happened to that battalion at that time. There is no doubt in my mind that the battalion was unquestionably fitter and better trained than anyone else there, way ahead in their ability to knock people down and with more ways of being able to do that than most. And so we had to stand fast . . . it was a galling moment, the war was effectively over, and the battalion had simply punched at air. It seemed as if all the training had been for nothing. The men had been denied a great victory. At first, the mood in the battalion was ugly, but it did not take long before the soldiers realised that no more lives would be lost, that they were alive, and that the 7th's enemy had been defeated.

We consoled ourselves with the knowledge that we were the people who should have gone into Stanley and taken it out, and gone on beyond. It would have been the sensible thing to have done *if* the Argentinians decided to make a fight of it. But they didn't, and the reason they didn't, as we found out two days later, was that they knew the Gurkhas were ready and waiting. They knew of the Gurkhas' reputation, which had been well broadcast in the previous few weeks, and they were simply not prepared to stand up to us. As one of the prisoners of war said: 'We did not want our heads chopped off.'

It is not a bad thought – that we can win battles by reputation rather than by killing people. Which, in a way, brings us back to the very foundations of the Brigade of Gurkhas. Their reputation has always run before them – but the Gurkhas have always delivered. They have always shown they have the mettle, the skills and above all the courage to fight to the last. This is the key to their future; the Gurkhas must always be able to prove they are a unique force otherwise they are dead. If the Argentinians had decided to make a stand at Port Stanley, the Gurkhas would have moved in and they do not mince their words when they come face to face with opposition. We would have socked Port Stanley with everything we had got. There would have been a hell of a fight and an awful lot of people would have died.

223

After a freezing couple of nights on the hills, the battalion was allowed to return to Goose Green, where the long-suffering inhabitants did their best to look after nearly 700 hungry, tired, cold and dirty soldiers. The postwar chaos was indescribable; steps had to be taken to clear the place up. It was during this period that the battalion's sole fatality occurred. While helping to clear the Goose Green battlefield and make it as safe as possible for the civilian inhabitants, Lance Corporal Budhaprasad Limbu was killed instantly when his spade struck an unexploded grenade embedded on the lip of the trench he was filling in. Two others in his party were injured in the explosion. Initially, Budhaprasad was buried just outside Goose Green in the village graveyard, but his body was later removed and sent back to the UK at the express wish of his father. His name is on the Roll of Honour in the crypt of St Paul's Cathedral.

Back at Goose Green, the 7th organised a party; the evening started with a Beating of Retreat with the Pipes and Drums marching in front of Falklands governor Rex Hunt and military top brass in the worst snowstorms experienced by the islanders for years. Then they were homeward bound aboard the *Uganda* in almost holiday mood. The liner docked in Southampton to a tumultuous welcome. Later, the battalion was greeted in spectacular fashion in the little town of Fleet, close to the Church Crookham barracks, on 9 August, 90 days after it had left on the *QE2*: 45 of those days had been spent at sea.

David Morgan, proud of his battalion's contribution to the British victory, went on record with a rejoinder that may well have been aimed at people in high places at the MoD: 'It must never be forgotten that the much-feared fighters from Nepal played a critical and decisive part in the final downfall of the Argentinians. It was the Gurkhas' reputation that helped win the war in the Falklands and thus brought about a conclusive victory, despite the problems of distance, weather and a harsh, forbidding terrain.'

CHAPTER SEVENTEEN

Decimated!

The end of the Falklands conflict, in which the Gurkhas had once again proved their versatility in and readiness for what Walter Walker always described as their 'fire brigade' role – go anywhere, do anything, fast – turned out to be, curiously enough, a defining moment in the future of the remaining battalions. Ahead lay almost a decade of relative calm around the world, ending with the collapse of Communism and the break-up of the Soviet Union. The need for fire brigades suddenly evaporated. There were a few areas of local difficulty, not least of which was Northern Ireland, but the Gurkhas had long ago been ruled out of any kind of military action within the United Kingdom, although many of its senior officers over the years believed they could have successfully carried out border and coastal patrols. Hong Kong continued to provide work on the Chinese border and general military duties there when the tension began to mount as the countdown began for the ending of British rule. There were also some large military NATO exercises in which the Gurkhas always played a substantial part, often being cast as 'the enemy'. But as the years of the decade passed with few arenas of real military action, the budget managers at the Ministry of Defence surveyed the best predictions of their Chiefs of Staff and levels of recruitment required to maintain an efficient modern army and their eyes fell on Nepal.

There, in the mid-1980s, were two quite luxurious recruitment centres whose intake of the hill boys in recent times had slumped to around 300 a year. The man who found himself in the role of axeman was none other than one of the Gurkhas' own stalwarts, David Morgan, who was posted to the Brigade of Gurkhas headquarters in Nepal. Little did he know it then, but the task he was about to undertake was but a beginning in a swingeing reduction of the Gurkhas' overall manning levels which, at the end of it, would see the total force reduced once again by more than half. David Morgan was there at the start of the procedure, much to his dismay, and in 1998 at his office in Glastonbury Abbey, where, in retirement from the military, he is custodian, he explained to me exactly what happened after his tour as commandant with the 7th ended in April 1984. He had spent some time in London and then a spell in Ghana before he returned to the Gurkhas:

> I was posted to Nepal as the local brigadier and unfortunately, and with great sadness on my part, my remit in due course was to close down one of the two Gurkha recruitment centres in Nepal, the one at Dharan, which took in hill boys from the east of the country. Dharan was the larger of the two because, at the time, it was also to be the brigade headquarters, although later this was moved to a purpose-built HQ in Kathmandu. It was a plush establishment set in the most marvellous estate of 750 acres [303 hectares], a magical place with a golf course, swimming pool, riding school, cricket pitches, football pitches, tennis courts, shops, school, churches, messes, bungalows, superb accommodation, its own power station and the most wonderful military hospital, one of the best in the whole of the British army's overseas possessions. And yet within a decade of its being built, the dramatic curtailment of British military presence in the Far East, the Middle East, the continent of Africa and elsewhere brought with it new thinking on manpower levels and the first wave of redundancies was being made in the Gurkha regiments. By the 1980s Dharan simply could not be justified and, marvellous though it was, one can understand why the closure was necessary. Since the amalgamation of battalions in the late 1960s and the planned reductions thereafter, two such places in Nepal was a luxury the army could not afford and, indeed, would have been ridiculed for keeping it on. By the mid-1980s the British army was recruiting around 250 to a maximum of 300 young men annually, and the numbers were falling. Of those, perhaps almost

two-thirds were being recruited in the west and assigned to Pokhara which, incidentally, was another landscaped oasis in the midst of that dramatic landscape. And so this place, tucked away in the eastern hills of Nepal, was being kept open for the recruitment of around, at best, 100 Gurkhas annually but falling. I could not see any case for keeping the military base open on such a scale. It was crazy. Even so, I did not enjoy the task to which I had been assigned, and I didn't like the way it was being done, and one of the key issues was the future of the hospital on the Dharan base.

The hospital was undoubtedly one of the best in Nepal. It was run by the Royal Army Medical Corps, with a lieutenant colonel in charge, and was staffed largely by British doctors and nurses, although it also employed a large number of local people. Local doctors used it both for in-patients and for out-patient treatment. The number of Nepalis treated at the hospital ran into thousands each year, serving as a community hospital for the whole region. In a country devoid of medical facilities outside the main centres of population, it was a godsend. But David Morgan's orders, dated October 1987, were to close the whole thing down, lock, stock and barrel, within a year – hospital included.

I protested and wrote back to the Ministry of Defence stating quite bluntly that we were pulling out far too quickly, storming out, in fact. It would leave a bloody great hole in the social and economic wellbeing of that region in particular and Nepal as a whole which, incidentally, had served us well with recruits for 160 years. It was not costing a huge amount, about £2 million a year. A Defence Committee with Winston Churchill and one or two others came out to have a look and they, too, could not understand why the hospital had to be shut. Eventually, I reached a compromise which was thanks entirely to Chris Patten, who was at that time Minister for Overseas Development. He paid us a flying visit. He arrived in Kathmandu and was given the tour and a flight around Everest by the ambassador. It was originally planned that he would come to Dharan for lunch, then we would show him around and explain the Gurkha Welfare Scheme. In the end he arrived so late in the day after his commitments in the capital that I could only take him to the hospital, where he was briefed by doctors of its importance to the community. We put up a pretty convincing case that there was no better community relations project than keeping this hospital open. The only way it could be saved was if the Overseas Development Agency took it on, because the military had said it was no longer in their budgets and had to close by October 1988.

Chris Patten agreed there and then to guarantee the survival of the hospital for three years, with 88 staff paid for by the ODA, and that's what happened. Eventually, it was turned over to the Nepal authorities, although today it has assistance and input from the Indian government. As for the base as a whole, it had to close and we pulled out inside the time limits I had been set by the MoD. Everything went, apart from the hospital and a small enclave which was to be used as our recruitment base and Gurkha welfare centre for the next two years. It was with great sadness, I can tell you, when the last British and Gurkha troops pulled away from that base. It was the end of an era. The place eventually became a university and community centre.

The importance of its original role in life was highlighted during the closure process when an earthquake struck east Nepal, causing substantial damage to the infrastructure and housing. It was to the Dharan base that thousands of people flocked for shelter, sustenance and treatment. The Gurkhas also arrived in force to help in the aftermath, for which the King and Queen of Nepal came to thank them personally and said Nepal would never forget their help which saved many lives. The Ministry of Defence, however, did not pay any heed to Mother Nature's last-minute interjection and the pull-out was completed within the time schedule. David Morgan remains convinced that it was a political error to have closed the hospital in the way that they did. A great deal of goodwill was cast away and an excellent humanitarian project scrapped for the sake of a couple of million pounds. And in fact the savings were not as great as originally estimated. A new headquarters for the Brigade of Gurkhas had to be built at Kathmandu, which was devised and planned during Morgan's time in Nepal at the end of the 1980s. It remains today the brigade headquarters in Nepal and the organisation of Gurkha hill selection, recruitment and initial training, with allied accommodation for Gurkha welfare schemes. Recruitment, thereafter, was centred on Pokhara in the west, and those recruited by the galla wallahs in the east are bussed cross-country for their final selection procedures.

As these changes were being completed in Nepal, the future shape of the Brigade of Gurkhas was becoming the subject for intense discussion in Whitehall. In 1989 the House of Commons Defence Committee produced a comprehensive review to which Brigadier David Morgan and Brigadier Miles Hunt-Davis made their contributions. Brigadier E.D. 'Birdie' Smith, former commandant of the 1/2nd Gurkhas and prolific brigade historian, was appointed unofficial adviser to the committee on all Gurkha matters. In its final analysis, the committee recommended that the brigade should be cut from its then manpower level of 7,500 down to 4,000. This, by and large, was accepted within the brigade itself as being in line with the changing times and the slackening of demand for 'fire brigade' forces, especially in view of the greater reliance now being placed on the SAS, the SBS and the Northern Ireland specialist 14th Intelligence Company which – with elements of the RAF – made up the Special Forces group. Later, the emergence of the European Rapid Reaction Force also had its effect on government thinking. And therefore 4,000 would have been an acceptable level if the Ministry of Defence had adopted the committee's figures.

But it didn't.

Gordon Corrigan picks up the story at this point because he, equally reluctantly, became the second axeman or at least the organiser of the way things would pan out once the axe had fallen. It is a sorry tale and he, like David Morgan, was only too sorry to be telling it; references to 'them' and 'us' and 'betrayal' littered our conversations with a certain bitterness while we were on the expedition to Nepal in October 1998 and later in the library at the former windmill on the South Coast which he and his wife made their home after he retired from the Gurkhas a year earlier. There was an odd correlation to the job he eventually had to do in performing the *coup de grâce* for the remaining Gurkha regiments in the early 1990s with what was happening when he first joined the 6th Gurkhas almost 30 years earlier, at a time when the two battalions had just amalgamated into one. That, oddly enough, presented great problems that were to be repeated years later when regiments – not battalions – were amalgamated and he was given the task of making it all happen:

> Although we were two battalions of the same regiment, the 1/6th and the 2/6th had never served together. There was no problem with the soldiers themselves when we merged but a tremendous problem with the British officers attempting to guard the traditions of their own battalions. Silly things occurred – such as one of the officers of one of the battalions buried all the silver of the other battalion in the garden. They even balked at sitting next to each other – and much the same happened when the mergers began to take place in the 1990s.

Gordon Corrigan served in the 6th until 1980, when he left the service to take up a civilian appointment in Hong Kong. He had been doing the job for seven years when, in 1986, he received a letter from the Ministry of Defence which stated that the army was desperately short of officers and they were canvassing those between the ages of 27 and 30 who had left but might consider returning. He was well outside that age bracket, in his 40s, and had been out for some years, but the brigade made it quite clear they would like him to return. Although thoroughly enjoying civilian life in Hong Kong, working for the Jockey Club, the idea intrigued him. The brigade gave him some interesting jobs, mostly independent of general routine, such as running the demonstration company. At one point, briefly, the Gurkhas were expanding again because the British army as a whole was having difficulty in recruiting. They were even looking once again at the Gurkhas providing a battalion of paratroopers . . .

> . . .their star was in the ascendancy at that point and then it all changed quite suddenly when the Russians came out with their hands up and the Berlin wall came down. A new defence policy was outlined in the Conservative government's now historical document, *Options for Change*, which – along with the eventual pull-out from Hong Kong – would enforce a dramatic reduction of the Gurkha establishment. The four remaining regiments (the 2nd, 6th, 7th and 10th) and their five Gurkha battalions were to be

amalgamated into one single regiment, the Royal Gurkha Rifles, with around 2,500 men. There was, of course, uproar and a great deal of bad feeling which permeated from the top down. Everyone was stunned by the sheer bloody extent of the cuts.

I drew the short straw, the organiser of this ground-shuddering event. I didn't want to do it. In fact, I refused to do it, sending my friends on redundancy, but my brigadier said: 'Look, you've been in the brigade longer than anyone, you know the people, you know the Gurkhas and they know you. The rest have already been promoted and gone on elsewhere. You are the one person they trust.' It was a bit of an appeal to my vanity, to be honest. It was a task I hated as a concept, but in the end I was glad to have considerable input in the way things were to materialise. I was able to curtail some of the demands of the influential old buggers in the shires of England – God knows what we would have ended up with if it had been left to them.

It was a situation packed with emotion, tradition and elements of military history that suddenly were to be thrown up in the air. Whereas the British army as a whole was to be reduced by 28 per cent, largely by voluntary redundancy, the Gurkhas were to be cut by 70 per cent – and it was all compulsory. The proposed cuts were eventually announced in 1991 and were to be achieved progressively over a period of three years from that date. Corrigan took over the role of administering the planning and was given 18 months to totally revamp the standing orders for the solitary Gurkha regiment in the British army.

It was an exceedingly sad time for all, not least myself, placed as I was in the position of being axeman to historical regiments and my very good friends. There were a lot of protests but no real fight from the colonels of the regiments, the generals. These were men who had jumped on the Gurkha bandwagon when our star was in the ascendancy, and as soon as it started to fall they all dived for cover. I made my own views known to each of them: 'General, you have got to get up and say why you believe it is unreasonable for the Gurkhas to be cut so drastically. We accept that redundancies are necessary, and we are willing to take our share, but a 70 per cent cut is totally unfair.' I could envisage some sort of public campaign, get it raised in Parliament and enlist the support of the very strong pro-Gurkha lobby, Gurkha fans no less, in the UK. But they would not fight it. They gutlessly accepted the cuts imposed by the MoD virtually without a murmur. One even suggested that the Brigade of Gurkhas had no wish to survive at the expense of a British regiment.

Meanwhile, the contraction itself was under way and was controversial at virtually every turn. Everything – from personnel, standing orders, establishment, money, uniform, dress, insignia – would be argued over. The men, by and large, accepted the redundancy and pension packages that were on offer; they didn't like it, but there was no alternative. The nitty-gritty, however, caused moments of high dudgeon and emotional outbursts, largely from people no longer serving in any of the regiments. The views of the serving officers and men had already been widely canvassed. Corrigan went around to discuss the future with all the battalions. They were scattered around the world, one in Belize, one in Brunei, two in Hong Kong, one in the UK. All the commanding officers were chums and, apart from quite a few technical difficulties to be resolved, the serving officers came to a measure of amicable agreements on most issues.

The trouble came sideways on from retired British officers who'd served perhaps four years with the Gurkhas thirty years ago and believed that they still had a right to say what would happen in the future in terms of reorganisation. They were fighting like hell with each other, and I got the most stupid, time-consuming reactions from some of them, particularly relating to dress. Every regiment had its own idiosyncrasies, and from the outset I attempted to keep as many items of historical importance as possible, regardless of which regiment it came from. We couldn't keep everything. I wanted to keep, for instance, the red piping around the collar because that came from the time of the Indian Mutiny, worn by what was then the Sirmoor Rifles (later the 2nd Gurkhas) and the first non-British troops to go into action against the mutineers. It was a significant moment in Gurkha history, the action that made the British realise the true value of Gurkha troops. So it was historically important, and even though I am personally a 6th Gurkha I felt we had to keep it and let it go forward to the new regiment. This single recommendation caused heart attacks in the shires.

The big issue of contraction seemed to get lost in the wake of internal feuding over comparative minutiae and Corrigan suffered numerous ear-bashings from retired and serving top brass alike whose only area of agreement appeared to be that he should be fired. They would call and threaten him until finally he had to tell them, 'General, you can huff and puff all you like. You can't do anything to me.' And they couldn't. He was out of the career rat race and knew he had the confidence of the electorate – the serving officers and men – behind him.

> These old buggers could threaten all they liked; it made no difference to me. What I was concerned with was getting the surviving elements established in the best possible order, bringing with it as much visible Gurkha history as possible regardless of these stupid inter-regimental spats. We ended up with a form of dress and standing orders that everyone in the Brigade of Gurkhas accepted, or at least felt were the best possible options.

Although the British government was less than generous in the first wave of redundancies in 1969, which caused a good deal of anguish among the Gurkhas, this time it was a far better package for those released between 1991 and 1996, which was a combined lump sum and pension, in which all those with more than ten years' service were deemed to have completed 15 years and thus qualify for their pension. They also set up an agency to help them find employment once they had been returned to Nepal which, by nature of the 1947 tripartite agreement, the British army was bound to do even though there was virtually no hope of work that would provide them with similar living standards in Nepal itself.

Those who returned and stayed had few options, and many were forced simply to go back to the land. But some joined international security organisations, which favour ex-Gurkhas, a large number were placed with mine-clearance companies, some took up jobs with shipping lines and cruise ship companies as on-board security officers, and another unexpected employer was the Royal Navy – taking them on as laundrymen, traditionally done by Chinese but less so since the pull-out from Hong Kong. It was a sad end to an action-packed career. There were even sadder cases of ex-Gurkhas working illegally in both Hong Kong and Japan in demeaning jobs. For many Gurkhas, redundancy and the curtailment of recruiting had a more poignant effect – that of the end once and for all of the family tradition of service with the Gurkha regiments.

One of those released under the redundancy scheme was Lieutenant (QGO) Lalbahadur Gurung, who was one of the new hill boys recruited into the 6th Gurkhas at the time Gordon Corrigan was in the regiment first time round. Now, 26 years later, Corrigan, in effect, had to fire him and a number of others who over the years had become good friends. And so . . . to the lieutenant's recollections, taped one evening in the shadow of Annapurna, not far from the village of Maniram Kanda, where he was a shepherd until he joined the army. Like most of his colleagues, his single ambition in life had always been to join the Gurkhas and reach officer status.

His grandfather was in the Indian army and his father was in the British army, in which he served for 23 years, reaching the rank of Gurkha major and winning seven medals. He also served at Buckingham Palace for 18 months and was awarded the MVO and later an MBE for his service in Indonesia and Borneo. Lal had a good start in life, better than most, although it did mean separation from his family.

A decent education was a priority; many children simply did not go to school and there was no school in my village, either, which is why my father took me to Hong Kong, where he was based. It was a great wrench because I had to leave my mother and I did not see her again for several years. My father wanted her to come too, because as an officer it was possible. But my grandfather, who was all alone, would not allow her to go because she was the only one there to look after our land and the cattle and sheep. I also had three brothers and three sisters so she had to stay. My father didn't see her for six years. I was around 12 years old at the time and was able to attend the Gurkha children's school, which was provided by the battalion.

Lal stayed in Hong Kong with his father for six years and when he was eighteen, in 1973, came back to Kathmandu to attend college. The political situation was very bad at the time, and the college was often closed so there seemed no point in staying on. In any event, he would soon be too old to join the Gurkhas, so without telling his family he presented himself at the Gurkha recruitment centre and, with his education and background, was accepted immediately. He joined the 6th Gurkhas, based in Hong Kong, although by then his father had retired and returned to Nepal.

This presented something of a shock on my first leave. He had bought a house in another village which I had never visited, so I did not know where my house was. I was lost and I did not get in until very late in the evening. In spite of all his years in the British army, he had quickly re-adapted to Nepalese culture, and when I arrived home I discovered that he had arranged for me to be married. I had never met the girl he had chosen. She lived in a village some miles away. That first night I was a little drunk from the celebrations of coming home and she was waiting for me, there. It was midnight when I saw. And when I saw her, I said 'Yes . . . she is lovely'.

Then I thought about it afterwards . . . it had been very dark and I had only seen her by candlelight. Also, I was slightly apprehensive about the prospect of an arranged marriage. When I left Nepal at the age of 12, I had been a shepherd boy. I had spent my life in the hills with only the animals for company, and perhaps in the course of things it would have been easier to accept a marriage which had been arranged for us. And then my father brought me to Hong Kong and I became a city boy. After that, I had spent three years in the British army, and all that goes with the social side of military life. Suddenly, on my first leave home, I am to marry a girl who had never been away from her village. It came as something of a shock, I don't mind admitting, but I could not go against the wishes of my father, whom I respected and loved. Now, as I speak, we have been married 20 years, we have four children and my eldest daughter is 19. She was born seven months after I had returned to my unit after that first leave, and so I did not see her or my wife again until three years later. She sent me tiny little pictures of our daughter, but when I came home on leave I did not recognise her, nor she me. I was walking towards my father's house and this little child ran past me. My sister cried out, 'That is your daughter . . .' and tears welled up in my eyes.

This is how it has always been for the Gurkha soldiers. Most of them married in this way. Believe me, although our image is one of fierce, fighting men, those occasions when we come home on leave and then have to return, leaving our wives, our children, our mothers at home, we are full of tears. It was very hard on the womenfolk and even now, when I talk of it to my wife – although I am retired from the British army – she cries. It brings back those memories of me leaving the village and returning to continue my duties in the British army.

Lal worked hard in the Gurkhas and was promoted to corporal and then made sergeant after ten years. His lifestyle improved and his wife and family were able to join him in Hong Kong. He took an officer's course and that, too, entailed much study. 'The tests and the skills required meant many hours of work, and one of the best things I discovered about this army is that the leader must lead. I liked that. I thought about it a lot. Even the word "lead" does not always mean exactly what it said; a good leader might not necessarily be at the front. It was curious; it took me some time to understand that word and how it was applied. The leader might stand at the side with a stick and bellow, "Go forward". That is not the Gurkha way. The Gurkha officer leads from the front. That is our way, and it is the tradition of the Gurkha regiments. The philosophy always is: I lead, you follow.'

Lal's father was overjoyed when he was promoted to the rank of lieutenant and took over as a platoon commander in Hong Kong, later training new recruits arriving to join the battalion.

It was a tremendous time in my life, and for my wife and family. It could not have been better for us – until suddenly we learned that there was bad news on the horizon. I was 37 years old and had been in the British army, the Gurkhas, for 21 years and was hoping to get further promoted when the announcement was made that there was to be further cuts in the number of Gurkha soldiers. The Hong Kong establishment was being closed down after the handover of the colony to China, and there would be redundancies across the board, all ranks. I was among the casualties. I had to accept the redundancy and retirement package, and I took a one-month resettlement course and a one-week reorientation course to prepare me to return to Nepal.

Everyone had to come back; the British army had to deliver you back to the place you came from, and I started my life of retirement. It is very difficult. Unlike myself who had left the hills when I was 12, many Gurkha soldiers had gone straight into the army from their villages. The British army had taught them skills and taken them around the world. It was once much easier to pick up, like my father did, back in the region in which he was born and become a farmer again. Now it is much more difficult. Perhaps one son may return to farming, but there is no land available for the others. It is difficult to make that adjustment now, in this modern age. From the 1996 neon city of Hong Kong, I and many like me were to be literally dumped back in our villages, where life has not changed much in decades. The simple things of life that we and my family had now become used to – like turning on the tap for clear drinkable water, like switching on the electric light, watching television, reading a newspaper every morning – would be banished from the lives of those who returned to the hills. And instead of riding on buses, on trains and in taxicabs, they would have to walk between villages, just as we always had, and perhaps two or three miles [three or four kilometres] to the nearest good water tap.

We are better off than most, of course, but with inflation and the whole business of returning in Nepal or finding alternative employment abroad is unsettling and expensive. The pensions that we Gurkhas receive in comparison to similar ranks in the rest of the British army are pitifully low. It is explained away by the lower cost of living in Nepal... these days, it is not a sound argument.

CHAPTER EIGHTEEN

A New Lease of Life or None At All?

Against the gloomy backdrop of cuts and redundancies as the 1990s dawned, it seemed that the very existence of the Brigade of Gurkhas was in doubt. Rumours abounded that at some point in the future it would simply cease to exist as a British military unit, and that possibility was only heightened as Britain prepared to pull out of Hong Kong in 1996, the last major area of traditional Gurkha deployment in the Far East apart from Brunei. As the full extent of the MoD's savage assault on their numbers began to sink in, the despair among officers and men alike was evident as long-established regiments finally vanished from the British military inventory. The 2nd, 6th, 7th and 10th Gurkha Rifles were formally wound up in 1994 and in their place came one regiment to be known as the Royal Gurkha Rifles.

It came into being initially with three battalions, but these were cut further after the retreat from Hong Kong to two battalions. The 1st Battalion, as these words are being written, was based at Church Crookham as part of 5th Airborne Brigade. The 2nd Battalion was in Brunei, where the defence agreement with the Sultan remains in force. The rest of what remained of the Brigade of Gurkhas was made up of the Queen's Gurkha Engineers, attached to the 36 Engineer Regiment, based at Maidstone, Kent, the Queen's Own Gurkha Transport Regiment, which eventually came under the auspices of the 10 Transport Regiment, and the Queen's Gurkha Signals (250 Squadron), which was linked to 30 Signal Regiment. In addition, there were two Gurkha Demonstration Companies – one at Sandhurst and one at the army's training centre at Brecon, Wales, and the last remaining Gurkha

239

band. There were also a small number of people in Nepal at the Pokhara Recruitment Centre and the Kathmandu brigade headquarters and transit camp, and a Gurkha support wing as part of the army personnel centre in Glasgow. By the mid-1990s the MoD target figures for Gurkha manpower were being met as the last Gurkhas were paid off from Hong Kong.

However, the story did not quite end there. Two things happened as these developments fell into place which began to swing the pendulum back in the Gurkhas' favour – the Gulf War and an across-the-board shortfall in recruits for the British army's mainstream regiments, combined with a higher-than-anticipated drop-out rate among those who did join up. Both offered a new dimension, and the Gurkhas, officers and men, snatched at the possibilities with both hands and came out fighting.

The Gulf War presented a scenario that pointed to future possibilities. The only Gurkha unit to be included in the British force shipped to Saudi Arabia was perhaps the least expected: the Signals Squadron. They surprised all onlookers with their skill and expertise in staking a claim for a piece of the action. Under the umbrella of the Royal Signals, the Gurkhas contributed to one of the most important areas of the new high-tech warfare graphically exposed on television in a conflict that relied for the first time so heavily on information technology and satellite communications. It was in the latter area that the Gurkhas were employed and gave a blemish-free performance.

In some quarters the very idea of Gurkha soldiers being involved at this level in vital and highly sensitive tasks, in which all crucial matters relating to the management and control of thousands of troops were disseminated, was viewed as a bit of a joke, that it was beyond them, coming as they did from a backward nation whose educational standards were still Third World. The doubters maintained that Gurkhas were historically an inflexible bunch who needed a total command structure; that, sure enough, they were loyal, obedient and brilliant infantrymen who would stay at their post to the death if necessary, but they simply weren't mentally equipped for modern warfare. Some military analysts – and not a small number of managers at the MoD – suggested that the Gurkhas and the style of warfare that traditionally engaged them were already dead, consigned to history with their collection of VCs.

Not quite! Once the shock of the scale of the redundancies had been overcome, their officers began to get pushy. They took a leaf out of the SAS handbook on how to make friends and influence people – they began touting for business, which was pretty well unheard of in the annals of Gurkha deployment history. As John Cross and others had been saying for years, they were able to move with the flow and demonstrate their versatility. It also so happened that in the 1990s the Royal Signals was one of the units of the British army which had the greatest difficulty in retaining its well-trained, well-qualified soldiers who, as soon as they reached this status, were then offered handsome packages outside the army by telecoms, communications and electronics companies. The army spent large sums of money training them only to see them depart into industry with their qualifications at the earliest opportunity.

As Gurkha management was not slow to point out, the skilled Gurkha soldier, once trained, will remain for 15 years, longer if he's promoted. There would be a cost-effective continuity in employing them in these roles, and consequently commercial pressure did the Gurkhas a good turn. So they picked up the challenge and showed they were perfectly capable of adapting to skills that are the key to a modern army. Communications is king. From the mundane management of stock control, gunnery supplies, general administration and on into the high-voltage world of frontline soldiers with laptops, fighter pilots with computerised targeting systems, missile delivery with pinpoint accuracy, troop movements steered by satellite – all heading towards virtual reality developments of being able to view the action in which they are involved unfolding on the screens inside their helmet visors, with command and control coming direct to their own personal headphones. It's all here, advancing with incredible pace and viewed time and again in the conflicts of the last decade of the twentieth century.

That their signals work in the Gulf and elsewhere must have been satisfactory is evident because in 1997 the order was given for the formation of a second Gurkhas Signals Squadron. It is possible that a third will be added later. This has not been without some effort. Only in recent years has English been included on the army's training syllabus, and now Gurkha soldiers proceed through an intense language course. Until then, it was not considered absolutely necessary for a Gurkha to speak English fluently because his superior officers would include many Gurkhas and, generally speaking, British officers spoke Gurkhali. 'They now have no problem in coping with modern technology,' said Gordon Corrigan, 'and if anyone wanted to do the research, they may well find that Gurkhas were better students, more receptive to further education and – embarrassingly – better educated than many of the British recruits. Certainly, the level of enthusiasm tends to be higher with virtually no challenge to the authority of officers and very, very few getting into trouble.'

The second event that ensured limited expansion of Gurkha numbers rather than further contraction was that of falling recruitment and retention levels in other British regiments in the 1990s. This reached such a pitch that several major regiments simply did not have enough men to fulfil existing commitments, let alone any surprises that came along. Basic training intakes were being cancelled because there were insufficient men coming forward to make them worth running, and in initial training alone 25.2 per cent of those recruits who began training in the British army failed to make it to pass-out. Those soldiers who did stay served for an average of just over four years.

In contrast the Brigade of Gurkhas was fully manned, had an endless supply of recruits and had a ridiculously low drop-out rate of around two per cent, compared with up to fifty per cent in some regiments. Furthermore, all soldiers served for a minimum period of 15 years. They were cheap to run, cost-effective and caused little trouble – all the kind of words that modern military managers like to hear. The Gurkhas were thus able to help the depleted mainstream regiments by supplying backup companies to fill the shortfall. By 1998 Gurkha reinforcement companies were attached to 1 Royal Scots, 1st Battalion, Princess of Wales Royal Regiment, and 2nd Battalion, Parachute Regiment.

Their versatility went beyond simply reinforcing other regiments and was once again on show when they were deployed to Bosnia for long tours during the crucial latter stages of the conflict and the implementation of the Dayton peace proposals. They secured roles that were well outside the 'normal' Gurkha remit of supplying the blunt instrument for such tasks as guarding key installations, which many considered was the level of their suitability. Again, the pushiness of the officers in discovering other areas of operations eventually led to the

Gurkhas experiencing a wide spectrum of activity, first under the auspices of the United Nations and later alongside both NATO's Allied Command Europe Rapid Reaction Corps (ARRC) at the time of the Dayton Peace Initiative and the American Psyops forces on their hearts and minds missions.

Bosnia became an important arena for the rediscovery of their talents. Regular British army units, unused to working with them previously because they were generally deployed overseas, found them willing, tough and capable. When a company from Royal Gurkha Rifles was deployed at seven days' notice for Operation Resolute, it was indeed given responsibility for guarding key installations. As the company's tour progressed, it provided security for Allied command and control headquarters in seven different locations, which allowed them to serve in Serbian, Muslim and Croat areas. Given the high alert on security issues prevailing at the time in every one of these areas, one of its officers, Major J. Robinson, reported: 'This required a very high standard of discipline and awareness from all concerned.'

Robinson and his fellow officers did not let matters rest there. Additional tasking was achieved through making contacts on their movement through the Bosnian military zones and blatantly offering themselves for employment – 'pushing for alternative tasks' was how the major described it – which is how they got involved with the US troops. The Gurkhas volunteered three-man teams with vehicles and communications at Sipovo and Banja Luka to assist the Psyops Patrols, which in time became one of their highest-profile roles, along with conducting weaponry inspections among the warring factions. The latter began at Banja Luka when the Gurkhas' commanding officer offered to take responsibility for inspecting three Serb army barracks when, as part of the peace process, the Serbs were required to remove all their weapons into compounds and declare locations and numbers.

This operation alone required tact, patience, determination and, later in the peace process, muscle. The Gurkhas' involvement expanded considerably when the deadlines set by the Dayton Peace Initiative for weapon disclosure approached. All heavy weapons, tanks, artillery pieces, small arms and air defence weapons were to be centralised at agreed depots and counted. The Serbs, in particular, were not only reluctant to comply with the rules of peace, but some generals kept some of their weapons back and even tried to retrieve others that had already been checked and surrendered to the compounds. There were several difficult confrontations at Serbian barracks and especially at the Vibras Military Academy, where, on a follow-up inspection, Major Robinson discovered seven large air defence weapons that had not been removed. He was informed that they were for training purposes only and they did not intend to release them. An impasse was reached. Major Robinson retreated to headquarters, whereupon he was ordered to return with backup riding in seven vehicles to confiscate the weapons. Back at the academy, he was met by a posse of senior Serbian officers who refused to budge; it was quite clear that they were prepared to use force to prevent the weapons from being removed. Major Robinson, treading the delicate path of strength combined with diplomacy, explained that he was under orders from General Walker in Sarajevo to confiscate the weapons because the Serbs had failed to comply with the peace process to which they were signatories. The Serbs refused to cooperate, and there were mutterings about force provoking force. Robinson withdrew in order to avoid an instant flare-up, and then entered several days of negotiations until a compromise solution was found and the Serbs were allowed to remove the weapons themselves.

Impressions were made, and the Gurkhas established for themselves another avenue of employment. The additional Signals Company and the provisions of reinforcement companies meant that the recruitment centre in Nepal was able to push up its quotas to 300 a year and in addition continues to supply a small number of recruits on contract annually to the Singapore Police Force. The overall establishment of the Brigade of Gurkhas by the spring of 1998 was 3,253, which was a few hundred more than originally envisaged in *Options for Change*. The tide had turned, or at least been halted, seemingly to provide an optimistic note on which to draw our story to a close.

Again . . . not quite! Other rumblings have crept up on the would-be saviours and the supporters of this great British military anomaly – and they revolved around money: pensions, pay and allowances, both for ex-servicemen and serving soldiers. What began as a humanitarian story about the plight of the VC survivor Lachhiman Gurung expanded into something much wider, picked up by honest campaigners and political activists alike. In Britain, there was good intent. As the fiftieth anniversary of VJ Day approached in 1995, Lachhiman and other

Gurkha veterans of the Second World War were invited to London to take part in the celebrations and to meet the Queen and Prime Minister John Major. My good friend Brian Hitchen, then editor of the *Sunday Express*, had the bright idea of sending a reporter to Nepal to discover the lifestyle of Lachhiman, long forgotten by all but his Gurkha regiment. Writer Deborah Sherwood flew to Kathmandu and on into the hills for the two-day trek to his village, Dahakmani, and found him living in the large, one-roomed mud hut built by his father and which he shared with three of his four sons, a daughter and their families. Not unlike the description in earlier pages of this book, Deborah described his surroundings – that he had no electricity, water had to be taken from a supply some distance away and the lavatory was a hole in a corner of their field and so on. This, to readers of Western newspapers, may have come as a shocking description of the living conditions of a hero honoured by Britain while in her service, but this is Nepal and thus it ought to come as no surprise. It is the lifestyle of the majority.

Similarly, Deborah Sherwood's revelation that Lachhiman received a pension from the British army of just £21 a month (including the extra for being a VC) sounded on the face of it to be pretty dire, and it was. Such a paltry sum for such a man may be regarded in Britain as nothing short of an insult. Furthermore, the only way he could collect his pension was for his son to physically carry him down the hillside to the area welfare office 22 miles (35 kilometres) of harsh countryside away – remembering, of course, that Lachhiman suffered severe wounds in his VC-winning exploits, losing a hand, the sight of one eye and was deaf in one ear. I have no criticism with the story. Everything in it was correct and factual, and if Britain needed a jolt into remembering the past heroics of its Gurkha force, then this was as good a way as any to achieve it. What was missing was a clue about the wider picture – that this state of affairs affected a vast section of the Nepalese community, who relied on Britain and India for a monthly pension cheque, and that even the seemingly simple act of collecting it presented many great hardships to be endured by most of the recipients.

Furthermore, many ex-servicemen did not receive a pension at all. Where were they to receive assistance in their times of hardship? That Britain was interested in their plight was demonstrated by the results of an appeal for the Gurkhas run by the *Express*. It raised £100,550, which was presented to Lachhiman by John Major at 10 Downing Street. It was a very satisfactory result for Lachhiman and the *Express*, but the wider implications were soon to become apparent and mushroomed into campaigns in the late 1990s on three fronts: first, improved pensions for both ex-servicemen and those yet to retire; second, welfare assistance from Britain for those ex-Gurkha soldiers who, for whatever reason, do not qualify for a pension; and, third, better pay and conditions for Gurkha soldiers in the British army.

Discontent on all three issues predated the *Sunday Express* focus on Lachhiman by several years, coming to the surface in 1991 at the time of the first round of redundancies. It was to some extent promoted by politically motivated activists in Nepal, on the warpath against a volatile and corrupt administration. With 50,000 ex-British Gurkhas in Nepal and 200,000 ex-Indian army Gurkhas, their votes were worth having. Having said that, there is no doubt that there was a sufficient justification on all three counts for the protests to gather pace.

The Ministry of Defence, in typical fashion, began by rejecting everything, claiming it was governed by the 1947 Tripartite Agreement between itself, India and Nepal, which pegs ex-British Gurkha pensions to the pension set by the Indian army. The agreement was, at the time, also meant to ensure that serving Gurkhas were paid the same amounts in both armies, although a series of allowances and other payments means that serving British Gurkhas receive significantly more than their Indian colleagues. Activists say the British are hiding behind an outdated deal, and even Nepali politicians in 1998 were calling for a renegotiation of the terms. Neither Britain nor India is keen to embark on such a project, since it would cost them dear – Nepal already takes in around £41 million a year in foreign currency, earned through its Gurkha salaries and pensions, which is another reason why the home-based politicians were beginning to get uppity – with that kind of money at stake, any percentage would improve their own desperately depleted coffers.

In 1997 two of the leading ex-Gurkha associations began to campaign heavily for a better deal. Retired Gurkhas, they claimed, received between £23 a month for a private to around £85 a month for senior officers, which in 'the worst-case scenario' was around one-twentieth the amount paid to their British counterparts. A Gurkha sergeant would receive around £40 per month pension, whereas a

British sergeant would get around £600 a month. One of the more vociferous campaigners called for equality. Even ardent supporters of the Gurkhas would agree that the claim is well over the top, given that in that year the average cost of living in Nepal was £150 a year and average incomes around £20 a month. With £600 a month, an ex-Gurkha sergeant would be exceedingly well off.

Secondly, they wanted better welfare benefits for the 15,000 Second World War veterans and 7,000 Gurkhas made redundant in the 1960s not entitled to any pension, although these figures are challenged. At present, these men are able to apply for welfare payments from the Gurkha Welfare Trust, an independent charity that spends more than £2 million a year in Nepal (see Appendix I). Pension and welfare payments were the key issues promoted by the veteran groups and perhaps may have been taken more seriously but for their links with political parties in Nepal. In its letter to the British Ambassador in Nepal, the Nepal Ex-Servicemen's Association pressed for an increase of about £100 a month on the basic pension, while the Gurkha Ex-Servicemen's Organisation wrote a more outspoken letter to the British Prime Minister demanding equality of pensions with British soldiers.

At the time of writing it was doubtful they would get either, although various MoD schemes are now in operation to assist in cases of hardship, both on an individual and community basis. 'My own view is that the pension system is fair,' Gordon Corrigan told me, and since he has been outspoken on virtually every other issue surrounding the decline of the Gurkhas' establishment, that view is the most honest we are likely to get.

Of course, it would be good to give them more money, but bearing in mind the treaty by which the British government is bound and the conditions in Nepal, the system is about the best that is available. It is now being topped up in cases of hardship, usually among those former Gurkha soldiers who for one reason or another did not qualify for a pension. Numerous schemes have been put into place independently of the MoD, and various employment agencies are now operating in Britain, Hong Kong, Nepal and elsewhere which are specifically geared to placing ex-Gurkhas in work when they retire. All in all, the package is looking much brighter. The chaps who go back to the hills find the pension a very useful supplement; the guys who go to Kathmandu find it goes much less towards maintaining the standard of living to which they have become accustomed. However, they are still better off than most, when you consider that few professions in Nepal qualify for a pension. There is no scheme for, say, an airline pilot. Many in government service will not qualify, and industry in general has very few pension schemes in operation. The so-called anomaly between pensions paid to British and Gurkha troops has resulted to some extent from political stirring in Nepal itself. What has happened now that they have a multi-party democracy is that certain political parties – such as the Maoist-inclined – have been pushing for the vote of ex-servicemen in Nepal, of whom there are many. To get their vote, they are promising to put pressure on the British government to pay higher pensions. It's Nepalese internal politics.

With most of its troops based in the UK by the end of the 1990s, the MoD meanwhile embarked on its first major review of Gurkha pay and conditions for almost 40 years and finally agreed a new structure, giving substantial rises to ranks and NCOs. Although a complex system which cannot be compared like for like, the Gurkha soldiers' pay through basic and allowances was brought more or less to the level of their British counterparts and gave those servicemen the chance to save much more of their pay. It also meant that those serving in Brunei accompanied by their families would have to take a pay cut.

The government also finally agreed to the Brigade of Gurkhas granting family permissions, i.e. soldiers being allowed to bring their families to Britain for the first time since it was briefly permitted in 1961. It took three years for the army and the Treasury to agree, the argument being, 'You have no recruiting or retention problems; why should we give you anything at all?' Accompanied service in the UK began on 1 July 1997, when the first families arrived to take up residence in married quarters at Church Crookham. The rules were the same as those that applied in the Far East: corporals and riflemen will normally be allowed just one family permission, which is one tour in which they are allowed to have their wife and children with them for a period of three years during their fifteen years' service. Colour sergeants and above may have their families with them permanently.

They will live wherever the soldier's unit is based, which today offers two options: the UK or Brunei. They also have the option of leaving their children in Nepal and educating them there at boarding-schools with the aid of a Gurkha education grant from the MoD. The difficulty in bringing them to the UK means they have to confront the language problem, which can set the child's education back, although generally speaking Nepali children are reaching a much higher standard of education more quickly nowadays and many already speak English. Having children educated abroad used to create an even bigger problem for the children when they were returned to their Nepalese schools after three years, although with English now becoming more generally used for a large part of the syllabus in their native country the difficulties are less pronounced. The choice is left to the soldier and his wife: they can bring them or make arrangements to leave them behind.

They are accommodated in married quarters on the base. The wives and children settled into their UK homes remarkably quickly, far better than in Hong Kong, where the Chinese were frightened of Gurkhas and offered little or no help to newly arrived hill wives trying to make sense of the Mass Transit Railway. Meanwhile, the Church Crookham camp took on the appearance of a smart Nepalese village, and the local Tesco had to send out for extra supplies of basmati rice.

It was, however, a temporary idyll.

What is left of the Gurkha organisation in the UK was about to be split up again when I visited the Church Crookham base in the spring of 1999. Plans were being finalised to close down the barracks that have been the Gurkhas' home in the UK for 28 years, sell off the land and disperse the various elements to other parts of the country. Local residents would be sorry to see them go.

The 1st Battalion, RGR, was heading for Brunei on a two-year assignment, and the 2nd Battalion then in Brunei was returning to the UK, taking up residence at the Gurkhas' new headquarters, a refurbished army barracks at Shorncliffe, near Folkestone. The Gurkha band will also transfer there. The Gurkha Training Wing, meanwhile, was to move to the British infantry training establishment at Catterick, which Gordon Corrigan described as being 'akin to telling the Foot Guards to hand over responsibility for Public Duties to the Boy Scouts'. The Headquarters Brigade of Gurkhas, a staff branch, was moving elsewhere; its new home had not been finalised at the time of writing. The brigade's three Gurkha Reinforcement Companies remained under the command of the host battalions, 1st Battalion, Royal Scots, in Colchester, 1st Battalion, Princess of Wales Royal Regiment, in Canterbury, and 2nd Battalion, Parachute Regiment, in Aldershot.

With the move the Brigade of Gurkhas, divided but not yet conquered, may have reached its long-term state: one regiment of two infantry battalions, three squadrons, two demonstration companies and a training organisation. However, nothing in the above summary of the upheaval and heartache suffered by the Gurkhas over the past decade, largely at the hands of merciless and faceless civil servants, gives cause for real optimism over their future. The pay reviews were virtually forced on them, and in the end it all smacked of parsimony, even though they will be financed for the next five years by selling off Church Crookham for housing. Somebody up there has no real feeling for the Gurkhas; they are a floating option in the British military, propping up other British regiments, plugging the gaps as they appear and putting a small number of their chaps into high-tech warfare. But is there any real commitment to the future? I fear not. The voices that might have been raised in the places that matter against shutting down the Gurkhas once and for all are becoming less vociferous, and the regimental bosses too few in number to matter. And if/when Northern Ireland frees up a chunk of its resident military might, the problems of under-manning in the army may yet be resolved. What will become of the Gurkhas then?

For the time being, the last remaining Gurkha elements in the British army appear safe although there is no guarantee that this will not change under some future government looking for another round of defence savings. The continued enthusiasm for their talents in times of major crises among the hierarchy of the British military, however, was no better demonstrated than in the early summer of 1999, during the Kosovo tragedy. Even as these words were being completed, the 1st Battalion of the Royal Gurkha Rifles, whose barracks at Church Crookham the author had visited only a few weeks before, were placed on alert. As part of the 5th Airborne Brigade, they were eventually shipped out to Macedonia as the NATO allies pursued their relentless bombing campaign against Serbia while the murderous troops and paramilitaries of Slobodan Milosevic forced hundreds of thousands of refugees out of the tortured Kosovan towns and villages.

As nations around the world watched the horrific drama unfold with scenes matched only by those of the Nazis in the Second World War, NATO ground forces massed along the borders waiting for the word to move in – either by way of a full-blown war or the preferred option of a peace deal. When the latter was finally agreed on 10 June, the Gurkhas were at the helm of 11,000 British troops, alongside the 1st Battalion the Parachute Regiment, the key elements of the 5th Airborne Brigade, waiting on the Macedonian border. They were the lead troops ahead of a 40-mile long British column preparing to enter Kosovo as part of Operation Joint Guardian and the first British uniformed soldiers to cross were indeed the Gurkhas. They moved cautiously ahead across terrain most probably mined to clear the road and secure the heights overlooking the crossover point and cut out any possible Serbian snipers. They also formed the protective guard around the brigade commander Brigadier Adrian Freer as he prepared to lead the first contingent of the massive force drawn up behind him across into Macedonia to begin the thrust towards Pristina and, hopefully, a resolution of the Kosovan nightmare. It was also a Gurkha officer, Captain Fraser Rea who experienced the first confrontation with the Serbs, and Boris Johnson wrote in the *Daily Telegraph*:

> . . . as one listened to his stand-off with the Yugoslav general one felt a ludicrous but irrepressible sense of pride. After all the madness of the war, the lies, the bullying, the cruelty, there was something in the civility with which this 27-year-old Sandhurst officer handled the Serb that made one feel that, well, the world wasn't all bad.

The Serb troops wanted to go one way in their huge articulated lorries, towards Skopje, to pick up some 'equipment'. The British Army wanted to go the other way, towards Pristina and, in a hurry, because the Russians had embarrassed everyone by installing themselves in the airport. The Serbs had their guns and the British had their orders. The Serbs stood in their hundreds and glared at the Gurkhas who had blocked the road with their Land-Rovers. The stand-off lasted an hour and Captain Rea kept his ground against the increasingly impatient

Serbian general hollering through the window of his white Mercedes which had no number plates. The Gurkha captain persisted, without raising his voice and, finally, got his way. And so, Johnson reported, the Gurkhas led the way for Her Majesty's forces to get to Pristina, 'past snow-capped peaks and hayricks and tidy fields. And past scenes of barbarism. They saw buildings burned, some reduced to piles of bricks and twisted steel. They went past plumes of smoke coming from fires that had been set only an hour or so before, as the departing Serb policemen and militia torched the buildings they had occupied – buildings once owned by Kosovo Albanians.' To the very last, and even as they proceeded towards their goals inside a country ripped apart, a military confrontation between Serbian and NATO ground troops was always a possibility.

There was, however, a tragic irony in these initial manoeuvres: the Gurkhas were the first NATO troops to suffer casualties on the advance into Kosovo, not from Serbian weapons but from cluster bombs dropped by their own war planes during the air campaign. Two members of the Queen's Own Gurkha Engineers were killed while clearing unexploded bombs from the village school at Orlate, south west of Pristina. Two members of the Kosovo Liberation Army were also killed and another injured in the incident. The Gurkha engineers, skilled in unexploded ordnance, had been given the task of securing the area to the west of Pristina airfield, including Orlate, which had been a major target for NATO in the previous weeks. Cluster bombs which are dropped in large numbers from a single bomb to cover a complete target area, had been heavily deployed and they are notoriously unstable. Most explode on contact but many fail to detonate. Military experts have estimated that almost 10 per cent of the thousands of cluster bombs dropped by NATO aircraft during the air strikes on Serbia and Kosovo failed to explode.

Villagers returning to Orlate found the surrounding fields littered with cluster bombs that had failed to explode. They had been bringing them to the school yard, miraculously without incident. Around 90 unexploded bombs had been gathered up and placed into heaps at the back of the school. Gurkha engineers planned a controlled explosion but agreed to move the bombs to a ditch on the edge of the school grounds to save the school building. They dealt with the first pile successfully but as they worked on the second pile, the tragedy happened, killing the four men. After their bodies were removed, a controlled explosion of the third remaining pile was carried out, leaving a crater three feet deep and eight feet across.

The two Gurkha engineers who died were British officer Lieutenant Gareth Evans, aged 25, from Bristol, and Sergeant Bala Ram Rai, 35, from Bhojpur in eastern Nepal, described by army colleagues as 'two high-fliers prepared to risk their lives for others'. Both President Clinton and Prime Minister Tony Blair expressed their condolences, paying tribute to the work of NATO combat engineers engaged in the highly dangerous work of clearing unexploded bombs and mines in Kosovo: 'brave men who were well aware of the dangers of dealing with explosives but were prepared to risk their lives to make life safer for others'.

Both the men were highly regarded among their colleagues. Lieutenant Evans was described as an 'excellent officer and a super bloke who loved working with his Gurkhas'. The son of a deputy headmaster, Lt Evans was an ambitious and inspirational officer who had joined his Gurkha squadron after training at Sandhurst and a spell at the Gurkha centre in Pokhara where he learned the language. He initially sought a career in the Royal Engineers and while still at school took work experience with the regiment, moving on to Exeter University where he gained his degree in engineering and computer science. He was posted to the 69 Gurkha Field Squadron, part of the 36 Engineers Regiment at Maidstone, Kent in 1997 and took an early appointment as squadron troop commander, with experience of exercises in Brunei and Canada before being deployed to Kosovo.

Sergeant Bala Ram Rai, the Gurkha soldier who died alongside him, was just five months away from completing 15 years' service with the Gurkhas. He was recruited by the galla wallahs from his remote mountain village of Bhojpur, six days' walk from the Dharan recruitment base, in January 1985. After basic training he was transferred to the Queen's Own Gurkha Engineers, based at Maidstone, Kent. He qualified as a combat engineer class one and saw service in the Falklands, Bosnia and Hong Kong. Gurkha Major Damar Ghale said: 'It is very tragic news for everyone among the Gurkhas. He had just returned from leave with his family in Nepal before he was posted to Kosovo. His career was outstanding. He was one of the high-fliers.' He had a wife and two children, who had remained in Nepal and as

253

fatalities among Gurkha soldiers were by then a rarity, veterans' groups in Kathmandu arranged an outstanding reception for his coffin bearing his body, with a vast escort of ex-Gurkha soldiers marching behind the cortège prior to his traditional cremation. The death of Sergeant Rai in such heroic circumstances brought fresh media focus on the Gurkhas in general, not least on the issue of pensions and the tripartite agreement between Britain, India and Nepal governing the qualification for a pension. Sergeant Rai's 30-year-old wife Asanta was found to be living in a tiny apartment in a poor neighbourhood of Kathmandu with their six-year-old son Salim and their four-year-old daughter, Ashmita. The pensions issue would come immediately to the fore, in that, as with most Gurkha soldiers, Sergeant Rai was the main provider and economic lifeline for his wider family circle in Nepal, with six members of his family dependent on his income. His monthly remittances home were sufficient to maintain his wife and children in their one-roomed flat in Kathmandu and his parents and his mentally handicapped younger brother in a small cottage near Dharan. Their prospects of continued security were high, since Bala Ram Rai was considered officer material with a good career ahead of him. The pension which his widow would receive, however, was criticised by politicians and veterans in both Britain and Nepal. It is linked to living standards in India and Nepal under the 1947 agreement, so that sergeant Rai's widow would receive around 7.5 per cent of what the widow of an equivalent British soldier would receive. She would recieve an immediate lump sum of £19,092 and a pension of £939.24 a year for the first five years and £771.48 a year thereafter. A British widow's equivalent would be £54,000 plus six months' pay and £15,192 a year pension.

The differences between the two had never been more evident. Gurkha ex-servicemen's organisations and political leaders in Nepal once again attacked the British Government for discriminating against the Gurkhas in terms of pay and pensions. The Ministry of Defence put forward the usual disclaimer about what it is allowed to do under the terms of past agreements and added its now familiar rider that in relative terms, Sergeant Rai's family 'are going to be wealthy people, which is not to suggest that any payment could compensate them for his loss'. British politicians, confronted by an immediate hostile media reaction to this now rather hollow defence in the days that followed glowing tributes to the Gurkhas, called for a review. Bruce George, Labour chairman of the Commons Defence Committee, responded to the urgings of other committee members, stating that he agreed the pensions for Gurkhas or widows were 'rather niggardly'. Tony Blair went further: as these words were being written, he promised a review of the whole system.

There could be no doubting the pleasure among Gurkha veterans and their supporters that at last a greater financial recognition of their collective service to the British crown, past, present and future, may yet be forthcoming. Behind the scenes, caution was urged. Somewhere down the line, some bright spark in the MoD faced with further demands for a tightening of belts, might be sufficiently emboldened by the power of office to risk public outrage and say: Let's call it a day. *Goodbye Gurkhas.*

That possibility may well have been lurking in the minds of some prior to the outbreak of hostilities in the Balkans. If it was, then for the time being they can forget it. The Gurkhas were once again given the opportunity to display their dedication. A potentially difficult challenge was presented and it was one which the Gurkhas – as part of the British armed forces under NTO control – were ready to meet. There can be no better or fitting conclusion to these chapters than that!

Units of the Brigade of Gurkhas at 1 January 1999

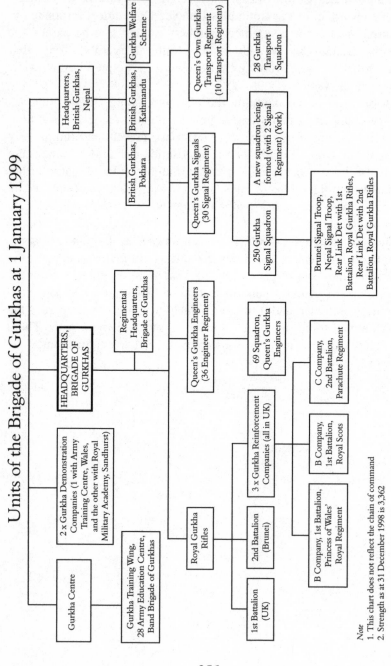

Note
1. This chart does not reflect the chain of command
2. Strength as at 31 December 1998 is 3,362

APPENDIX I

Gurkha Welfare Trust

'If there was a minute's silence for every Gurkha casualty from World War 2 alone, we would have to keep quiet for two weeks. But silence will not help the living, the wounded and disabled, those without military pensions following World War 2 service or redundancy, or those left destitute by ill health or natural disasters.'

So says the Gurkha Welfare Trust which was established in 1969 for the relief of poverty-stricken Gurkhas and their dependants. It enjoys the patronage of Prince Charles. It aims to provide financial, medical and community aid to alleviate hardship and distress among Gurkhas and their families when they leave the British army. With their dependants, they number many thousands. They live in conditions hardly imaginable to Westerners, with no National Health Service, no public housing, unemployment benefit or general welfare services.

In a country that suffers from many natural disasters, such as earthquakes and landslides, their plight is made all the worse. There is very little industry and roads are scarce. It is a harsh environment in which to live, and the work of the Gurkha Welfare Trust is crucial. The Trust operates 24 welfare centres throughout Nepal. These are manned by retired Gurkhas who investigate cases of hardship and distress and recommend appropriate aid. The average payment to destitute Gurkhas or their families is just £10 per month, currently being received by around 12,000 veterans and widows who have no service pension. Medical treatment is provided for about 58,000 of them and their dependants each year. In addition, about 3,000 hardship grants are awarded annually to alleviate destitution following natural disasters (fire, flood, etc.). The cost of education is paid by the Trust for around 650 children each year and, although the Trust is making a substantial contribution, it acknowledges that it is still nowhere near enough.

A key source of income comes from the Gurkhas themselves. Every serving officer and soldier in the Brigade of Gurkhas contributes a day's pay each year, while the administrative costs in Nepal are paid by the Ministry of Defence. The Trust still needs to find about £2 million a year simply to honour its existing commitments. Like all charities, it needs a constant income from donations to continue its work and to help destitute Gurkhas break out of the cycle of poverty, disaster and disease that so often blights their homecoming to Nepal. At present, the Trust's commitment stretches for many years into the future; thus, the cash is in a way already spent before it is received. A shortfall would mean the dilution of existing aid.

Brainchild of Major General A. Patterson, the then Major General, Brigade of Gurkhas, the Trust's formation followed the discovery of the desperate plight of many Second World War veterans and others who were discharged from the British/Indian army with less than 15 years' service and who therefore did not qualify for a pension. Many additional men who left the British army on redundancy without a pension in the late 1960s also fell on hard times (and are continuing to do so). The key difference between those Gurkhas and their British contemporaries, many of whom also received no military pension, was that the British lived in a welfare state which provided old-age pensions and a health service. No such luxuries exist in Nepal.

The headquarters of the Trust's field arm, the Gurkha Welfare Scheme, is based at Pokhara in western Nepal. The majority of current welfare pensioners are Second World War veterans and widows. Recipients of welfare pensions are restricted to those who do not already receive a service pension. Medical aid is a vital part of the Trust's work and in 1998 was also provided for 58,489 treatments at an average cost of £2 per treatment, a number so large and increasing that the Trust has its own medical orderly based at each centre who treats the simple cases. More serious ones are treated by local Nepalese civilian doctors retained by the Scheme who call at each area welfare centre each week.

In addition to the education grant paid individually for Gurkha children, the Trust has built ten school buildings in the hill areas of Nepal devoid of any education facilities. But perhaps one of the Trust's most vital tasks is the provision of one thing that Westerners take for granted – clean water. It has laid on village taps where previously none existed to hill communities, though many remain unconnected. It has also helped in the construction and repair of bridges and walkways across deep gorges which may cut many miles off a journey from the hills.

The author visited one of the Trust's centres at Gorkha, which is in the front line of the fight against poverty and hardship, but once again it is the statistics which show the extent of the difficulties faced. The centre is staffed by an area welfare officer and his assistant, along with a medical orderly. The Gorkha welfare centre, 89 miles (143 kilometres) west of Kathmandu, looks after two districts, with 90 villages spread over the hillsides of the Himalayas stretching up to the Chinese border. Around 4,000 ex-servicemen live in the area. About 90 per cent resumed their place in the community as farmers. The area covered is 1,393 square miles (3,610 square kilometres), and the population of that one region is 300,000.

There are two categories of welfare aid. One is individual aid; the other is community aid. Currently, four types of aid are being administered to individuals. First is the welfare pension, usually around £10 a month to men over the age of 65, which is paid to those who did not, for various reasons, qualify for a pension from the army. If his wife is still alive, a further allowance of £5 a month is paid, although also she has to be over 65 years to qualify. This amount increased to £12 a month from 1 January 1999. Those under 65 may qualify for a reduced pension. There are also hardship grants to relieve destitution or particular hardship brought about by illness or natural disasters. Small grants, left to the discretion of the area welfare officer, may be made up to 2,000 rupees (around £20). Major grants, which may be as high as the equivalent of £1,000 in extreme cases, are decided on by regional officials.

Community aid is divided into four main categories: first, the provision of a drinking-water supply to a village; second, building bridges across gorges; third, schools projects; fourth, agricultural projects for community farming. In the Gorkha region, 38 water projects were completed . Two schools have been built and forty-seven minor projects, to buy books, equipment or carry out repairs to existing buildings, have been approved.

The area welfare centre is also used as a distribution centre for service pensions. This has eased the burden considerably for pensioners who previously had to make a long journey to either Pokhara or Kathmandu in order to collect their pensions – a two-day walk instead of a five-day journey. The centre also acts as a meeting point and information centre for former serving soldiers.

The Trust is now running a sponsor a veteran scheme, pointing out that £20 provides enough food for a month. The address is: The Gurkha Welfare Trust, PO Box 18215, 2nd Floor, 1 Old Street, London EC1V 9XB. (http://www.gwt.org.uk).

APPENDIX II

The Regiments and Battle Honours

1st KING GEORGE V'S OWN GURKHA RIFLES
(THE MALAUN REGIMENT) Formed 1815.
Transferred to Indian army at the time of partition and Indian independence.
Bhurtpore, Aliwal, Sobraon, Afghanistan 1878–80; Tirah, Punjab Frontier; Givenchy, Neuve Chapelle, Ypres, St-Julien, Festubert, Loos, France and Flanders 1914–15; Megiddo, Sharon, Palestine, Tigris 1916; Kut-al-Amara, Baghdad, Mesopotamia 1916–18, North-West Frontier, India 1915–17; Afghanistan 1919; Jitra, Kampar, Malaya 1941–3; Shenam Pass, Bishenpur, Ukhrul, Myinmu Bridgehead, Kyaukse 1945; Burma 1942–5.

2nd KING EDWARD VII'S OWN GURKHA RIFLES
(THE SIRMOOR RIFLES) Formed 1815.
Remained in existence until 1994, then Royal Gurkha Rifles.
Bhurtpore, Aliwal, Sobraon, Delhi 1857; Kabul 1879; Kandahar 1880; Afghanistan 1878–80; Tirah, Punjab Frontier, La Bassée, Festubert, Givenchy, Neuve Chapelle, Aubers, Loos, France and Flanders 1914–15; Egypt, Tigris, Kut-al-Amara, Baghdad, Mesopotamia, Persia 1916–18; Baluchistan 1918; Afghanistan 1919; El Alamein, Mareth, Akarit, Djebel el Meida, Enfidaville, Tunis 1942–3; Cassino, Italy, Monastery Hill, Pian di Maggio, Gothic Line, Coriano, Poggio San Giovanni, Monte Reggiano 1943–5; Greece, north Malaya, Jitra, central Malaya, Kampar, Slim River, Singapore Island, Burma – north Arakan, the Irrawaddy, Magwe, Sittang Arakan Beaches, Chindits 1942–5.

261

3rd QUEEN ALEXANDRA'S OWN GURKHA RIFLES (KEMAON BATTALION)

Formed 1816.

Transferred to Indian army 1947.

Delhi 1857; Anmed Khel, Afghanistan 1878–80, Burma 1885–7; Chitral, Tirah, Punjab Frontier; La Bassée, Armentières, Festubert, Givenchy, Neuve Chapelle, Aubers and Flanders 1914–15; Egypt, Gaza, El Mughar, Nebi Samwil, Jerusalem, Tell-Asur, Megiddo, Sharon, Palestine, Shargat, Mesopotamia 1916–18; Afghanistan 1919; North Africa, Monte della Gorgace, Il Castello, Monte Farneto, Monte Cavallo, Italy 1943–5; Burma 1942–5: Sittang, Kyaukse 1942; Imphal, Tuitum, Sakawng, Bishenpur, Tengnoupal, Meiktila, Rangoon Road, Pyawbwe, Pegu 1945.

4th PRINCE OF WALES' OWN GURKHA RIFLES

Formed 1857.

Transferred to Indian army 1947.

Ah Masjid, Kabul 1879; Kandahar 1880; Afghanistan 1878–80; Waziristan 1895; Chitral, Tirah, Punjab, China 1900; Givenchy, Neuve Chapelle, Ypres, St-Julien, Aubers, Festubert 1914–15; Gallipoli 1915; Egypt, Tigris, Kut-al-Amara, Baghdad, Mesopotamia 1916–18; North-West Frontier, India 1917; Baluchistan 1918; Afghanistan 1919; Iraq, Syria, North Africa 1940–43; Trestina, Monte Cedrone, Italy 1943–5; Pegu 1942; Chindits 1944; Mandalay, Burma 1942–5.

5th ROYAL GURKHA RIFLES (FRONTIER FORCE)

Formed 1857.

Transferred to Indian army 1947.

Peiwar Kotal, Charasiah, Kabul 1879; Kandahar 1880; Afghanistan 1878–80; Punjab Frontier, Helles, Krithia, Suvla, Sari Bait, Gallipoli 1915; Suez Canal, Egypt, Baghdad, Mesopotamia 1916–18; North-West Frontier 1917; Afghanistan 1919; North-West Frontier 1930; North-West Frontier 1936–9; Caldari, Cassino II, Sant' Ángelo in Teodice, Rocca d'Arce, Rippa Ridge, Femmina Morte, Monte San Bartolo, Italy 1943–5; Burma 1942–5; Sittang, Kyaukse, Yenangyaung, Stockades, Buthidaung, Imphal, Sakawng, Bishenpur, Shenam Pass, the Irrawaddy 1942–45.

6th QUEEN ELIZABETH'S OWN GURKHA RIFLES
Formed 1817.

Remained in existence until 1994, then Royal Gurkha Rifles.

Burma 1885–7; Helles, Krithia, Suvia, Sari Bair, Gallipoli 1915; Suez Canal, Egypt, Khan Baghdadi, Mesopotamia, Persia 1916–18; North-West Frontier 1915–17; Afghanistan 1919; Coriano, Sant' Ángelo, Monte Chicco, Lamone Crossing, Gaiana Crossing, Italy 1944–5; Burma 1942–5; Shwebo, Kyaukmyaung Bridgehead, Mandalay, Rangoon Road 1945; Chindits 1944.

7th DUKE OF EDINBURGH'S OWN GURKHA RIFLES
Formed 1902 as a battalion of the 8th Gurkha Rifles.

Remained in existence to 1994, then Royal Gurkha Rifles.

Suez Canal, Egypt, Megiddo, Sharon, Palestine, Shaiba, Kut-al-Amara, Ctesiphon, Baghdad, Sharqat, Mesopotamia 1915–18; Afghanistan 1919; Tobruk 1942; North Africa 1942; Cassino, Campriano, Poggio del Grillo, Tavoleto, Montebello-Scorticata Ridge, Italy 1943–4; Burma 1942–5; Pegu 1942; Kyaukse 1942; Shwegyin, Imphal, Bishenpur, Meiktila, Rangoon Road, Pyawbwe 1945; Falkland Islands 1982.

8th GURKHA RIFLES
Formed 1824.

Transferred to Indian army 1947.

Burma 1885–7; La Bassée, Festubert, Givenchy, Neuve Chapelle, Aubers, France and Flanders 1914–15; Egypt, Megiddo, Sharon, Palestine, Tigris, Kut-al-Amara, Baghdad, Mesopotamia 1916–18; Afghanistan 1919; Iraq 1941; North Africa 1940–43; Gothic Line, Coriano, Sant' Ángelo, Gaiana Crossing, Point 551, Italy 1942–4; Tamu Road, Bishenpur, Kanglatongbi, Mandalay, Myinmu Bridgehead, Singhu, Shandatgyi, Sittang, Imphal, Burma 1942–5.

9th GURKHA RIFLES
Formed 1817 as Fatchgarth Levy.

Transferred to Indian army 1947.

Bhurtpore, Sobraon, Afghanistan 1879–80; Punjab Frontier 1914; La Bassée, Armentières, Festubert, Givenchy, Neuve Chapelle, Aubers,

Loos, France and Flanders 1914–15; Tigris, Kut-al-Amara, Baghdad, Mesopotamia 1916–18; Afghanistan 1919; Djebel el Meida, Djebel Garci, Ragoubet Souissi, North Africa 1940–43; Cassino I, Hangman's Hill, Tavoleto, San Manno, Italy 1943–5; Greece 1944–5; Malaya 1941–2; Chindits 1944; Burma 1942–5.

10th PRINCESS MARY'S OWN GURKHA RIFLES
Formed 1866.
Remained in existence until 1994, then Royal Gurkha Rifles.
Helles, Krithia, Suvla, Sari Bair, Gallipoli 1915; Suez Canal, Egypt, Sharqat, Mesopotamia 1916–18; Afghanistan 1919; Iraq, Deir ez Zor, Syria 1916–18; Coriano, Sant' Ángelo, Senio Floodbank, Bologna, Sillaro Crossing, Gaiana Crossing, Italy 1944–5; Monywa, Imphal, Thitum, Tamu Road, Shenam Pass, Litan, Bishenpur, Tengnoupal, Mandalay, Myinmu Bridgehead, Kyaukse 1945; Meiktila, the Irrawaddy, Rangoon Road, Pegu, Sittang 1945; Burma 1942–5.

QUEEN'S GURKHA ENGINEERS
Formed 1948 as Royal Engineers, Gurkha; remains in existence but reduced to one squadron attached to 36 Engineer Regiment.

QUEEN'S GURKHA SIGNALS
Formed 1948 as Royal Signals, Gurkha; remains in existence but reduced to one squadron attached to 30 Signal Regiment.

QUEEN'S OWN GURKHA TRANSPORT REGIMENT
Formed 1958 as Gurkha Army Service Corps; remains in existence but reduced to one squadron attached to 10 Transport Regiment.

ADDITIONAL UNITS
11th Gurkha Rifles was a temporary regiment formed for the Afghan conflict in 1919 and disbanded 14 months later. Gurkha Military Police formed 1949, disbanded 1965. Gurkha Parachute Company formed 1961, disbanded 1970.

THE GURKHA CONTINGENT, SINGAPORE POLICE FORCE
Formed in 1949 from ex-British Army Gurkhas, the unit was raised to replace a Sikh unit which disintegrated during the Second World War.

Today, they are taken as new recruits, supplied under contract from the British army recruitment centre at Pokhara. The Gurkha contingent is an integral part of the Singapore Police Force, largely as a specialist guard unit for government and VIPs. In times of crisis it can be deployed as an impartial reaction force. During the turbulent years before and after independence, the Gurkhas received high praise for their actions during outbreaks of civil disorder in which they 'displayed courage, self-restraint and professionalism'. In later, more peaceful years the Gurkha Contingent has continued to play a key role in Singapore law enforcement, as for example mounting the entire security cover for the 1998 World Trade Organisation Ministerial Conference. As with the British arrangement, once their period of service is completed, they are returned to Nepal with a pension for life.

APPENDIX III

Victoria Cross Awards

(Only British officers in Gurkha regiments were eligible for the award until 1911)

Rank (at date of action) and name	Regiment	Date of Action	Campaign
LIEUTENANT J.A. TYTLER	Bengal Staff Corps attached 66th or Goorkha Regiment, later 1st King George's V's Own Gurkha Rifles (The Malaun Regiment)	10 February 1858	Indian Mutiny
MAJOR D. MACINTYRE	Bengal Staff Corps attached 2nd Goorkha (The Sirmoor Rifle) Regiment, later 2nd King Edward VII's Own Gurkha Rifles	4 January 1872	Looshai
CAPTAIN G.N. CHANNER	Bengal Staff Corps attached 1st Goorkha Regiment, later 1st King George V's Own Gurkha Rifles	20 December 1875	Perak
CAPTAIN J. COOK	Bengal Staff Corps attached 5th Goorkha Regiment, later 5th Royal Gurkha Rifles (Frontier Force)	2 December 1878	Afghanistan
CAPTAIN R.K. RIDGEWAY	Bengal Staff Corps attached 44th (Assam) Regiment of Bengal Native (Light) Infantry, later 1st Bn 8th Gurkha Rifles	22 November 1879	Naga

Rank (at date of action) and name	Regiment	Date of Action	Campaign
LIEUTENANT C.J.W. GRANT	Indian Staff Corps attached 12th Burma Infantry commanding a detachment of 43rd Gurkha (Rifle) Regiment of Bengal Infantry, later 2nd Bn 8th Gurkha Rifles	27 March 1891	North-East Frontier
LIEUTENANT G.H. BOISRAGON	Indian Staff Corps attached 5th Gurkha (Rifle) Regiment, later 5th Royal Gurkha Rifles (Frontier Force)	2 December 1891	Hunza
LIEUTENANT J. MANNERS-SMITH	Indian Staff Corps attached 5th Gurkha (Rifle) Regiment, later 5th Royal Gurkha Rifles (Frontier Force)	20 December 1891	Hunza
CAPTAIN W.G. WALKER	4th Gurkha Rifles	22 April 1903	Somaliland
LIEUTENANT J.D. GRANT	8th Gurkha Rifles	6 July 1904	Tibet
RIFLEMAN KULBIR THAPA	3rd Queen Alexandra's Own Gurkha Rifles	26 September 1915	France
MAJOR G.C. WHEELER	9th Gurkha Rifles	23 February 1917	Mesopotamia
RIFLEMAN KARANBAHADUR RANA	3rd Queen Alexandra's Own Gurkha Rifles	10 April 1918	Palestine
SUBADAR LALBAHADUR THAPA	2nd King Edward VII's Own Gurkha Rifles	6 April 1943	Tunisia
HAVILDAR GAJE GHALE	5th Royal Gurkha Rifles (Frontier Force)	27 May 1943	Burma
LIEUTENANT M. ALLMAND	6th Duke of Connaught's Own Lancers attached 6th Gurkha Rifles	23 June 1944	Burma
RIFLEMAN GANJU LAMA MM	7th Gurkha Rifles	12 June 1944	Burma
RIFLEMAN TULBAHADUR PUN	6th Gurkha Rifles	23 June 1944	Burma
JEMADAR NETRABAHADUR THAPA	5th Royal Gurkha Rifles	26 June 1944	Burma
RIFLEMAN AGANSING RAI	5th Royal Gurkha Rifles	26 June 1944	Burma
CAPTAIN F.G. BLAKER, MC	Attached 9th Gurkha Rifles	19 September 1944	Burma

267

Rank (at date of action) and name	Regiment	Date of Action	Campaign
RIFLEMAN SHERBAHADUR THAPA	9th Gurkha Rifles	18/19 September 1944	Italy
RIFLEMAN THAMAN GURUNG	5th Royal Gurkha Rifles	10 November 1944	Italy
RIFLEMAN BHANBHAGTA GURUNG	2nd King Edward VII's Own Gurkha Rifles	5 March 1945	Burma
RIFLEMAN LACHHIMAN GURUNG	8th Gurkha Rifles	12 May 1945	Burma
LANCE CORPORAL RAMBAHADUR LIMBU	10th Princess Mary's Own Gurkha Rifles	21 November 1965	Borneo

APPENDIX IV

Select Bibliography

Allen, Charles, *The Savage Wars of Peace*, Michael Joseph, London, 1990

Bellers, Brigadier, E.V.R., *The History of the 1st King George V's Own Gurkha Rifles*, Vol. 1, Gale & Polden, Aldershot, 1956

Biggs, Maurice, *The Story of the Gurkha VCs*, The Gurkha Museum, Winchester, 1993

Calvert, Michael, *Prisoners of Hope*, Jonathan Cape, London, 1952

Chapple, John, *The Lineages and Composition of Gurkha Regiments in British Service*, Gurkha Museum, rev. Edn, 1984

Cross, J.P., *The Call of Nepal*, New Millennium, London, 1996

Farwell, Byron, *The Gurkhas*, Allen Lane, London, 1984

Gurung, Chandra Bahadur, *British Medals and Gurkhas*, Gurkha Memorial Trust, Kathmandu, 1998

Lewin, Ronald: *Slim: The Standard-Bearer*, Leo Cooper, London, 1976

Lunt, James, *Jai Sixth*, Leo Cooper, London, 1994

Limbu, VC, Rambahadur, *My Life Story*, Gurkha Welfare Trust, Kathmandu

MacKay, Colonel J.N., *History of the 7th Duke of Edinburgh's Own Gurkha Rifles*, William Blackwood, Edinburgh, 1962

McAlister, Major General R.W.L., *Bugle and Kukri*, Vol. II, Regimental Trust, 10th Princess Mary's Own Gurkha Rifles, 1984

Masters, John, *Bugles and a Tiger*, Michael Joseph, London, 1956

Messenger, Charles, *The Steadfast Gurkha*, Leo Cooper, London, 1985

Mullaly, Colonel B.R., *Bugle and Kukri, The Story of the 10th Princess*

Mary's Own Gurkha Rifles, William Blackwood, Edinburgh, 1957
Pocock, Tom, *Fighting General*, Collins, London, 1973
Smith, E.D., *Britain's Brigade of Gurkhas*, Leo Cooper, London
   Valour: A History of the Gurkhas, Spellmount, Staplehurst, 1997
   The Autumn Years, Spellmount, Staplehurst, 1997
   Malaya and Borneo – Counterinsurgency Operations, Ian Allan,
   London, 1985
Tuker, General, Sir Francis, *The Story of the Gurkhas of Nepal*,
   Constable, London, 1957

INDEX